With Hearts and Minds

Maillardville, 100 Years of History on the West Coast of B.C.

A.J. Boire

To Shirley!
Hope you enjoy!
Al B
11/08/16

Book Layout © 2016 BookDesignTemplates.com

With Hearts and Minds/ A.J. Boire -- 1st ed.
Published Al Boire 2016
Print Edition ISBN 978-0-9952550-0-5

In 1907, A.D McRae, a wealthy businessman and entrepreneur, has come to the west coast of British Columbia to build the Fraser River Lumber Company into one of the largest operations in the British Commonwealth. But McRae has a problem. At a time when anti-Asian sentiment is at fever pitch in Vancouver, his mill is populated with Chinese, Japanese and East Indian workers. Determined to correct this "intolerable" situation he sends two recruiters, a Catholic priest and a night-watchman, to Ontario and Quebec to lure French Canadian lumbermen to his mill to displace the Asians.

Promised higher wages, land and lumber for house and church the first contingent arrives at Millside station in September, 1909. The great experiment to displace the Asian labour force begins. It is an experiment watched closely by the provincial government, the Catholic Church and the entire lumber industry in BC and across the nation.

Will McRae be successful? Will the French Canadians prosper in their new English world?

This is the exciting story of Canada's two founding nations in the far west of the country coming together to form the quintessential Canadian experience in the early twentieth century.

Set against the backdrop of many of the major events of the times, this epic 100 year history is sweeping in its scope as it examines racism and multiculturalism, the growth of the lumber industry, grass roots union movement, communism and the Catholic Church.

Above all, the history of Maillardville, BC is a bright illustration of that elusive and sometimes tragic Canadian ideal of "two founding nations".

Dedication

"Mon Canada, je l'aime. But don't let Maillardville disappear!"
Johnny Dicaire

In researching and writing this history of Maillardville, I rediscovered a part of my own nature that had remained buried since childhood. A pride and love for the French language and culture was rekindled and a new admiration for those men and women who came to the west coast to found Maillardville was born.

This work is dedicated to:

My parents, Gerard and Cécile Boire, who managed to instil in me, though it lay dormant for many years, a deep and abiding connection to the Francophone culture.

To Mr Jean Lambert, a true son of the pioneers and a living link to the fortitude and the joie de vivre that they brought with them. For over 70 years, through his work with the French Scouting movement, numerous committees and organisations and with Les Jammers, Jean has embodied the essence of their existence: devotion to the Catholic Church, love of the French language and a determination to build up the Francophone culture in Maillardville.

I have a great admiration for him, and he has been an inspiration in the writing of this book.

Finally, to all those Maillardvillois and Maillardvillians, past, present and future, who have offered their hopes and tears, their work and devotion to keep alive the dream of a bilingual life on the west coast of Canada.

Introduction

A celebration of 100 years is a noteworthy event in the life of any community. It is of particular significance in the 2009 centenary of Maillardville. To have established and maintained a visible French community for 100 years in the westernmost part of our vast country is a truly remarkable achievement. But there is so much more to the story! From the very beginning, Fraser Mills, Maillardville and Coquitlam have been rooted in many cultures. English, French, Chinese and Japanese, East Indian and eventually Scandinavian people have all been a part of the ongoing cultural development of this area. Thus Maillardville and the greater Maillardville area becomes a microcosm of Canadian life and culture. What a truly fascinating study!

The early 20th century was marred by racist overtones…"No Asian labour!" to take away jobs from our own! It was in this vein that the management of Fraser Mills sent two intrepid scouts (with their own agendas) to the east to recruit a stable work force to support the burgeoning industry at Fraser Mills and to displace the "Asians". And so they came. In 1909 and 1910, pioneer families from Ontario and Quebec arrived at Millside, in the wilderness, to establish a new life for themselves. The new arrivals were full of hope for a future abundant in opportunity. Perhaps they did not realize the long road ahead. Whatever their first impressions, their stalwart spirit drove them on.

This story is about the life of Maillardville, from the beginning a mix of people and races, but overall about a French community that has survived against all odds. It is the story of a hearty and intrepid people who, over the decades, understood that survival depended upon the need to nurture and preserve their culture, transplanted from such a distant part of Canada and indeed to another time and place.

How did this fragile seed survive? The story of Maillardville is a testament to the fortitude of a people who were brought together by the call of opportunity at Fraser Mills.

A community of people who, isolated within an English world, were left to mature and grow strong to prepare for the trials ahead. It is about a community bound together by the strong influence of the Catholic Church. It is the saga of French Canadians whose fierce pride in their culture, their language and history, has time and again over the decades responded to outside threats by establishing francophone initiatives to keep alive at all costs "La Francophonie". And it is a portrait of the joie de vivre and humour of this people.

So the story of Maillardville is really the story of many things. Without Fraser Mills, there is no Maillardville. Without Maillardville, the early history of Coquitlam is significantly diminished. Without the efforts of so many individuals, both great and small, Maillardville would not have survived.

It is also the story of the growth of the lumber industry, of unionism and communism and of grass roots movement. It is the story of racism and multi culturalism.

A surprisingly large body of research and documentation about the history and evolution of Maillardville already exists. It is the objective of this project to bring together much of this knowledge of our community into one resource and (we hope) to add to it by lending the reader a perspective of Maillardville that goes beyond its own borders and examines the community in relationship to the "outside" world of which it is a part.

This is the story of two founding nations on the west coast of Canada...

NB This history is based upon events and the development of Maillardville rather than people or families.

NB The spelling of A.D. McRae's name appears differently in quotes from newspapers and magazines (McCrae) The spelling McRae is taken from documents of the Canadian Western Lumber Company. The author has chosen to use "McRae" in the text of this work and to leave "McCrae" in quotes from newspapers and magazines.

List of French Canadian Settlers Arriving
September 27, 1909 and May 28, 1910

On June 1, 1910 Théodore Théroux wrote a letter to Premier Richard McBride updating him on the status of the "colonization" project at Fraser Mills. With his letter, he included a complete list of the settlers and their families for both the 1909 and 1910 groups. Here is that invaluable list reproduced in its entirety.

nb The names and line spacing are per the original document

September 27, 1909

Sherbrooke

Théodore Chevalier
Mrs. Louise Chevalier
Wilfred   20 years
Joseph   17
George   15
Helen   13
Jules   11

Louis Couture
Mrs. Eva Couture
Almanda   12 years
Lola   9
George   7
Anna   1

Victor Gaboury
Mrs. Aurore Gaboury
Georgine   7 years

Milien Richard
Mrs. Victorine Richard
Edmond   11 years
Wilfrid   9

Vidal Therrien
Mrs. Vitaline Therrien

Alfred McNeil
Mrs. Delia McNeil
Oscar   1 year

Joseph Deschènes
Joseph Fortin
Mrs. Louisa Fortin

Henri Morin
George Paquet
Arthur Doyer

Quebec

Louis Boucher
Mrs. Leodia Boucher
Francois   14 years
Edmond   12
Raoul   5
Agnes   3

Ernest Gagner
Mrs. Victoire Gagner
Jesephine   13 years
Alphonsine   11
Catherine   8
Josaphat   6
Cordelia   4
Edmond   2

Joseph Joncas
Mrs. Olive Joncas
Edmond   1 year
Alice   1

Wilfred Grenier
David Hebert
Mrs. Louisa Hebert

Edward Robinson
Mrs. Olive Robinson
Edouard   20 years
Alice   18

Mrs. Ella widow 28 years
Charles   14
Helen   12
George   4

Louis Landry
Paul Girard
Narcisse Drolet
Leon Tallbot
Claude Tallbot
George Richard
J.B. Lachance
Ovide Lachance
Ernest Blouin

Quebec

Leon Lajeunesse
Adelard Trepannier
Ernest Bell

Grand Mère

Stanislas Tellier
Alcide Tellier
Mrs. Corrianne Tellier

Montreal

Pierre Gagnon
Mrs. Rose Gagnon
Ernestine   28 years
Ernest   24
Zacharie   22
Raoul   12

Joseph Pigeon
Mrs. Eva Pigeon

Edouard   3 years
Alphonse   1 ½

Montreal

Joseph Harmer
Mrs. Florida Harmer
Denis   14 years
Louisa   12
Eva   10

Arthur Lebel
Mrs. Lisa Lebel
Joseph   8 years
Olive   6
Edmond   4
Josephine   2

Paul Gauthier
Mrs. Milina Gauthier
Joseph Desjardins
Alex Dufresne
Edmond Kelso
Ernest Dion
Oswald Vallières
Demetrius Vallières

Montreal

René Vallières
Mrs. Rose Vallières
Donat   4 years
Elmina   2

Seraphin Major
Henri   19 years

Charles Lavigne
Arthur Fournier
Eugene Dupont
Louis Dhrean
Vincent Michel

Mederic Laverdure
Mrs. Florence Laverdure
Joseph   12 years
Marie   10
Alphonse   8

Josephine	6 years
Arthur	4
Oscar	2

Ernest Desprès
Adolphe Fournier
Mrs. Alma Fournier

Bernard Atoch
Mrs. Anna Atoch
Josephine	4 years
Edward	2

Eugene Dupont
Charles E. Lavigne

George Noël
Mrs. Lena Noël
Joseph	22 years
Elisabeth	16
Edouard	12
Elgerine	9

Rockland, Ont

Arthur Martin
Eugene Beaubien
David Seguin

Rockland, Ont

Jean Rochon Snr
Mrs. Mathilda Rochon
Jean Jnr	20 years
Eloise	17
Willie	15
Jeanne	13
Johnny	11
Alphonsine	9
Joseph	7
Anna	5
Louise	3
Wilfrid	1

Pollidore Gauthier
Mrs. Mathilda Gauthier
Gertrude	18 years
Whilemine	16 years

Alma	14 years
Arthur	11
Mary Ann	8
Josaphat	6

Cleophas Leblond
Mrs. Oliva Leblond
Catherine	16
Edmond	8

Joseph Mailhot
Mrs. Albertine Mailhot

Felix Dinel
Mrs. Rose Dinel
Josephine	6 years

George Martin
Charles Martin
Mrs. Jeanne Martin

August Dherun
Mrs. Alphonsine Dherun
Eloise Giraldi
Laurent Giraldi
Joseph Giraldi
Emmanuel Pasquie
Pierre Podio
Albert Sarault

Hull, PQ

Charles Bouthot
Mrs. Marie Bouthot
Charles Jnr	24 years
Thomas	22
Pierre	20
Jacques	18

Louis Lafrance

J.B. Dicaire
Baptiste Dicaire
Mrs. Anna Dicaire
Alfred	12 years
Joseph	8

Moise Coutu
Mrs. Eva Coutu
Josehine   16 years
Olive   14
Alphonse   12
Aime   10
Henri   8
Marie   4

Albert Deschamps
Mrs. Louisa Deschamps
Alfred   12 years

Adolpe Goulet
Mrs. Marie Goulet
Eugène Boileau
Adolphe Lamoureux
Arthur Lamoureux
Mrs. Louise Lamoureux

Moise Martin
Mrs. Eva Martin
Albert   10 years
Albertine   8

Alphonse Boileau
E. Charles Martin
Mrs. Marie Martin
J.B. Martin

Total 219 Souls

May 28, 1910

Rockland

Henri Hammond
Mrs. Leonora Hammond
Joseph   8 years
Graciosa   7
Beatrice   6
Lorenzo   4
Anayse   2
Julia   3

Joseph Boileau
Mrs. Beatrice Boileau

Arthur Viau
Mrs. Louise Viau
Estelle   7 years
Arthur   2 ½
Dorima   ¼

Mrs. Eug. Boileau
Marie Anne   17 years
Bernadette   13
Rodolphe   12
Eugene   7

Moise Grottier
Mrs. Emela Grottier
Albert   2 years

Jacques Cayer
Mrs. Alexina Cayer
Ermani   3 years
Noel   9

Jas Beaulieu
Mrs. Roxina Beaulieu
Joseph Jnr   25 years
Dolphis   20

Stanislas Goyer
Mrs. Melnia Goyer
Charles   13 years
Isidore   11
Stanislas Jnr   19

Rockland

Antoine Mantha
Mrs. Poline Mantha
Alda   8 years
Herve   3

Dolphis Payer
Mrs. Julie Payer
Wilfrid   8 years
Alphonse   5
Josephat   4
Areme   1
Mrs. P. Auger

Jean Laroque
Mrs. Lavina Laroque
Regina   12 years
Germina   12
Eugene   4
Florentine   2

Ben Marcellin
Mrs. Gelia Marcellin
Remi   8 years
Eva   7
Herve   5
Bertha   3
Leo   2

Napoleon Cayer
Mrs. Rosina Cayer

George Wright
Mrs. Melina Wright
Gedeon   5 years

Athanase Villeneuve
Mrs. Clementine Villeneuve

Isidore Lacasse
Midas Hammond
Geoff Hamelin
Jaques Schryre
Ovila Provost

Hull

Philippe Gauthier
Mrs. Rosalie Gauthier
Emile   21 years
Arthur   19
Donat   17
Xavier   16
Napoleon   13
Eugene   9
Albert   7
Edgar   4
Delisca   2

Baptiste Picard

Pierre Bouthot
Mrs. Eva Bouthot

Gilbert Cadieux
Mrs. Elise Cadieux
Rose   23
Gilbert Jnr   21
Gabriel   17
Elia   14
Bertha   11

Henri Cormoux

Joseph Parent
Mrs. Helene Parent
Joseph Jnr   16 years
Rose   8
Lorette   3

Ovila Leblanc
Mrs. Emilie Leblanc
Rosa sauve   5 years

Xavier DesOrmeaux
Mrs. Philomene DesOrmeaux
Lorenzo   8 years
Morel   2
Wilbrid   1

Geo. Benoit

Eugene de Repentigny
Jules Gravelle
Loyal Pansot
Eug. Consiveau
Nap. Belanger
Xavier St, Armand
William St. Armand
Stanislas Villeneuve
Geo. Lebel
Epbem Ouellette
Eug. Regenbal
Joseph Gibatieault
Henri Huvand
Philippe Regenbal
Peter O'Brien
Theo Benoit

Sherbrooke

Jean Mannone
Mrs. Mannone

Albert Boldue
Mrs. Boldue
child   8 years
child   5
child   1

Jos. Gilbert

Alphonse Bearbieu
Mrs. Bearbieu
child   12 years
child   10
child   9
child   7
child   5
child   3
child   2
child   1

Hilaire Pare
Donat Pare

Vitalien Pare
Mrs. Pare
child   5 years
child   4
child   3 years
child   1

Emery Pare
Mrs. Pare
Antoinette   17 years
Emery Jnr   15
Alex   11
Yvonne   9
Jeanette   5
Eva   3

Ph. Bedard

Napoleon Remillard
Mrs. Remillard
Joseph   11 years
Edmond   8

Ernest Desrochers
Thomas Scully
Arthur Rodrigue
Alphonse Rodrigue
Josepf Suinotte
Geo. Proulx

**Total 166 Souls
including 49 fathers of families and
72 lumbermen.**

Acknowledgements

In researching and writing this 100 year history of Maillardville, I was very fortunate indeed to receive the kind cooperation of so many people, whose invaluable help have made this work possible. I would like to acknowledge the staff at:

Coquitlam Public Library
Terry Fox Library
Our Lady of Lourdes Parish
Société Place Maillardville
Mackin House Museum
Club Bel Âge
CBC Radio Archives
City of Coquitlam Archives
Royal B.C. Museum and Archives

Emily Lonie at the City of Coquitlam Archives: her good will and efficiency was of great assistance. Her insatiable curiosity led her to examine old maps of the municipality to discover that Fraser Mills was actually a part of New Westminster before 1913, a key piece of that particular puzzle. Good one Emily!

Diane Johnston and Claudia Lemay: their enthusiasm for Maillardville history was inspiring. I am grateful for their knowledge and the resources at Centre bel Age that they freely gave.

Mr. Bernie Théroux who generously shared his own research of Théodore Théroux. That part of this history would have been significantly diminished without his assistance.

Mr. Maurice Guibord and the Société historique francophone de la Colombie-Britannique for their support and for sharing their resources. Maurice offered the invaluable service of providing the index for this work. In doing so he also became a de facto editor. His experience, knowledge, suggestions and enthusiasm have contributed greatly to the quality of this book. Merci Maurice!

And finally I gratefully acknowledge and thank Victoria for her editorial and proof reading skills as well as her unfailing patience in the face of my endless excursions to libraries, interviews and museums.

With Hearts and Minds

Maillardville, 100 Years of History on the
West Coast of B.C.

A.J. Boire

Table of Contents

One

Beginnings

The enigmatic village of Maillardville B.C. A small and relatively insignificant neighbourhood of the City of Coquitlam, the history of Maillardville is inseparably bound to that of Fraser Mills and of the city. From the beginning, it established its own unique heritage. The success of the French settlement founded in 1909 is rooted in its initial physical isolation and the strong influence of culture, language and religion characteristic of French Canadians of that era. Paradoxically, the early recognition that their language and traditional way of life were threatened by the cultural isolation of living in a predominantly English society also drove the development of the colony. In addition, the secession in 1913 of Port Coquitlam and Fraser Mills paved the way for a new city hall to be located in Maillardville.

The unique strategy implemented by the Fraser River Lumber Company to import and indeed transplant an entire community into a foreign environment was the first step toward the conception and birth of Maillardville. One hundred years later it continues to exist and, in some ways, to flourish. What was behind this strategy, what benefits did the Company hope to gain and where did it find its beginnings?

The Ross-MacLaren Mill was established in 1889. An ambitious venture for its day, it suffered a number of obstacles that included poor deep water access on the Fraser River and a decade of unusually cold temperatures that hampered transportation even further. After a few short years, the mill closed and lay idle until a new group of investors took over the operation in 1903. It re-opened in 1905 as Fraser River Mills. Although the mill enjoyed some greater success, it continued to be challenged by transportation issues on the Fraser.

After another change in ownership which renamed the operation "Fraser River Lumber Company", a consortium headed by A.D. McRae and Andrew Davidson bought the firm in 1907. A.D. McRae had previously enjoyed tremendous success as one of the principals of the Saskatchewan Land Company that had bought up and was now selling thousands of acres of land across the prairies. So successful was this venture that the Federal government of the day credited the firm with being instrumental in opening up and helping to populate the vast Canadian plains.

McRae eventually moved to the west coast of British Columbia, and one of his primary goals was to purchase a lumber mill with which to feed the prairies' building boom that he had helped to create. Armed with many high level contacts, both business and political, his group of investors completed the purchase of the Fraser River Lumber Company. McRae's vision and organizational skills would transform the mill into one of the largest and most modern operations in the world. In 1910, they incorporated as the Canadian Western Lumber Company. McRae, using his political contacts, spearheaded a group of like-minded entrepreneurs from New Westminster who successfully lobbied the federal government to dredge the Fraser River from its mouth all the way up to the town of Langley. Finally the river access so vital to McRae's plans was provided for. In 1908, after upgrading the facility with a substantial injection of capital, McRae offered a tour of the "new" mill to local politicians and businessmen. The Columbian of November 1908 was on hand to record that day's events and offer readers an insight into the wonder of that modern day marvel:

*"**Businessmen Inspect Mammoth Sawmill Plant**   With more than 3,000 horsepower sending life through its veins of steel, with its whirl and whir of shaft and pulley, its impression of vast and majestic strength the mammoth fabric of the Fraser River Lumber Company compelled the interest and the admiration of the eighty or more businessmen who yesterday responded to the invitation of the president, A.D. McCrae, to visit the mill. And few left that monument to the enterprise of modern businessmen without a feeling that here indeed was the foundation on which would grow the future of New Westminster as an ocean port....The Trip The party left the city on the 3:20pm train...Arrived at the mill offices,*

2

*the party was received by Mr. McCrae, president and managing direc-
tor, W.S. Rogers, manager of manufactures, R.L. Craig, treasurer and
H.J. Mackin, sales manager, who then guided them through the intrica-
cies of the mill. First, the big burner was visited and the draft and side
doors thrown open to give a view of the roaring furnace within. The
burner is over 100 feet in height and 33 feet in width, built of steel and
firebrick and weighing in all over 800 tons. The party was then given a
lesson in economy at the boiler house. Sixteen boilers were seen in the
battery, eight on either side connected overhead by the smoke tubes,
which in turn joined the great smokestacks, each 8 feet in diameter and
50 feet in height. A steel platform extends above the boilers and on this
the visitors stood in the glow of heat that caused J.C. Armstrong to re-
mark that this was a glimpse of a future home for some who stood there.
Above each boiler appeared a circular hole leading to the furnace
through which could be seen the flames below, from above trickling a
stream of sawdust from blower pipes feeding to the fire constantly and
with no manual labor. A visit to the engine room was next in order
where three great engines developed the 3000 horsepower animating the
mill. The largest of these is a veritable Goliath, the flywheel giving a
good idea of the dimensions of the whole, being eighteen feet in diameter
and 62 inches in width. The engine is a Reynolds Corliss twin.
Throughout the basement of the mill a maze of pulleys and shafts, the
party went ducking and dodging, noting with interest that every part was
so arranged as to be easily accessible and when they reached the mill
above they found that the plant had been so arranged that all the shaft-
ing was underneath, away from the workers of the mill itself. The great
jack chain which drew massive logs from the river as though they were
scantling aroused much interest but still more were they struck by the
celerity with which the same great logs were torn apart by the saws on
reaching the mill. Reaching the skidway, and it was about as large a log
as can be seen on the coast that the visitors were fortunate enough to
observe, the log was seized by a steam operated canthook and turned
over until the side reached was in place then a kicker came forward
pushing the log tight on the carriage. All this was done in a second. The
three band saws ripped the logs apart as though they were paper, sending the plank and board on moving rollers to the trimmers and edgers. It
was most notable that although more lumber was being cut there than in
any other two mills combined, there was scarcely a movement on the
part of a man and absolutely no work that required bull strength and
awkwardness....The full capacity running several shifts amounts to
100,000 feet every 24 hours. After viewing the mill proper, visits were
paid to the wharves, the boarding houses of the men and the town."*

Conceived originally as a means to supply lumber to the booming prairies, the expanded and modernized mill soon began to meet those expectations. Indeed the Columbian of August 1909 reported that:

*"**Record Established In August By the Fraser River Mills In Business By Rail**   During August, the Fraser River Mills established a record in the shipment of lumber by rail. During the month between 240 and 250 car loads were shipped from this mill eastward to the prairies. As each car held roughly speaking 22,000 feet of lumber, it is estimated that over 5,000,000 feet of lumber was shipped to the prairies."*

With vastly increased production, the shortage of skilled labor became acute. Other influences also at work led to the decision to import a labor force that would suit the needs of management. At the time, British Columbia was experiencing considerable racial tension. McRae and his family moved to Vancouver in 1907, a time punctuated by Vancouver's infamous race riots and the existence of the Asiatic Exclusion League. The young province was full of opportunity for industrial interests including logging and milling. The labour shortage suffered at Fraser Mills was typical of operations throughout B.C. To resolve this, many companies used workers from Japan, China and India. Eventually the numbers of immigrants grew to a point that the local population perhaps felt threatened. It was believed that while "taking away" jobs from the locals, the immigrant workers contributed very little to the local economy, preferring instead to send their earnings back to family in their countries of origin. Although the Fraser River Mills Company under new management in 1905 declared that "*no Mongolian labour would be hired*", they also admitted that they would be hard pressed to keep the Mill operational without them. There are many allusions to the undesirability and unreliability of the so-called "oriental" labor force. Appearing before the B.C. Forestry Commission McRae, now himself a member of the Asiatic Exclusion League, made the following statement as the Columbian, September 1909 reported:

"McCrae made a striking statement in regard to Oriental labor. He said that they found that white labor, even at a greatly increased price, was much cheaper in the end, and for that reason they were bringing in families from the East."

Also from the Columbian, August 1909, in an article anticipating the arrival of the French Canadians:

4

"The directors and officials of the company express the greatest abhorrence of the habits of the Asiatics they are compelled to employ on the rough work around the mill and are anxious to see them displaced. The men are filthy in their personal habits and send the bulk of their money to India and China instead of spending it in the country where they reside. They are also in the hands of unscrupulous bosses who take a percentage on all the earnings of the men and boys."

Under these circumstances, management conceived a plan to resolve this unrest and unpredictability by the creation of a stable white work force. Skilled lumbermen from the east of the country, white, French Canadian Catholics were ideal for the purpose. The need to guarantee their religious, linguistic and cultural rights was also recognized.

Business, the B.C. government and the hierarchy of the Roman Catholic Church watched the "experiment" of importing the white labor force carefully. This article from a Toronto newspaper in September 1909 illustrates further the conditions surrounding the unfolding strategy being implemented by McRae:

*" **French Canadians For The Coast** The step taken by the Fraser River Lumber Company in the direction of substituting French Canadians for the Japs, Chinese and Hindus in their mills is meeting with a great deal of commendation among the people of Vancouver. French Canadians are being brought from Quebec to replace the Orientals who number about one half of the force engaged at the firm's mills near New Westminster. From the outset the hiring of Orientals has been an unpleasant necessity. The Hindus employed in the mills are said to have been remitting about $7,000 a month to India and the Chinese and Japanese do the same thing to a greater or less degree.*

The plan of the management of the Fraser River Company is to replace these Orientals gradually. The working out of the plan has been placed in the hands of Father O'Boyle, parish priest of New Westminster, and Mr. Théodore Théroux of the Fraser River Mills, who recently left for Quebec to bring out the first detachment of 100 men. In order to secure these men they are going into the lumbering districts of Quebec and thoroughly acquainting the lumbermen with the conditions existing on the coast. It is hoped that in the end some 500 expert mill operatives and loggers will be induced to go to the West, the married men taking their families with them. The company expects to have to pay larger wages to

*the French Canadians than the Orientals, but at the same time they ex-
pect that they will secure much better work and also furnish employment
to a better class of people, who will spend their money in the country
instead of sending it to their families in other lands."*

The *Canadian Lumberman and Woodworker* magazine in its July 1909
issue was also monitoring the progress of the experiment and the broad
interest being shown:

*"Other employers of Oriental labor on the coast will watch the experi-
ment with a great deal of interest. If it proves satisfactory, it will
probably be adopted by others. It is believed that in this way one of the
most serious problems at present facing mills of British Columbia will be
solved satisfactorily."*

The stage is set and the story begins. The Fraser River Lumber Company, located several miles from New Westminster, purchased District Lot
46 from the Corporation of the District of Coquitlam. This wilderness
land was located upon the hill north of the mill. It was bought to fulfill
that part of the agreement that ensured land would be made available for
the homes and church of the newcomers. At the mill site, the area known
as Millside, visible and distinct communities of Chinese, Japanese and
East Indians had sprung up forming what was then known as "Oriental
Town". All this was situated within an English dominated society. The
introduction of the French Canadians to this mixture, therefore, created
an almost perfect microcosm of Canada with both founding nations represented in quasi-correct proportion. This picture of Canadian dualism
and multiculturalism is completed with the presence of both indigenous
populations and the diversity of the above mentioned ethnic groups.

In 1909, the Company assigned their night watchman, Théodore Théroux, to embark upon a recruiting mission to eastern Canada. There, the
logging industry was flagging and experienced men, for lack of work,
were looking elsewhere for opportunity. Théroux, in cooperation with
Father William Patrick O'Boyle, O.M.I., Saint Peter's Parish in New
Westminster, embarked upon a dual mission. The first objective was to
import a stable work force for the mill. Secondly, they saw an opportunity not only to propagate the Catholic faith and the French culture in
British Columbia but also to help stem the flow of French Canadians that
were heading south into the U.S. from eastern Canada in search of new
opportunities.

The pair departed for Ottawa. Their intention was to work through the French Catholic parishes looking to entice loggers and mill workers to the west coast with the promise of good wages, land and a more temperate climate. Their first contact in Ottawa was with Jean-Baptiste Dicaire, a young man selling newspapers at the train station. Noting his bilingualism, they asked him if he knew where they might find the type of men they were looking for. The young man quickly led them to his own relatives and to the local Catholic parish and the recruitment effort began. Fr. O'Boyle has been described as a charming and persuasive speaker and in short order they had a group of men interested in their proposal. When they expressed their need to be able to practice their religion and educate their children in the Faith, Fr. O'Boyle was a sympathetic listener. The would-be pioneers were promised raw land and materials to build church and school. Here again the Columbian of July 1909 offers a glimpse into the past:

"Eighty French Canadian mill hands will be imported from Eastern Canada to work in the big sawmill of the Fraser Lumber Company at Millside, near New Westminster. This is the plan that the management has decided to adopt in an effort to solve the labor problem. If the experiment is successful, additional French Canadians will be engaged.

Negotiations for the batch are in progress between Mr. A.D. McCrae of Winnipeg, president and general manager of the company who is in Vancouver, and a well known French Canadian Member of Parliament. The company will agree to prepay the railway fairs of the workmen and their families, guarantee steady work at ruling wages and provide each family with a cottage and a garden. Eighty acres have been reserved for this purpose. The company will also build a Roman Catholic church on behalf of its employees of that faith."

Father O'Boyle was, in fact, the representative for the Roman Catholic Archdiocese of Vancouver in this endeavour. Letters[1] dated June 11 and August 3, 1909 between O'Boyle and A.D. McRae outline the agreement:

"The Company agrees:

---

[1] Archives Roman Catholic Archdiocese of Vancouver

a) *To substitute, as much as possible, good, honest, French Canadians for Oriental labor,*

b) *To give continuous work the year round at a minimum wage of $2.00, per day, to 200 men or more if they can be had,*

c) *To reserve 80 acres of the best residential portion of townsite, have same surveyed in half acre lots. Said lots to be sold to bona-fide colonists at $150.00, on long time payment at 6 per cent interest,*

d) *To advance lumber necessary for building, the cost price of the lumber with the price of the lot to be put in the shape of an agreement of sale, extending payments on total from five to eight years at 6%, giving the man an opportunity to pay it off as soon as he desires, when he will receive a deed in fee simple,*

e) *To advance the one half fares of children between 5 and 12 years and the fares of children between 12 and 18 years,*

f) *To deed the church an acre and one half of ground free for church, school and other necessary buildings, also to furnish lumber from stock gratis. "*

Following meetings at parish halls in Hull, Sherbrooke and Rockport, the first contingent from those cities assembled in September of 1909 and left by rail for parts unknown. The recollections of one who made that long and likely uncomfortable journey across our vast country tell us that the trip was made more enjoyable by the shared anticipation of what the unknown would bring. Much of the time was passed by the playing of music and singing. The children themselves were most in awe as the train made its way through the Rocky Mountains.

The pioneers arrived at Millside station next to Fraser Mills on September 27, 1909. Their arrival was anticipated as the "Columbian" reported on September 23, 1909 and headlined:

"COMING ON SPECIAL TRAIN *Five Hundred French Canadians Have Left Montreal Yesterday For the Fraser Mills"*

The newspaper goes on to say:

"A special C.P.R. train left Montreal yesterday bearing 500 French Canadians bound for the Fraser River Mills at New Westminster. The party is in the charge of Mr. Théodore Théroux representing the company and Rev. Father O'Boyle, the parish priest at New Westminster. The special

train is composed of 13 cars and will be sent through to their destination as rapidly as possible. The party is expected to reach here by September 28......Liberal terms have been offered these people and Mr. Théroux and Father O'Boyle experienced little difficulty in persuading them to make the change.....Elaborate preparations have been made for the accommodation of so large a number of new settlers and Millside has been growing rapidly as a consequence. Thirty two new dwellings have been built near the mill and will be ready for occupancy by the time the party arrives here."

Again, the "Columbian" commenting in their issue dated September 27, 1909

"At 12:30 today a special train composed of nine coaches including baggage cars reached the Fraser River Mills bearing some 250 French Canadians who have been brought out from the province of Quebec to work in the mill ....A large number of the employees of the Mills were assembled to welcome these new settlers today.........All brought plenty of household furnishings and in a few days will be settled in their new homes in a new country. There are 110 workmen with the party and these will start work on October 8. In the meantime the Japs, Chinese and Hindus are working along in a stolid fashion though they know that this means that in a short time they will have to look for work elsewhere."

And from one of the first to step off the train[2]:

"Departing from Ottawa, we arrive here on the 27 of September, at noon. And the train pull into Fraser Mill the whistle had just blown to start work...Someone noticed that there was a train arrived, the whole mill stopped working" and " We were kinda scared...there was all Chinamen, Hindus and Japanese that met us...but they were friendly."

These were true pioneers. Although the mill operation was one of the largest and most modern in the world, it was nonetheless largely isolated in a wilderness. The accommodations promised them were not complete, and many had to live on the train for several months. The men were quickly put to work at the mill. They worked ten-hour days, six days a week. With lumber and land supplied by the Company, they set about

---

[2] Vancouver Oral History, Coquitlam Public Library

building their homes and their church. In 1910 a second contingent arrived, many of them relatives of those who came earlier.

That the fledgling French community was physically isolated is noteworthy. Their basic needs of food, clothing, hardware and so on, were provided at the Company's town site that included a general store, hotel and meeting halls. Anything further that was wanted could be had in New Westminster. At that time, the tram's eastern terminus was the village of Sapperton and a walk of a mile or so along rough trail was required to complete the journey to Fraser Mills making shopping in the "big city" an occasional event. Although economically attached to the Fraser Mills Company, the social and spiritual life of the French Canadians remained separate. This early isolation must have had a "cradling" effect on the French settlement, binding the newcomers even more closely by ties of language and religion.

Almost by definition the newcomers, being French Canadian, were Catholic. Father O'Boyle continued to oversee the goings on among his new charges, including the building of the new church and convent in 1910 and 1911 respectively. A letter from the assistant secretary of the Canadian Western Lumber Company dated September 22, 1911 states that A.D. McRae's promise for land and materials for a church were fulfilled. As of this date, Father O'Boyle was still the main liaison and Father Edmond Maillard, the first priest assigned to the settlement, had already been moved from the new parish and replaced by Father Pelletier[3].

"Reverend Father W.P. O'Boyle, New Westminster
copy to Reverend Father Pelletier, Fraser Mills

Dear Sir,

In accordance with the promises made to you by Mr. McCrae concerning the material in the Church building on the French Townsite, I have to advise that on this day we have credited their account with the sum of $1912.86. This represents the amount of the lumber which we furnished for the church building and which Mr. McCrae agreed to donate free."

---

[3] Archives, Roman Catholic Archdiocese of Vancouver

The letter goes on to request payment for other services and materials including:

"a statement for the lumber gotten by Reverend Father Pelletier and used in the construction of his residence. This amounts to $702.71"

Although Father William Patrick O'Boyle typically receives most of the credit in the recruiting process, Théodore Théroux may have been the catalyst that inspired the scheme to bring Francophone immigrants to Fraser Mills. Mr. Théroux was no stranger to colonization. Théodore Francois Théroux was born in Quebec in 1863. He became a teacher and moved west, teaching for a time at Mission, BC in 1891. In 1894, while in Calgary, Alberta, a chance meeting with two other men, Joseph Poulin and Benoît Tétrault, led him on a quest to found a new Francophone village in the Vermillion River valley. From completely uninhabited land the village of Vegreville would spring. Mr. Théroux was their first schoolteacher in an independent Catholic school. Théroux kept a diary of the early years of Vegreville's birth, with much emphasis on both the notion of founding a Francophone village and the close ties the Catholic Church had in that process. He would participate in an almost identical process 15 years later at Millside in British Columbia. Clearly, this man had a deep and abiding love for the French culture and the Roman Catholic faith. He brought the tools necessary with him: his passion, his education and his experiences in Vegreville to the Fraser River Lumber Company. He was employed as night watchman.

What an interesting turn of events: A.D McRae, the brilliant and visionary businessman, came to the west coast to buy a mill to supply lumber to the booming prairies. Théodore Théroux found himself at the very mill bought by McRae, who had determined to resolve the "problem" of Asian labor. Théroux was uniquely qualified to offer a solution he was already familiar with and passionate about, namely the importation of French Canadians (and Francophone culture) from Quebec to the west. It is interesting to speculate about the interaction these two unique and strong individuals may have had. Was Théodore Théroux the instigator of the scheme to import French Canadian lumbermen from the east? In any case, he clearly played an important role and he believed that the "experiment" had implications that went far beyond the concerns of the Fraser River Lumber Company.

After the arrival of the first of Maillardville's pioneers, he corresponded with then Premier Richard McBride, keeping him updated on progress and imploring McBride to support the project further. His letter dated June 1, 1910[4] also included a complete list of "colonists" from the arrivals on September 27, 1909 (219) and May 28, 1910 (166):

"To the Hon. Richard McBride
  Prime Minister
  Victoria, B.C.

Hon and dear Sir

I beg to call to your attention the successful results of our campaign in the east for French Canadian Colonists for Fraser Mills, and to suggest that in view of further encouragement your kind grant of a few months ago be supplemented.

I have every reason to believe that the presence of an official Government Agent either on the Coast or in Montreal or even better in the New England State U.S.A. would help especially in the matter of handling correspondence.

Please find herein the names and numbers of French Canadian Colonists delivered to Fraser Mills, B.C. September 27, 1909 and May 28, 1910.

> *I am*
> *Honourable Sir*
> *Your Obedient Servant*
>   *Théodore Théroux"*

Théroux also emerged as an early leader in the new French community as a liaison with both mill management and local politicians. He remained in Maillardville until, in 1913, he took up a new post at Essondale (renamed from Mount Coquitlam in honour of Doctor Henry Esson Young), the nearby hospital for the mentally ill. The French settlement was eventually named for Father Edmond Maillard, the first priest assigned to the colony. However, history has shown that, as he

---

[4] GR-0441,Box 39,File 1,Letter 372/10 courtesy of the Royal BC Museum and Archives

was a part of the founding of Vegreville in Alberta, so Théodore Théroux should also be considered a founding father of Maillardville.

Responsibility for the parish was initially handed to that young Oblate priest, Father Edmond Maillard, from St. Louis College in New Westminster. In his first document, the baptismal registry, the priest refers to the "Paroisse (parish) de Fraser Mills"[5] Soon, the Catholic community was consecrated to Notre Dame de Lourdes. From the accounts of those who knew him, he was a "good man" "not very strict" and "could preach a good sermon" He was certainly deeply involved in the building of his community and became a very well loved and respected leader. Under his guidance, a church was built at what is now known as Laval Square and Mass was celebrated there for Christmas 1910.

Father Maillard himself remains something of an enigma. Very little information remains to reveal the man, the extent of his impact on the fledgling community or his very sudden removal as parish priest after so short a stay. Of course, naming the village after him speaks eloquently to the fact that he did indeed hold a special place in the hearts of his parishioners. Father Edmond Maillard was born in France on January 31, 1880. He was ordained in 1900 and came to New Westminster in 1906 where he resided at St. Louis College. Named as first parish priest for the French Settlement, he set about building up the new parish with a zeal for both faith and culture.

In a letter to Father A. Fréchette in 1959 on the Parish's fiftieth anniversary, Father Maillard recounted the time when then Archbishop of Vancouver Neil McNeil visited the new parish. According to Father Maillard, Archbishop McNeil was very interested in this "frontier" parish and visited frequently. Apparently impressed with the young Oblate who was often to be found with pick and shovel working hand in hand with the men of the parish, the Bishop presented him with a gift of a new pair of boots. It seems clear that Father Maillard was a well-loved man. The recollections of those who knew him, the kind and very complimentary letter sent to the Parish from his Superior on his death and even the fact that the local papers kept track of him over the following years are all testament to the character of this man for whom the village would be named. He was abruptly removed from the parish in 1911. Again, from

---

[5] Archives, Our Lady of Lourdes Roman Catholic Church

his 1959 letter[6], Father Maillard describes the suddenness of his removal:

"En 1911, un certain jour je faisais le tour du village pour quêter pour l'école. On me dit qu'un Prêtre me cherchait, c'était l'Abbé Pelletier porteur d'une lettre, dans laquelle Msg. McNeil me disait que ce Prêtre est nommé curé de la Paroisse. Avouez que le coup fut rude-le soir même je rentrais à New Westminster."

"In 1911, on a certain day, I was making the rounds of the village raising funds for the school. I was told that a priest was looking for me, it was Father Pelletier carrying a letter in which Msg. McNeil told me that this priest has been named as parish priest. Admittedly the blow was harsh, that very night I was back in New Westminster."

He remained at St. Louis College until 1914, occasionally filling in at his old parish when the priest was away or ill. In 1914, he was given the opportunity to return to Notre Dame de Lourdes, but from his letter:

"En Février 1914 tout m'allait pour le mieux et Msg. McNeil me demanda de retourner à mon ancienne paroisse-je refusais et le Père Provençal me nomma Supérior de la mission du Cariboo où je restais douze ans »

« In February 1914 everything was going well with me and Msg. McNeil asked me to return to my old parish-I refused and our Father Provincial named me Superior of our Cariboo mission where I stayed for twelve years."

The reasons for his removal remain obscure, as is his refusal of the Archbishop's request to return. That these events were painful for Father Maillard is highlighted in a letter[7] from his Superior to the parish of Notre Dame de Lourdes on his death in 1966:

" Le Père Maillard pensait souvent à Maillardville, il aimait peu en parler car cela faisait souffrir son Cœur; mais il collectionnait tout ce qu'on lui envoyait sur la vie de son site....Je sais qu'il avait été invite en 1959 pour les fêtes du Cinquantenaire...il n'avait pas osé y aller : un trop

---

[6] Archives, Our Lady of Lourdes Roman Catholic Church
[7] Archives, Our Lady of Lourdes Roman Catholic Church

long voyage, trop d'émotions...Mais il vivait souvent en pensée avec tout ce qu'il avait laissé là-bas. »

« Father Maillard thought often of Maillardville, he didn't like to speak of it as it caused him a sadness of heart; but he collected everything we sent him on the life of his village...I know that he was invited in 1959 to the Fiftieth Anniversary celebrations...he didn't have the desire to go: too long a trip, too many emotions...But he often lived with the thoughts of all of the things he left there."

Father Edmond Maillard, OMI returned to France in 1937 where he died peacefully on August 3, 1966.

Father Maillard was followed by a succession of priests starting with Father Charles Pelletier. The loss of their founder priest notwithstanding, there was an incredible zeal to see the new community built. By as early as 1913, Maillardville was recognized as the leading French settlement in Western Canada. As quoted from the Coquitlam Star, July 2, 1913:

"Maillardville is now recognized as the leading French Canadian settlement of British Columbia and consequently a large number of people of that nationality are coming into the town regularly, the present population being estimated at 400"

Also from the Coquitlam Star on October 1, 1913 headlined

"Maillardville Shows Remarkable Growth"

"The population of Maillardville, the thriving young village, has increased from practically nothing to 525 in three years according to Municipal Chief of Police Paré, who is at present taking a census of the population of the entire Coquitlam Municipality....In addition to the population, Mr. Paré reckons that there are 115 families varying in size from three to five members and an equal number of residences....Three years ago the town site, known as Block 46, was nothing but forest, but since the coming of the first batch of French Canadians under the auspices of the Canadian Western Lumber Company, the population has increased by leaps and bounds, and Maillardville is now regarded as the leading French Canadian settlement in British Columbia; in fact in Western Canada"

By 1912/13 water and electric lighting were supplied to the village. On March 26, 1913 the Coquitlam Star reported that:

"after long delay, the electric lights are now installed and in use in "Frenchtown" or Maillardville, the Western Canada Power Company having now completed operations on the Pitt River road and Church street....Unavoidable delay was caused last year by the non-registration of District lot 46... The registration of the same lot will have a further important result, as the residents are now enabled to purchase their holdings ......This will give them the right to register as owners of land in the municipal voters list."

Also in June of 1912, the B.C.E.R opened the new extension of its tram-line into Millside, making the trip into New Westminster much more accessible to the citizens of "Frenchtown".

The Star reported on April 16, 1913 that:

"The population of Maillardville was augmented last week by the arrival of five new French Families from Ontario. Many new houses are going up for residents, among whom are Messrs. H. Charland, O. Leblanc, E. Leblanc, H. Sabourin, R. Hudon, O. Vallière, W. Dunbar, L. Boileau and J.P. Paré."

The new village offered a sight unique in this part of the world and its inhabitants carried about them a certain mystique and an aura of ro-mance. In referring to the "inmates", the settlers were described thus:

"They have been brought out by the company from time to time to work in the mill. It will be remembered that the habitant is the coureur de bois, the pastmaster in woodcraft, whose progenitor was the first to carve roads in Canada" Star, May 8 1912

Even the settlers' new homes seemed to have something of the exotic about them: Coq. Star 1912

"Their homes are pitched for the most part on the rise of the hill beyond Mr. Roger's charming dwelling. Land there is still in process of being cleared and the numerous pretty, artistic residences peep out from among the green pines and the brown timbers, making the most pictur-esque corner of the district. It is to be hoped when Coquitlam starts in to

build in earnest that it will be with some regard for form and color, as has been the happy inspiration here."

Names were soon being considered for the various streets. Again, the filament of Catholicism and French patriotism ran through the thoughts of the pioneers as they chose names to honour both Church and cultural icons. An article appeared under the headline "What's In A Name" in the Coquitlam Star, June 1914:

"The names bestowed on Maillardville by its residents exhibit patriotism and theocracy. Cartier and Laval Streets represent the names of great French Canadian explorers, Bégin was a cardinal and Casey, the philanthropic Archbishop, formerly of Vancouver and now of Toronto, is still the generous friend of Maillardville and its residents. It was found impossible to change the name of the portion of Pitt River Road running through the burg to Quebec Street, but an agitation is on foot to name the pound Paré Square and the lock up cell's Emilie's (Emeri?) mansions."

Everything that was needed to accommodate the French community was established almost immediately. Besides home and church, a convent was built to house the sisters in their mission to teach the young ones. Of course, Millside School had been built in 1907 and by this time was a two-room facility. Children of Fraser Mills attended Millside and a diversity of ethnic backgrounds coexisted there. The Star, May 22, 1912 mentions:

"The public school at Millside is situated at the end of the French Settlement, rather far from the houses of the Protestant section of Millside but having the advantage of being on higher ground. It contains two large fine rooms and the playground is being got into order. There are 42 pupils covering many nationalities and Americans of a somewhat migratory disposition."

Although some of the French settlers sent their children to Millside, for reasons of economy or a desire to ensure their children were fully integrated into their new world, most were sent to the French Catholic school.

Fire was always a hazard and the local paper reported on numerous incidents of buildings being destroyed, perhaps none as dramatic as that of the church fire of December 24, 1913 as chronicled by the Coquitlam Star:

"Was Burned to Ground at Maillardville"
Roman Catholic Church Gutted by Fire on Eve of Christmas Mass Celebrations

"The Roman Catholic Church at Maillardville was burned to the ground early on Saturday morning, three hours after the residents had finished decorating the church ready for the Christmas mass celebration arranged for the next day. The fire was first noticed by a neighbor who raised the alarm. Chief Paré entered the burning belfry and tolled the bell until his hands were scorched by the roaring flames. All the residents turned out. By an almost superhuman effort the convent and priest's residence were saved by the men preventing the spread of the flames with a chain of pails of water. The entire contents of the church, valuable ornaments, the organ and priestly robes were demolished. All that remains is a mass of charred timbers. The church was built about three years ago and is in the charge of Rev. Father Garon. Much credit is due to the Reverend Father who was burned slightly when trying with the others to save the sacred edifice, while Chief Paré was a tremendous worker. On Sunday the services were held in the moving picture theatre."

Nevertheless, this community full of strong willed and dedicated citizens did not look back. Abandoning the old foundations, they erected a new building to the east of the Rectory. On February 21, 1914, Father Émile Garon, the parish's third priest, celebrated the opening and dedication of the new church.

For the French Canadians, Catholic education of their children was essential. The first teacher in the colony was Adrienne Blancard, and she was stationed at Notre Dame de Lourdes for a very short time. Soon the "Soeurs de L'Enfant Jésus" "Sisters of the Child Jesus" from New Westminster took up that duty. At first, the daily trip brought them to Sapperton by tram followed by a two-mile walk to Fraser Mills along rough trails. A convent was soon built at Laval Square. These faithful women would serve the needs of the parish for the next 42 years. Again, outside observers were most impressed with the very satisfactory schooling being provided and the excellent behavior of the children. A

Coquitlam Star article, May 8 1912, describing the village includes the following first hand witness of school life at the convent:

"Behind these stands the convent of the Sisters of the Child Jesus. One is kindly allowed to visit the school. The portress, wearing the quaint old dress of the mediaeval order, opens the door and welcomes the visitor to a Spartan side room which is the Sisters' sitting room. She fetches a teaching Sister, who is pleased to show the sewing class. The muddy boots of the children, says the Sister, have made havoc of the floor. Upstairs are some 25 to 30 girls in a well lighted room busy sewing under the supervision of a young brown-eyed Sister. They are old fashioned children who rise politely when visitors come. The work is crochet with white cotton and wool, knitting of stockings, small embroideries, such as collars, and one girl is busy lace-making with pillow and bobbins. They gave us a little singing. Three times a week the girls put in an extra hour to take their sewing lesson. This is all the time devoted to that work. The rest of the school is closed, the boys having gone home. Reading, writing and arithmetic, English language, are the subjects chiefly taught, and half an hour a day singing, the Mother Superior says. Six girls learn to play the piano, and religious teaching is kept well to the fore. The children, of whom there are about 115, boys predominating, pay 50 cents a month for their schooling, and these small payments make the entire income of the establishment. The school receives no state aid. The equipment much suffer under such conditions and it behooves good Roman Catholics to give their support and an occasional visit to this isolated school.

The sisters, of whom there are five, including the Mother Superior come from France and devote their lives to the work of teaching. One would like to thank them for their kind welcome and their manners of gentlewomen. It may be that the sectarian school is doomed in the development of the centuries. If so, it were well to incorporate some of the best features of the old Orders in educational work."

So it was that life in the French settlement unfolded. The men, for the most part, worked at the mill. The church burned down in 1913 but was soon rebuilt. Father Maillard was replaced by Father Charles Pelletier and then by Father Emile Garon. Garon was instrumental in the choosing of the name "Maillardville" named in honor of le Père Maillard after considering, and rejecting, such possibilities as "Cargo" and "Rosetown". The Coquitlam Star reported on July 3, 1912 under the headline:

"A Flourishing Community Adjoining Fraser Mills- A New Name Wanted"

"There is a flourishing French Settlement adjoining Fraser Mills commonly known as "Frenchtown". But, although its "habitants" are nearly all French-Canadians, they are not entirely satisfied with this designation and have decided to be known in future as "Mayor" a name which is not only that of a former priest of the settlement, but that of an important functionary of a town. At least, that is the name which during the last few days has been tentatively decided upon by residents of the place."

The article goes on: *"There is now a Catholic church and school and several stores. Application has recently been made for a post office which is likely to be opened within the next few weeks at the store of Mr. J.H. Proulx, on Pitt River Road. The lots on which the houses or cottages are built are sold by the Western Canadian Lumber Company, Fraser Mills, for $250 the half acre, paid at the rate of from $5 to $10 per month. The lumber and the paint are supplied by the Fraser Mills."*

Reporting in this instance was not entirely accurate. According to Johnny Dicaire, present for this important event, Father Garon originally suggested that the village be named "Maillard". It is easy to see how an Anglophone reporter, hearing the French pronunciation "My-yar", might mistake that word for "Mayor" thus the article reported above. However, it was later suggested that the name "Maillard" could be improved upon by the addition of "ville". This, of course came to pass. It was in 1912 that the village was recognized by the granting of a post office under the name of Maillardville. The pronunciation was to be a challenge then as it is today. The Star reported on July 24, 1912:

"Milliardville" The Name

"It has been decided by the post office department, Ottawa, to establish a new post office to be known as Milliardville, at what is more familiarly known as French Town, on the Pitt River Road, opposite the Fraser Mills. The new office will be established on August 1st and will be of great convenience to the residents of that section……..The proper way to pronounce Milliardville is as near as possible, "Meyardville"

The Postmaster General, Louis-Philippe Pelletier, a relative of Father Charles Pelletier, was responsible for the creation of the new facility. It opened on the first of September, 1912 under the name of Maillardville. George Proulx was its first Postmaster and he served until 1924. Wilfred Duplin followed him from 1925 to 1930. Henry Thrift held the position as postmaster from 1930 until his son Frank took over in 1957. Frank Thrift was Maillardville's last Postmaster. The branch closed in 1972.

In 1912 the area from Port Moody to Pitt Meadows was in a fever of incorporation. The residents at Westminster Junction moved to secede from Coquitlam and in 1913 became Port Coquitlam. Fraser Mills followed eight days later and incorporated as the District of Fraser Mills. It has been suggested that Maillardville also applied to incorporate but the effort was unsuccessful. The reason given is that the Government was not keen to allow a permanent French township to be established. This may be true, but there seems to be little evidence to support the notion. The efforts of Port Moody, Port Coquitlam, Fraser Mills and Pitt Meadows to incorporate were all reported in the papers, but there are only a very few oblique references to any notion of incorporation for Maillardville. Some clues to the mystery may be found in the events that followed the successful incorporation of Port Coquitlam and Fraser Mills.

As the District of Coquitlam, the city offices were located at Westminster Junction (Port Coquitlam). After secession Coquitlam needed to accommodate temporary Council Chambers and West Coquitlam seemed to be the obvious choice, being more commercially active and in closer proximity to developed areas such as New Westminster. Even before the secession was complete, however, debate raged as how best to serve both ends of the sprawling new district. The east versus west controversy would not really be resolved and would manifest itself in the late fifties with a serious attempt by the "east side" to secede and join Port Coquitlam. The west seemed fated to be the location of the new City Hall, and Burquitlam emerged as the early front-runner. The Agricultural Hall was a ready-made location, and area residents set about to enthusiastically increase their activity at and around the Hall. The Star, February 26, 1913 relates that:

*"**Burquitlam Headquarters of Coquitlam District**   Now that the new municipal centre of Coquitlam is being shifted to Burquitlam, the Agricultural Hall on Austin Road is becoming the scene of great activity,*

*both in Municipal affairs and in many other directions...It has been de-
cided that the new Coquitlam Ratepayers' Association will have their
headquarters at the Burquitlam Agricultural Hall...Another important
organization to be started at Burquitlam is the Ladies' Institute. At the
annual meeting of the Coquitlam Farmers' Institute held in Burquitlam
Agricultural Hall last Thursday night the president informed the meeting
that there was a movement afoot to form a ladies' institute in Burquitlam...*"

As a very vibrant and fast growing community, Maillardville had its own
strong views on the subject. Council meetings were dominated by the
debate that followed. Eventually it was announced that the City was to
purchase a large building from the estate of S. Lamoureux in Maillardville and the matter was settled. Furious debates, accusations of
"railroading" and the threat of lawsuits resulted. At one meeting, a Burquitlam proponent, referring to the pre 1913 status as the District of
Coquitlam declared:

*"the West End sat on the tailboard while the Junction drove the team.
This is now being done by Maillardville!" A resident of Maillardville,
Mr. Beaulieu stated that "It was impossible now for that settlement
(Maillardville) to incorporate with Fraser Mills, as an application to do
so had already been refused" (Coquitlam Star)*

Later, it was discovered that the Lamoureux property, which had been
purchased from the Canadian Western Lumber Company, was not held
in free title and came with land use restrictions. Council Chambers was
not listed among the permitted uses. Council asked the management of
CWLC to waive that clause but they refused. In the end, temporary offices were located in the house of Police Chief Émeri Paré, to the dismay
of some citizens from Burquitlam. On September 17, 1913, the Star reported:

"Municipal Offices Found In Maillardville"   *At a meeting held on
Saturday afternoon the special committee appointed by the Coquitlam
Municipal Council to secure temporary administration headquarters for
the Municipality selected two rooms in Chief of Police Paré's house at
Maillardville. Inclusive of light and fuel $15 a month will be paid for the
place. The rental also includes the fire hall and stables for Municipal
police horse, both of which stand on Mr. Paré's property."*

This arrangement was in place until the first City Hall was built in 1920 at the corner of Brunette Avenue and Marmont Street.

Is the statement noted above: *"It was impossible now for the settlement to incorporate with Fraser Mills as an application to do so had already been refused"* evidence that the residents of Maillardville sought to incorporate as a part of Fraser Mills? Is this the source of Maillardville's alleged attempt to incorporate on its own? Were their solicitations declined? Do that and the mill management's failure to waive the land use clause on the Lamoureux property suggest that the new Municipality of Fraser Mills was not keen to have Maillardville as an established "City Centre" encroaching on its borders?

By October of 1912, the effort by Fraser Mills to incorporate was well under way, and the idea that Maillardville would remain a part of the new District of Coquitlam was, apparently, a given. The Star reporting on Fraser Mills progress on October 30, 1912:

"The required notice has now been published of the proposal to incorporate Fraser Mills as a Municipality. Outside of ``Frenchtown`` or Maillardville as it is more properly called, which contains about 85 families, the population of the Company`s domain is very considerable...Maillardville will remain as it is now a portion of the Municipality of Coquitlam".

Were there other reasons that Fraser Mills might have declined a proposal to accept Maillardville as a part of their new Municipality? The likely reason is that it may not have been technically possible for the two areas to merge. When the Fraser River Lumber Company bought District Lot 46 in 1909 in order to provide land for the newcomers, the transaction was never registered. On paper at least, neither Fraser Mills nor the French settlers owned the land. The matter of registration would be resolved later in 1913, but this may have been an impediment to Maillardville`s failed attempt to merge with Fraser Mills if that attempt was actually made. In addition, the Fraser Mills land itself was a part of New Westminster while District Lot 46 was a part of the Municipality of Coquitlam.

Another possibility may have some connection with the notion that Maillardville was denied because of race. The new Municipality of Fraser Mills was unique in that it was the smallest in B.C. (500 acres approximately) and aside from a small portion that belonged to dairy farmers A. Bréhault and R. Booth, the company owned all of the land. The inclusion of an additional 85 landowners of French Catholic background who would likely band together to safe guard their interests may not have been compatible with the Company's plans.

Perhaps more clues await discovery. However, the important outcome of all of this is that Maillardville did in fact remain a part of Coquitlam and that the new City Hall was established there. New energy was provided to the growing community and its importance as the centre of Coquitlam was assured.

Meanwhile the new Municipality of Fraser Mills was seen to be in an enviable position and once again, the vision of A.D McRae was instrumental in the creation of a progressive community to be located there. The Star April 16, 1913:

"This new municipality starts out with every prospect of a bright future and if all that is promised comes true it will be an enviable place to reside in. The area incorporated is largely owned by Col. A.D. McCrae who is the principal owner of the huge lumber mills situated at that point, probably the largest mill of its kind in the world and we understand the reason for incorporation was the desire on the part of the Western Canadian Lumber Company and its employees to establish a model village at that point. Being one of the richest, most fortunate, busiest, albeit it is the smallest municipality in Canada, it offers a splendid opportunity for the carrying out of ideas which its promoters have before them. We believe that a scheme is already in hand for the laying out of the community on progressive, up to date and model lines, with a park and public sports grounds, stadium etc. It is the desire of the Company to give its employees an environment that shall be a stimulation to greater happiness and efficiency and this could only be accomplished by its incorporation."

In the aftermath of those turbulent times, the village at Maillardville was slowly consolidating. After a quick succession of priests, Father Alexandre DeLestré was assigned to the Parish and stayed from 1916 to 1929. Perhaps one of the first to feel anxious about the preservation of faith, language and culture, Father DeLestré held a very hard line when it came to the Faith, and he often admonished those whom he heard speaking English in the streets. Father DeLestré was the first "long term" priest for the French parish providing a stability and continuity that had not previously existed. However, he would eventually leave Notre Dame de Lourdes after parishioners petitioned the Archbishop of Vancouver for his removal.

The new District of Coquitlam needed to establish services such as police and fire department. In this endeavor, an early leader emerged in Émeri Paré. Many members of the Paré family had moved to the French settlement and took an active role in the life of the new community. Even before the secessions that took place in 1913, Council at Westminster Junction had already singled out Paré as a special constable. The Star reported on October 7, 1912 that:

"E. Paré and Mr. Hart were engaged as special constables at $10 per month and they will be paid 40 cents per hour when called out for duty."

Not only did Mr. Paré become the first Police and Fire Chief, he became involved in every aspect of community life. He is often referred to in the newspaper of the day as a congenial, well-liked man and many deeds of compassion and charity are ascribed to him. Johnny Dicaire, who was to become known as "Mr. Maillardville", also emerged as a real leader. He embodied the fortitude and good nature of his people. It was Father O'Boyle who had stated on his recruiting trips that he had a cure for homesickness and that it was *"fun, fun and more fun."*[8] These good humoured and high-spirited people needed little prompting. A band was formed named "Fanfare Canadienne Française de Maillardville". It was greatly anticipated and reported on regularly. The group held many euchre parties to raise funds as well as a successful "*box social*" that "*realized about $60. One box, suspected of containing exhilarating refreshment and smokes fetched $7.50*" The group eagerly awaited the arrival of their new instruments (16) from Toronto and the community looked forward to their first concert in the "moving picture hall" Even Postmaster General Pelletier offered his warm congratulations on the proficiency of such a newly formed band.

Dances were held. February 28, 1912 edition of the Coquitlam Star:

"Hier au soir a eu lieu dans la jolie colonie naissante de Fraser Mills une grande danse dans la salle de Mr. S Lamoureux. La partie a été très

---

[8] Man Magazine, 1911

réussie. On y remarquait à présence de Mr. et Mme. S. Lamoureux, Mr. et Mme. E. Beaulieu, Mr. et Mme. O. Leblanc, Mr. et Mme. E. Leblanc Mr. et Mme. Jos. Boileau, Mme. J. Dicaire, Mme. R. Boileau, Mme. P. Peterman, Mme. W. McBaine, etc. Les demoiselles Mary Anne et Bernadette Boileau, Mary et Myrtle Peterman, J. Pickering, Ernestine Gagné, Regina et Germaine Laroque, etc. etc. Messieurs J. Dicaire, L.Boileau, A.Roi, Z. Coutes, H. Albert, J. Arseno, B. Marcelin, M. McBaine, A.Bell etc. etc. Mademoiselle Alva Paré et Mr. Richard Lehoux nous ont donnés les meilleurs morceaux de leur répertoire. Les demoiselles Bernadette Boileau et Regina Gauthier sont chargées pour collecter pour l'achat de deux tableaux pour l'église de Fraser Mills."

Picnics at the nearby Booth Farm, bazaars and sports including baseball and lacrosse all contributed to what was a very rich and vibrant community life. Times were hard of course, and, according to interviews with some of the pioneers, the winters were definitely colder than today. Skating at Como Lake was not uncommon. The Fraser River occasionally froze over. After the Church burnt down in 1913, the old foundation would be flooded and made into a skating rink.

The women of the community are not to be forgotten. They were noted regularly in the Coquitlam Star for their many fund raising activities, dances and concerts in aid of the Parish as recounted in the Star February 14, 1914:

"A musical and dramatic social will be given by the ladies of Maillardville on the 17th in aid of the building fund of the new Roman Catholic Church"

In 1917 "Les Dames de Sainte Anne" was formed.

Nineteen fourteen saw the advent of World War I. Some sons of Maillardville were called to serve Canada in the "Great War" and Émeri Paré was responsible for recruiting.

The Star on August 29 and September 12, 1914:

"Although Chief Thomas and his seventy five men of Port Coquitlam have not yet shown up in New Westminster, Chief of Police Paré, of the municipality, who is a quiet and unostentatious public servant, induced

some thirty men to enroll with the 104 (New Westminster) Regiment last week." And:

"Chief of Police Paré, who has been patriotically acting as recruiting agent for the 104 Regiment at Maillardville, on Tuesday sent eight recruits including two of his sons and a brother, to New Westminster. Almost an entire company has been recruited among the French Canadians since the war started. The men are Émeri Paré, Alex Paré, Donat Paré, Richard Lehoux, Charley Lafleur, John Dicaire, Joe Parent and Zavier Desormeaux."

For those who remained, according to comments from our pioneers, life remained much as it had been. By the end of the decade, another important transformation was taking place. A commercial and social hub was consolidating in the area of Brunette and Laval. At that intersection, were located two general stores, a post office, a liquor store and a barbershop and pool hall. Tremblay Hall was the location of many of the village's social gatherings.

As Maillardville approached a new decade, it found that much had been accomplished. What had been untouched wilderness a mere ten years earlier was now a strong hub that continued to serve the needs of the French Canadian community and was, indeed, the seat of governance for the District of Coquitlam. The Fraser Mill was the economic centre of the lives of the "settlers". Maillardville had a defined core that included residences, businesses and government services. It also continued to attract new residents, many of them French.

Two schools were established as well as the Parish church around which much of the life of the community revolved. To the east of Schoolhouse Road, the Booth Farm was very much a part of life in Maillardville. A portion of that land was given over to vegetable farms from which was offered fresh produce, sold door to door by the Chinese farmers. Coquitlam City Hall was established in Maillardville. Therefore, the rapid transformation from wilderness to "French Town" to Maillardville is a striking testament to the spirit and dynamism of those men and women who braved the unknown to settle here and create a new life for themselves.

Two

The Good Old Days

The roaring twenties swept down upon North America in a tradition breaking decade of loose morals, flappers, jazz, consumerism and boosterism. But the glitz and glamour of life in the big city was a world apart from rural existence in Coquitlam. In Maillardville, the exhilaration and challenge of building the infant community gave way to a new decade that was characterized by a more rhythmic and established way of life. What did the village look like? What sounds, sights and smells filled its daily life?

To the south were the mill and the River. East of the mill, was the "oriental" town. Here were located its low-slung red buildings, cookhouses, gambling parlours and Hindu Temple. From upon the hill in Maillardville, flames from Hindu funeral pyres were a common sight. The mill whistle, heard as far as New Westminster, sounded the wakeup call early in the morning urging the shift to another workday. The smell of smoke and cedar and the sounds of heavy machinery rumbled up the hill to blend with everyday life in the village. Up King Edward came the familiar clip clop of the Clydesdale teams pulling the "Circle F" wagons delivering firewood and lumber around the community.

On the east side of town was the large dairy operation known as the Booth farm, which predated the French settlement. Here also were the gardens run by Chinese farmers, the produce sold door to door in Maillardville, Fraser Mills and other parts of Coquitlam.

29

To the west was New Westminster. The city served many of Maillard-villes's needs. Goods not to be had in the village or at Fraser Mills could be bought here. Movies, dances and beer parlours provided special occasion entertainment. In between Maillardville and New Westminster was that "other" main employer; Swift's Packing House. The Coquitlam Times reported:

"An industry of great importance is to be shifted from the New Westminster side of Brunette Creek to the Coquitlam municipality side. As is now pretty well known the Canadian Swift Packing Co. has absorbed the Vancouver-Prince Rupert Co. in the same line with its abattoir and other properties. In addition, the new concern has purchased in all about 30 acres of land in Coquitlam in an ideal situation for their purposes......Surveyors have been on the ground recently and plans and specifications are in the course of preparation for the erection of the finest and most up to date abattoir and packing plant on the Pacific Coast. Approximately the new scheme will cost from three quarters of a million to one million dollars. Some asset for old Coquitlam"

To the north was Burquitlam, a quilt work of agricultural operations, chicken farms and greenhouses that originated along the North Road built by Colonel Richard Moody. This community also predated the French settlement. The Agricultural Hall and the Vancouver Golf Club were located on Austin Avenue. Far from the isolation of the previous decade, the residents of Maillardville were becoming a part of the larger world around them. More frequent interaction with the "outside" brought new ideas and influences and helped shape Maillardville's future.

Although the village was not the rural settlement of a decade earlier, its core and commerce were still minimal. With most goods and services available either at Fraser Mills or in New Westminster, commercial development in Maillardville remained limited to the service of daily needs and to entertainment enterprises. Perhaps this is why a strong town centre with enduring architecture was never truly developed. Nonetheless, Maillardville was not without its amenities and charms. The "hub" of course consisted of Laval Square with the church, convent/school and priest's residence. Encircling the "square" were a number of charming homes with wraparound porches and balconies. The original commercial core dominated the corner of Brunette Avenue and Laval Street and included the Proulx store and post office, Pett's Meat Market, the pool hall and liquor store and Grevelyn's shoe repair. The Tremblay hall, site of much of the community's social life, stood over all.

The roads were gravel and required periodic oiling. Sidewalks, where they existed, were constructed of wood. Brunette, east and west of Laval was dotted with a growing number of large, picturesque and colourful homes. At the corner of Marmont and Brunette, a new City Hall was being built. The great arch of the Canadian Western Lumber Company framed the entrance to Fraser Mills at King Edward. On either side of King Edward Street were the stately residences of the mill manager and the mill president. Present day Mackin Park was a field where cows grazed. South of the field, the Company maintained their own baseball park. Some building, residential and commercial, was beginning to take a firm hold on Brunette west of Marmont. Before the end of the decade, this part of town would see a gas station, pool hall and bakery.

As of 1922, Canadians were required to drive on the right hand side of the road, conforming to North American standards. This change likely had little impact in Maillardville, as automobiles were few. Émeri Paré remained as Chief of Police until, in 1926, the Municipality engaged the BC Provincial Police to provide that service. Chief Paré joined this force and remained as the city's law enforcement until 1929 when the BCPP transferred him to Mission. If any doubt remains as to the extent to which this man was involved in the life of Maillardville, the Coquitlam Times in 1917 reports that at a Council meeting:

"On the motion of Councilor Mars the providing of a new auto for the Chief of Police was left in the hands of Reeve Philp and Councilor Neelands, chairman of the Finance Committee. It was considered that without an auto the chief, with his multiplicity of offices, as the municipal blacksmith, fire and police chief, jailer, dog and road tax collector, school board commissionaire, water inspector, charity commissioner-a sort of Coquitlam Pooh-Bah- would be shorn of much of his usefulness"

The measure of a community is the strength of its institutions. They are the pillars that serve as its foundation and framework. When sheathed and clad with the good will and dedication of the people they form the strong and reliable edifice of a healthy society. Thus, the decline of a community may also be gauged by the weakening of those same institutions.

At the least, the transfer of Chief Paré to Mission was the end of an era for Maillardville. Since the inception of the new District in 1913 until his transfer, Emeri Paré was a constant in the community. Moreover, he was one of Maillardville's own; a pioneer, a French Canadian. In the late forties, in a letter to Archbishop W. Duke[9], Father O. Meunier, pastor of the newly formed parish of Notre Dame de Fatima would refer to him as:

"The famous Emery Paré, the terror of the pastors of Maillardville, the great trouble shooter..."

The history of Maillardville's cultural community is closely tied to the rise and fall of its own institutions. Perhaps the end of "in house" policing as symbolized by the work of Éméri Paré was a first step in that process.

Firefighting was still primitive and done on a volunteer basis. Late in the previous decade, three "fire stations" were set up. The Coquitlam Times 1917 reported:

"This village now boasts a volunteer fire brigade, and the following stations have been selected to more expeditiously take care of any fires that may take place. At each of these points there will be kept three hundred feet of hose, reel and other necessary equipment. No.1 shed (headquarters) will be at the Municipal offices, Pitt River Road; No. Two, corner of Begin and Cartier Streets. No. Three, on Laval Square. Each of the sheds will contain 300 feet of hose and reel and other equipment. Different fire alarms will signify to the men where they shall muster. All told, the men aggregate a dozen and will be under the command of Chief of Police Paré. Drills will be held every Wednesday evening until the brigade is pronounced efficient"

Some hydrants and standpipes were installed in the twenties but a permanent, paid fire department was still a long way into the future.

Life in the village had taken on a rhythm and charm of its own: the early morning smell of fires for cooking and heating, the mill whistle calling and the men discussing the day's events as they walked in groups to and from their shifts, horses pulling carts and Chinese vendors calling out their wares. And of course, there were the sounds of children doing what

---

[9] Archives, Roman Catholic Archdiocese of Vancouver

children have always done. Although there were many different nationalities represented, there could be no doubt that this was a French
Canadian village with its church Square and large homes built for large
families. In the background was the ubiquitous and delightful hum of the
spoken French language.

The men were employed in a variety of jobs throughout the area but Fraser Mills remained the economic nerve centre of Maillardville. The mill
had a history dating back to 1890, but until 1907, it never fully achieved
the productivity expected of it. Uncertainty in the labour force and an
elusive commitment from the Federal Government to dredge the river
for deep-water access contributed to the failure to realize its full potential.

Enter A.D McRae who, along with his consortium of investors, brought
fresh and substantial capital to the operation. And it was Alexander
Duncan McRae's organizational genius, political connections and truly
visionary presence that set the Fraser River Lumber Company on the
path to remarkable success.

McRae it was who played a key role in the creation of the Saskatchewan
Valley Land Company at the turn of the century. It was this company
that was a recognized catalyst in the populating of our Canadian prairies.
The scheme was so successful that McRae came to BC to seek opportunities to supply the booming prairies with lumber to build their towns.
And he became involved with the struggling mill on the Fraser River. In
the early years, after the company incorporated as the Canadian Western
Lumber Company, fully 80% of its product was shipped to the prairies.
With the advent of WWI, McRae was called upon to use his organizational skills in aid of the Canadian war effort. Over the years, the
management of the mill fell largely upon H.J. Mackin. Mackin rose from
the position of sales manager in 1907 to become the mill manager in
1914 and eventually president. By 1920 the Columbian newspaper, reporting on productivity statistics in the lumber industry in BC, cited
Fraser Mills as number one in productivity, nearly doubling the output of
its nearest competitor:

***"Fraser Mills Plant Produced Double Cut Of Any Other B.C. Mill"* "**
*The Canadian Western Lumber Company at Fraser Mills led the field
among British Columbia mills during 1919 in respect to cut, the Circle F
plant almost doubling the cut of any other mill in the province. No less*

*than eighty million feet of lumber was turned out last year. The nearest
competitor to this figure is the Hastings Mill with fifty million."*

On average, wages gradually rose through the decade. Nonetheless, de-
clining demand in the market, a scarcity of raw materials due to forest
fires and challenges in transportation contributed to a decrease in production and eventual wage cuts by the Crash of 1929.

In the midst of this, Maillardville continued to flourish. The location of
City Hall in Maillardville was still contentious in 1920. The Coquitlam
Times on January 10 reported the following exchange at a Council meet-
ing:

*"Opposition developed later on in the meeting when a considerable
amount of questions were leveled at the old council, who are all seeking
re-election. A ditch on Walker Road led to some discussion but the main
bugbear of the evening was the selection of the new Municipal hall site
at Maillardville. Coun. Whiting stated that he had previously gone on
record of having the people decide upon the site to which Reeve Marmont replied that the deal was carried out on a vote by the council, four
of whom were in favour of purchasing the new site opposite the Fraser
Mills entrance."*

The hall was built for a projected cost of $16,000. The Columbian re-
ported on March 29, 1920:

*"Coquitlam Hall Contract Awarded"   "Maillardville, March 29-   The
contract for the new municipal hall was let at a special meeting of the
council this afternoon. Messrs. Sloan and Harrison of New Westminster
were successful in their bid for the carpentry work. Mr. J. McKay of
South Vancouver will do the masonry work, while Spring and Sibley of
New Westminster were the successful tenderers for the plumbing and
heating. The cost of the building, which was designed be Messrs. Gardi-
ner and Mercer, will be in the neighbourhood of $16,000."*

With the seat of governance located in the heart of the former "French
Town", Maillardville's residents began to serve in local politics. In 1917,
Amédée Allard was elected as a counselor, the first in a long line of
Frenchmen who would follow. He served two terms before he tragically
lost his life in a logging accident in 1918. The Times marked his death:

"Lamentable Death Of Mr. A. Allard- Well known District Councilor Succumbs to Injury Received In Woods- Man of Sterling Worth" "To the deep regret of all who knew him Councilor Allard died in the Royal Columbian Hospital. His funeral took place this morning from Maillardville after a requiem mass in the church of Notre Dame de Lourdes...Councilor Allard met with his fatal accident on Tuesday afternoon in the Burquitlam woods whilst he was superintending a logging operation....Mr. Allard was standing on what is known as a spring board, affixed to a tree trunk some seven feet from the ground, witnessing the felling of a tree. When the tree hit the ground it hit the end of another tree lying athwart a fallen trunk at an upward angle. The force of the impact raised the butt of the transverse tree which struck with great violence the underside of the platform upon which Mr. Allard was standing, propelling the unfortunate gentlemen into the air. In his fall he must have struck some obstacle, for it was found later that he has a broken bone in his neck and badly injured his spine. The lower part of his body was paralyzed....The deceased leaves a widow and grown up family. He was a native of Montreal and came to Maillardville several years ago. He was a gentleman in every sense of the word. His shrewd and kindly humour made him popular with all with whom he had dealings. His absence at the Coquitlam Council table will be deeply regretted, for there was no man better liked and respected."

George Proulx also entered the political arena and was elected Reeve in 1923. Increasing traffic on the Pitt River "corridor" from Port Coquitlam, Essondale and Colony Farm en route to New Westminster brought new concerns for Council under the watch of Reeve Proulx. The Coquitlam Times reported in 1923 that:

"The 60% share of the expense of maintaining the Pitt River Road between New Westminster and Port Coquitlam was represented to the government heads in Victoria as a manifest injustice by Reeve Proulx and a deputation from Coquitlam municipal council last week. The points emphasized by the Reeve are that a great part of the traffic passing over the western end of the Road was from Fraser Mills, a separate municipality, that government owned land on each side of that portion of the highway and paid no taxes of course. That 50% of the traffic originated at the eastern end from Essondale, another government owned institution, Colony Farm ditto, which also contributed no taxes....The reeve reported that his arguments appeared to impress Dr. Sutherland, Minister of Public Works who promised them careful consideration with

his colleagues. The plea of the Reeve that the government should maintain the road without burdening the Municipality will also be deliberated..."

In addition, E. Girard served as councilor for much of the decade and Tom Allard was elected in 1929.

Businesses such as the Proulx Store, Pett's Meat Market and Thrift's Groceries thrived. The story of Henry Pett is noteworthy. An immigrant from England, he spoke not a word of French. He, his family and their Saint Bernard dogs set up shop in the heart of Maillardville in 1919. They not only succeeded but their business flourished until 1947. Henry Pett also held the distinction of owning the first neon store sign in Coquitlam. Bewildered residents, at first seeing this new technology, reported that the building was on fire!

Mr. Pett was not the only non-French to do business here. The Chinese farmers were very much a part of the economic scene in Maillardville. They went about town selling vegetables and fish and offering laundry services. The most well known and fondly remembered from that community is Lum King, from the "west side" of Maillardville. King Street is named for him.

The daily life of Maillardville's residents was coloured by many "non francophone" encounters. But the social, cultural and religious life continued to be the glue that bound the community and the rock upon which its Francophone heritage was founded. All of these elements were bound together on the most intimate level-one did not exist without the other.

The Church continued to play a central role and by the end of the decade, the burgeoning Paroisse Notre Dame de Lourdes was outgrowing the second church building. Maillardville continued to follow the traditions of the Catholic Church and expressed its devotion through the celebration of significant religious events. Christmas Eve (midnight) Mass was followed by "la reveillon". This was a celebration that included traditional food such as tourtières, singing and music and above all a meeting of family and friends. Processions honouring "Le Fête Dieu" the "Blessed Sacrament" and celebrations for the children's first communion were traditions that endure to this day. These colourful and elaborate processions began from the Square and proceeded around the village, stopping to visit with parishioners who had decorated their house for the occasion. The school and its children were an integral part of community life. The boys were recruited as altar servers and the children entertained with concerts and plays. One such event is reported here from the Coquitlam Times:

"A bilingual concert and variety entertainment was given by the pupils of the Convent school on Monday night. Gauthier's hall was crowded and the children showed marvelous talent in their musical numbers and dramatic sketches. The acrobatic feats of a young gentleman not 6 years of age gave the audience fits. They ranged from ring performances to tumbling to standing on his head and walking on his hands. Rev. Father DeLestré thanked the audience in French and English for their presence and encouragement"

But all was not well at Notre Dame de Lourdes. Growing dissatisfaction with Father DeLestré's pastoral leadership eventually resulted in a request to Archbishop Casey and Father W. O'Boyle for his removal. In a letter dated May 1, 1926 and signed by 22 parishioners, it was stated that[10]:

"there has been a general dissatisfaction, with the exception of five or six families, for the last three years, spiritually, financially and faithfully."

Allegations ranged from a refusal to allow a church choir, insufficient financial support for the school and a lack of opportunity for parishioners to participate in the financial decision making of the parish. This may have been a particularly sore point with some of the original settlers as a committee under DeLestré's predecessor, Father E. Garon, in fact, helped govern the parish.

Apparently no action was taken and in February of 1929, another appeal was forwarded, this time to the newly appointed coadjutor Bishop W.M. Duke. Interestingly, the document opens with a statement about the authors themselves:

"Your Grace, We the undersigned French Catholics, residents of Maillardville, the only "Colonie Canadienne" in this protestant province, desire to bid you welcome among us…"

---

[10] Archives, Roman Catholic Archdiocese of Vancouver

The letter goes on to describe some of the long-standing concerns the majority of parishioners had regarding Father DeLestré and adds a respectful request to remove him from the parish. The desired change still did not take place and it took a final, more strongly worded letter, this time signed by 134 parishioners, to finally accomplish their goal:

"Nous soussigné, paroissiens de Maillardville, sommes convaincu être priver de nos droits come paroissiens, et voyant et sachant que la situation deviant déplorable et dangereuse pour nos enfants par le surexcitement des esprits en ce moment, donc pour le bien-être de cette paroisse, tout qu'au point de vue spirituel et matériel, et en plus pour faire cesser cette propogande de haines et de malice contre les uns et les autres, causé sous la direction du Rév. A.L. DeLestré, curé ici. Nous vous demandons et insistons auprès de Votre Grace de retirez d'ici le Père DeLestré.

Les signatures ci-inclu sont convaincu que cette procédure seule sera effective, nous espérons que vous ne tolererez pas cette guerre paroissiales, qui déja est connu parmi toute la Province."

"We the undersigned, parishioners of Maillardville, are convinced that we have been deprived of our rights as parishioners, and seeing and knowing that the situation is becoming deplorable and dangerous for our children by the highly charged spirit of this time, for the well-being of this parish from the point of view of both the spiritual and material, and also to put an end to this propaganda of hatred and malice against each other caused under the direction of Rev. A.L. DeLestré, pastor here. We request and insist that Your Grace remove from here, Father DeLestré.

The signatures here included are convinced that only this action will be effective, we hope that you will not tolerate this parish war, which is already known throughout the Province."

Father DeLestré was finally removed and replaced by Father F.X. Teck.

The social life of Maillardville expressed itself in varied ways. The Tremblay Hall at the NE corner of Laval and Brunette provided the venue for many activities from dances to weddings, and picture shows to boxing matches. Weddings were celebrated more or less by open invitation as everyone knew everyone else. One practice at the time was to impose the "chivaree" upon the newlyweds. The point of this particular exercise was to employ whatever means necessary to keep the bride and groom up all night thus denying them the consummation of their newly formed union. Although it was a hardship for the newlyweds, it was considered an insult if this particular tradition was not observed.

The Fraser Mills baseball team, the Circle F team, was a regular source of excitement not only for the locals but also for fans from all around "Greater Vancouver". Sundays saw packed attendance at the Fraser Mills ballpark. In fact, Mill management imported "ringers" from the States to stock their team. These men were hired at the mill, but did little work. Sending one of their own down in the morning, he would punch the clock for all of them. Clearly, a winning team was of great importance to the movers and shakers of the day.

Picnics at Ralph Booth's farm also formed a part of the most cherished memories of so many of the original settlers. These gatherings were opportunity for shared food, music, games, races and romantic encounters for the young.

The wilderness and clear running streams provided much opportunity for hunting, fishing and swimming. In the village itself, throughout much of the previous decade and well into the twenties, Maillardville had its own grand master of entertainment, Arcade Paré. Organizing musical and dramatic productions was his particular passion. Writing and producing most of his own material, he contributed to the preservation of French culture in Maillardville.

Billiards was also a popular pastime. Two halls were located at the hub. There was also a barbershop, liquor store and confectionary. Louis Boileau cut many a head of hair in his shop. He is reported to be of the "old school" of the rough handling barber, but by all accounts, he was indeed a kindly gentleman. Later, a third pool hall would be located at the west end of Brunette.

On the subject of liquor, Maillardville was not exempt from the effects of prohibition in BC from 1917 to 1921. According to several pioneers, moonshine from clandestine stills was not unknown and the Chinese Town could always be relied upon to provide prime bootleg whiskey. An interesting side note is that in Canada, prohibition was a provincial concern. It is a small insight into the French Canadian Catholic population of Maillardville to know that the Catholic Church in BC was opposed to prohibition (they favoured a general regulation of alcohol instead) and that the province of Quebec never did impose it. Sacramental wine for the Church and alcohol for medicinal purposes were exempt. A study of the period revealed that doctors' prescriptions for medicinal alcohol went up significantly during those years. In any case, prohibition in BC defined alcohol as over a 2.5% content. This gave rise to a product that was sold in Maillardville as "Near Beer"... beer under 2.5% alcohol!

Life in Maillardville throughout the twenties appears to be one of relative peace and contentment. Indeed, in the recollections of many, a commonly expressed sentiment is "Those were the good old days". Life unfolded in a pleasant way. People were friendly and ready to lend a hand. A close-knit community had developed that individuals relied upon. Yet as the decade ended, the fortitude of the people was about to be tested by the hardship of the "hungry thirties".

Three

Strike and Depression:
A Community Comes Together

In spite of the crash of 1929 and the onset of the Great Depression, the thirties were, ironically, also a period of growth and revitalization for Maillardville and the French community. The Canadian gross national product plummeted by 40% in the first years of the Depression and unemployment soared to 27%. This dark time in Canadian history spurred a chain of events in Maillardville that galvanized the French community and brought new life to it.

The deepening gloom of the early thirties was not able to completely dampen the spirit of the villagers. People continued to socialize, play sports and work as and where they could. The life of the Church community not only survived the decade, but also saw strengthening and growth. Young couples were married in the Church, children baptized. One such occasion, the wedding of Romeo Couture (son of pioneer Louis Couture) to Olida Messier in 1930:

"A pretty wedding took place on Wednesday morning in the Church of Our Lady of Lourdes when Miss Olida Messier, daughter of Mr. and Mrs. Zoel Messier, became the bride of Mr. Roméo Couture, son of Mr. and Mrs. Louis Couture, Brunette Street East. The ceremony was performed by Rev. Father F.X. Teck. The bride, who entered the church with her father to the strains of Mendelssohn's wedding march played by Miss Bertha Marcellin was attired in white crepe de chine and georgette, with hat to match and carried a bouquet of white carnations

and sweet peas. Miss Juliette Couture, sister of the groom, who was bridesmaid, wore a gown of pink crepe de chine and georgette, with hat to match, and carried a bouquet of pink carnations and sweet peas. Mr. Exias Messier, brother of the bride was best man. During the service in the church which was attractively decorated with white roses, ferns and sweet peas, solos were sung by Mrs. W. Dicaire, Mrs. Joe Sauvé, Mrs. R. Bellerose and Miss G. Thomas. Mr. and Mrs. Romeo Couture will take up residence on Nelson Road."

Circle F baseball was still a popular diversion and followed closely in the papers. The Columbian, September 11, 1931:

"FRASER MILLS AND CAFE MEET ON WEDNESDAY   Fraser Cafe and Fraser Mills will meet in the second contest of the three game series for the city senior B baseball championship and the Homer Leash cup Thursday evening. The game will be at Queen's Park at 5:45pm Fraser Mills won the first game by one run. The box score of the initial contest follows."

That box score showed the game was won by Circle F, 5-4 with Boileau scoring two runs, LeRoux and Sauvé with one apiece.

Nonetheless, Maillardville would not be spared the trials of the depression. An early consequence of it was that Fraser Mills, the mainstay of Maillardville's financial livelihood, fell on bad times. With few orders on its books, management initiated a series of wage cuts that eventually led to the strike of 1931.

The strike of 1931

It is important to note the context within which the strike took place. Wage cuts brought on by a worsening economy, unsafe work conditions and no overtime pay all contributed to discontent among the workers at Fraser Mills, making it fertile ground for action. The twenties and thirties were also a time of heightened activity for the Communist Party of Canada. The drive to organize labour swept North America, driven in large part by communist interests. The lumber industry of the Pacific Northwest and BC was a particular target of these forces. As one might expect, there was a serious backlash to this movement by government, business and the Catholic Church. There is no doubt that outside forces instigated the Fraser Mills strike. According to an interview[11] with Harold Pritchett, a key strike organizer, it was at a meeting in New Westminster in early 1931 that the plan to organize and strike at Fraser Mills found its beginning:

"Executives of the Lumber and Sawmill Workers Union came out from Vancouver and distributed a leaflet at the gate when we were coming out of work and the leaflet called for a meeting at the Labour Temple in New Westminster behind the courthouse and set the time and date. And I went to that meeting. And one of the members of the executive...called the meeting to order and made a short speech on the importance of organizing a union. I would judge about 50 or 60 Fraser Mills workers showed up at the meeting...I walked to the front and signed the first card and all the rest followed. That was in the early part of 1931."

Pritchett himself allegedly had close ties to the Communist Party of Canada, although he denied membership. After several meetings, the recruitment of members and the formation of a strike committee headed by Pritchett, the fledgling union was ready for action. On September 16, 1931, they presented a list of demands in the name of the Lumber and Agricultural Workers' Industrial Union (affiliated with the Communist controlled Workers Unity League). They included a 10% wage hike, equality in wages regardless of marital status or race, and above all, recognition of the union. The owners and shareholders, represented by H.J. Mackin, refused all demands. On September 17, the workers went on strike. The Columbian Daily ran the headline:

*"**Big Fraser Mills Plant Closed as Men Call Strike**   700 workers idle and Company Management states that no attempt will be made to resume operations--Walk Out follows unsuccessful attempt by Employees to secure wage increase after series of slashes--Firm contends Vancouver Agitators responsible--One man dragged from vehicle by Crowd--Automobile of H.J. Mackin stoned--Many Police dispatched to Mount guard--Members of Unemployed Organization active in Proceedings."*

Throughout the strike, support from other trade unions was actively sought and given. Mass demonstrations by hundreds of the workers and their families in front of City Hall and at the mill gates highlighted the strike. Many on the picket line were unemployed workers from Vancou-

---

[11] Vancouver Oral History Project

ver. The strike was also marred by early violence and the arrest of ten people, including four from Maillardville.

The spectre of the "Red threat" was a tool used by both management and the Church in an effort to get the men back to work. In addition to the alleged ties Harold Pritchett had to the Communist Party (he would later run as a candidate for them in a federal election), an interview[12] with a native of Maillardville states that there were some thirty local residents who became card-carrying members of that party. The priest at Our Lady of Lourdes, Father F. X. Teck, apparently preached against the evils of communism, exhorting his parishioners to turn in their union cards. Failing this, Father Teck refused to offer Sacramental absolution. According to Pritchett, this difficulty for the many Catholics among the strikers was overcome by sending the men to the church in Sapperton. The priest there had agreed to hear their confessions.

After the early violence and arrests, a large contingent of armed police, both foot and mounted, were brought in to keep the peace and remained for most of the strike.

Because only union members could participate, the initial strike vote was taken among only 210 of the mill workers from a potential of around 650. The vote was 130 to 80 in favour. Mackin pointed out that this represented about 20% of the workers and called for a secret strike ballot to be taken. After initial agreement by the strike committee, the members chose not to participate. The company went ahead with the ballot, but it failed miserably with only109 votes cast. Of these 104 were in favour of a return to work. Of those who voted, forty were white men and the rest Orientals. The union ignored the vote. Membership in the union quickly grew. On October 7, the Company softened its stance and proposed the following settlement as reported in the Columbian:

"...upward adjustments An increase in the rate for shingles by 2 cents a thousand on #1 shingles and 3 cents a shingle on #3. The manufacturing plants to work not more than 48 hours a week for any one month. The Company to meet a committee of its own employees to discuss matters affecting its men at any time...." But on October 10:

---

[12] Vancouver Oral History Project

"MILL OFFER REJECTED BY STRIKERS-- *Statement from strike headquarters asserts "Vote showed workers 100% against accepting terms"...Decision made after inflammatory speech"*

The Company thus began preparations to shut down the mill indefinitely. Office staff was given notice and an estimated 350 men from logging camps supplying the Mill were put out of work. The strike committee leveled various accusations at Canadian Western management and Mackin denied these in a statement to the papers on October 31. A significant portion of that text from the Columbian newspaper is included here not to skew the reader's bias but rather as a convenient method of presenting some of the issues brought forward:

"...On September 16 at 9:30 in the morning, the company was presented with certain demands, as per copy attached. The company was unable to meet these demands. The union referred to, we understand, was only at that time being organized, and the company could not consider recognizing the union, and the following morning the plant was picketed by several hundred men, largely from Vancouver, and men who, we are now given to understand, were members of some unemployed union. At the first meeting of the committee of the strikers, it was stated by their chairman that the strike vote calling out our employees was 130 for the strike and 80 against, which clearly shows that less than 20% of our employees voted for this strike...It is not now claimed by anyone that the standard of wages which we are prepared to pay the men is lower than the wages prevailing at other mills, and in fact the wages, generally speaking, are higher than those prevailing at many of the mills and are substantially higher than are being paid at a great many mills at in the states of Washington and Oregon...For the past six months this company has been operating at a tremendous loss and were the company's officials only considering the 3500 shareholders who own this company, the manufacturing plants would have been shut down some time ago, but the company has felt a responsibility for employing as many men as possible during this severe depression, and at a sacrifice of the shareholders interest, has continued to operate and was willing to continue further, but of course could not continue indefinitely to pay out one dollar for every 90 cents it receives. Many mis-statements have been made in connection with some of the details of this company's operations....the strike committee has stated that men were working here for as low as 14 cents an hour, but when the names of the parties have been supplied, we have found in every case the strike committee's information was not only in-

correct, but in most cases maliciously incorrect. Further it has been stated that we have an Oriental contract system. This is wholly untrue- we have no contract system whatever. The question has also been raised as to the rental charged for Orientals, particularly one Mari Yama. The facts are that this man has a four or five room house and his rental depends on the hours that he works averaging 6 to 8 dollars per month. For this he secured free of charge electric light, water and fuel. In connection with the other Orientals, we charge what is about the equivalent of 4 cents per hour on their labour for rent which includes free of charge electric light, water and fuel...As a matter of fact, apart from probably half a dozen Orientals, there has been no complaint on the part of the Orientals...This company also operates a general store for the convenience of its employees and it has been stated that the company has insisted on its employees trading at the store...at no time has any employee of this company been requested to trade at the company store...As the situation exists today, the company has no orders on its books and it is very doubtful whether the plant could secure orders with which to operate were a settlement effected. I am attaching hereto, for your information, a copy of the offer made by the company."

Negotiations continued for a time, but the position of the strike committee was weakening. Another vote was taken on November 21. The result was an overwhelming decision in favour of terminating the strike. The mill resumed operation on December 1, 1931. They had gained little. In fact, they settled for what had been offered on October 7th. Even this small victory would soon fade. A letter dated June 13, 1932 from the company directed Mackin to:

"...substantially reduce wages and salaries of all employees of the company and all other expenses will have to be reduced to a minimum."

Ultimately, some of the strike leaders were "blacklisted", a particularly hard fate during the depression. A partial roll of those blacklisted includes many members of the French community...J. Dicaire, R.Marcelin, J.Chabot, L.Canuel and A.Laverdure. The decade saw several more demonstrations and another strike at Fraser Mills but none like this first attempt at organizing labour in September of 1931. Fraser Mills' management eventually recognized the union. Harold Pritchett himself went on to become the first president of the International Woodworkers of America.

Although little was gained in terms of concessions to the workers' demands, it was a first step in the effort to organize the lumber industry in BC. The strike is also remarkable for its galvanizing effect on the French community of Maillardville. French Canadian solidarity was evident from the earliest beginnings of the French settlement. They were not only tightly bound by language, culture and religion, but they were tied even further by intermarriage. The strike enjoyed widespread support among the workers at Fraser Mills. However, the organization and life of the strike coalesced around the close-knit group in Maillardville. Support for the strike came in many different forms. According to Harold Pritchett, the strikers received donations of money as well as goods from sources across Canada and the US. The women ran a soup kitchen on Cartier Avenue. It was supplied with vegetables and fish from the local Oriental community and by farmers from around British Columbia's Lower Mainland. The strength of the group was also manifested by the actions of the women. They took part in the regular mass demonstrations that occurred in front of City Hall, went into Vancouver on "bumming" expeditions to raise strike funds, and made presentations at City Hall. Mrs. Y. Hammond appeared before Council on October 26, 1931 on behalf of a large delegation and council minutes records the following:

"A large delegation of Ratepayers and residents attended the meeting. Mrs. Y. Hammond addressed the Board on behalf of the delegation and made the following demands:

1. Relief for all unemployed at five days per week at Union wages, or if no work available the equivalent in cash

2. Free housing, light, fuel, water and clothing for all workers and dependents.

3. That no one destitute be imprisoned or deported.

4. Non contributing state insurance for unemployed.

5. Absolute and non conditional and immediate release and charges withdrawn of all class war prisoners...."

It is difficult to measure the intangible effects that the strike of 1931 had on the community. The event, for some, remained a vivid defining point in the life of Maillardville. Council minutes show that delegations headed by people from Maillardville appeared regularly before Council for the remainder of the decade, pleading the cause of the unemployed and destitute. In this, perhaps one outcome of the strike was to bring the community ever more tightly together to meet the trials of the Depression and the cultural threat that loomed as thousands came to the west coast in search of work.

Maillardville during the Depression knew privation yet, overall, fared better than many. In spite of labour unrest, the Mill remained open throughout the thirties. Many were able to supplement low wages by growing their own vegetables and by hunting and fishing. Gathering bark to be sold at Buckerfield's for 12 cents per pound was a common activity. Trapping licenses were granted and muskrat pelts could be sold for 25 cents each. The soup kitchen remained open after the strike and offered aid not only to its own community, but also to those drifters who wandered in from other parts of the country. Those who had no means of income were granted relief in exchange for labour. Single unemployed men had to go to the relief camps, also known as "prison camps". Relief was not granted automatically. In addition to having no means of income, one was not permitted to own or operate certain items while on relief. For example, when E. Leroux asked at a council meeting why his relief had been cut off, council responded:

"Councilor Clark explained that he was operating a motor vehicle and that he had held up his cheque. Mr.Leroux said his wife had bought the car for 15 dollars while he was working at the Fraser Mills. moved by Co. Sipprell, sec. by Co. Hart that no one on relief be permitted to operate an auto without the permission of the Chairman of the Relief Committee. Carried".

Although some in Maillardville really fell on hard times, many who lived through it recalled the Depression years as a time of poverty but not destitution. The strength of the French community again proved its value, as family and neighbours pulled together to make the times as bearable as possible. The Church remained the focal point of the community. Many of the men were members of the Catholic Order of Foresters. This item appeared in the Columbian September 11, 1931:

"Stanley Lamoureux was installed as chief ranger of St. Anne's Court of the Catholic Order of Foresters at the election of officers held at the home of Mr. L.A.Paré, Laval Square September 2. The other officers

elected were secretary A.Sabourin, Treasurer L. Duplin, speaking con-
ductors Dan Amero, H. Racine and L. Racine. L.A. Paré is state officer
and Rev.Father F.X. Teck is chaplain. The society consists of 50 adult
members. Many new juvenile members have been enrolled. After the
business of the meeting the wives of the members entertained at a jolly
social."

The Order of Foresters engaged in charitable activity in the Parish, but a
key value offered by the National organization was a group insurance
scheme. Given the date of the above-mentioned meeting, it is intriguing
to consider the possibility that Fr. Teck promoted this movement in response to what he may have known about the coming attempt to
organize labor at the mill.

The women continued to work for the parish through Les Dames de Ste.
Anne. The school was flourishing with upwards of 200 children enrolled
and as many as ten Sisters of the Child Jesus teaching them. Sr. Augustin
served continuously from 1917 to 1950 and became known as "Ange de
la Paroisse" ("Angel of the Parish").

After the difficulties of the 1931 strike, Father Teck continued his work
among the people, appearing several times before Council in support of
parishioners in need. He also lobbied for other interests. In September
1938, foreshadowing the school strike of 1951, Father Teck appeared
before Council asking for the provision of schoolbooks. The Coquitlam
Herald describes the response he received:

"Father Teck spoke on a petition which was largely signed by Roman
Catholic Ratepayers. The petition requested that council make a grant or
supply school books to children attending separate schools. There are
200 children attending. The Council held it was out of their jurisdiction
so were unable to do so."

Still, there were those who truly suffered, especially in the early thirties.
The names of Pritchett, Lanoue, Laverdure and Hachey appear regularly
in Council minutes, pleading for individuals or presenting demands on
behalf of the National Unemployed Workers Association. In April, 1932,
a special Council meeting was held at the request of the NUWA. It was
moved that the following telegram be sent to the Provincial Secretary:

"Referring to our letter of the 20th inst., to the Provincial Secretary, 111 families with 309 dependents without food, Municipality has no funds, What are we to do, Advise, Urgent."

The Great Depression saw its darkest days in the early to mid-thirties but the struggle to survive lingered throughout the decade. One consequence of these times was to open the floodgates to what is sometimes called the Great Migration. Canadians in other parts of the country, and particularly those on the prairies suffering the additional trial of severe drought began an exodus in search of work. This prompted a wave of migration from these hard hit areas to the west coast that continued through World War II and into the fifties. Naturally, people who were farmers were attracted to the rural life found in Coquitlam. Thus began a new influx of people into Maillardville. Indeed, the French village attracted many of their own during this time, bringing new life and vigour to the community. However, many others also came to settle here. We will see later that as this phenomenon continued over the decade, it gave rise to new movements and institutions designed specifically to protect the French culture.

Life in thirties Maillardville unfolded in a surprising way. Because of hardship and deprivation, the workers were actively organizing to protect their rights, the Church community flourished and the village was experiencing a burst of new growth. Council minutes show that there were continual requests for the subdivision of properties, for new roads to be built and for old ones to be either hard topped or oiled. Moreover, the growing town put more and more pressure on an inadequate infrastructure. The regional medical officer, Dr. Cannon, in his annual report of 1938, condemns the overburdened septic system as unacceptable as effluent bubbled to the surface and found its way into open ditches. This dangerous problem is mentioned many times in Council minutes. Serious illness was also a concern as reported by Doctor Cannon in his 1936 summary:

"showed that there had been considerable scarlet fever, some twelve families having been affected, 8 cases of mumps and 1 of typhoid. The water supply was good but the sewerage was very poor."

The water supply system got a passing grade from the Doctor, but the delivery system was also hard pressed. It is often reported that six, eight or in one case twelve buildings were supplied by a single half inch line.

The French Canadians continued to be active in politics. Tom Allard, following his father's example, served on council throughout the thirties. In 1935, Councilor Allard was given responsibility for:

"organizing a volunteer fire brigade and purchase a siren, expense not to exceed $75."

He was defeated in his bid to unseat Reeve R.C. Macdonald in 1938, by a vote of 536 to 384. Allard and Councilor Thomas Douglas both supported of the strikers in 1931. The community was shocked when Mr. Douglas was shot and killed at his gas station on North Road July 13, 1934. The killer, a man known to Mr. Douglas, had apparently first gone in search of Harold Pritchett and not finding him home, went on to the gas station. It was alleged that the killer was motivated by Douglas' "communist" sympathies. This was never proved.

During these years, Maillardville also saw a considerable increase in commerce by both builders and merchants. Among the more active builders, we can include the LeBleus, the Allards, M. Filiatreault and Ben and Fred Quadling. Father Teck should also be mentioned in the builder category, albeit as a special case. As evidence of the growth of the Parish, the church built in 1913 (present day St Anne's Hall) had become inadequate. In 1929, a structure was built upon the original church foundation. This served as the main church for a time. It became the basement of the present day church that Father Teck designed and had built and was consecrated in 1938. The BC Catholic reported November 12, 1938:

*"**New Church Blessed At Maillardville**   One of the most beautiful little Churches in the Archdiocese of Vancouver dedicated to "Our Lady of Lourdes" was blessed last Sunday at the historic town of Maillardville by His Excellency Archbishop Duke... At the conclusion of the Mass His Excellency congratulated Rev. Fr. Teck and the parishioners of Maillardville saying in part "The beautiful Church you have erected for the worship of God and in honour of Our Lady of Lourdes will ever remain a monument of your faith, and of your work, and of your alms. It is a beautiful, solid and useful construction of which all of you can justly feel proud."... Rev. Fr. Teck was the recipient of hundreds of congratulations. This being his seventh successful attempt to finance and build a Church"*

Service enterprises began to multiply as well. The Quadling brothers opened "Home Gas" at Quadling's Corner, while Al Best provided competition with Standard Oil opening in 1936 at 945 Brunette. The decade also saw the establishment the Wood's and the Jubilee Hotels. The Filiatreault barbershop now became something of a beauty salon with the arrival of Anne Protheroe. Anne, as all would know her for many decades, eventually bought the entire operation and established Trev's Fountain Lunch, named for her husband. Trev's became a true community icon. Besides delicious coffee and pies and the availability of an amazing array of sundries, Anne "did hair" for several generations of women wanting to look their best for those special occasions.

Harry Thrift not only provided the services of his store for Maillardville but also took part in the life of the community itself. Mr. Thrift would often transport groups of young people to dances held at the agricultural hall in Burquitlam. While there, he provided free hot dogs and coffee and then drove everyone back home. In time, Harry Thrift would emerge as a real pillar of the Maillardville community.

Lest we give the impression that Maillardville was becoming "New York West", it must be pointed out that life in this little corner of the world was still very much rural. Council meetings could be amusing at times. Here it was that citizens voiced their concerns and opinions. For example, there was a demand from "seven determined women" complaining that a certain dairyman's cows were being left to roam freely on Cartier Avenue. The cows were grazing and otherwise trampling their lawns. Then there was the gentleman from Alderson Avenue who asked if it was:

"lawful to use eighty two sticks of powder to blast a stump. A neighbor had done so and a big chunk of wood had been blown onto his place injuring his little girl's knee. Constable to notify him not to do it again."

A clue is also provided to the never-ending question of "borders" in Maillardville. The Herald of September 1935, reporting on a Council meeting discussing insurance rates:

"...a reduction of 15 cents a hundred would be granted west of Nelson Street. East of Nelson, the village of Maillardville, the same rate would be continued but no extra charge would be made where new buildings were erected."

It appears that the city in 1935 considered the western boundary of Maillardville to be Nelson Street, representing an expansion west of Marmont from the original 1912 subdivision.

Finally, the passing of some of our pioneers was noted in the Coquitlam Herald and included an obituary for Théodore Théroux in 1938:

"Théodore F. Théroux, 75, passed away on Wednesday at the Royal Columbian Hospital. Mr. Théroux was one of the founders of the French Canadian Colony of Maillardville. He was night chief at Essondale Mental Hospital for 23 years, retiring three years ago. He is survived by his wife, one daughter, Yvonne, and three sons George, Albert and Arthur, all at home. High Requiem Mass will be celebrated by Rev. Father Finnegan, at 9am Saturday at St. Peter's Church. Internment in St. Peter's Cemetery, New Westminster."

The tide of life in Maillardville ebbed and flowed. Its people, bound by their common dreams and aspirations, faced the challenges of the times as a strong and unified community. As the thirties ended, the economy began to accelerate and the Big Mill went into full production once again. Nevertheless, the dawning light of hope was soon dimmed by the approaching darkness of World War II.

Figure 1 A.D. McRae

Figure 2 First church c. 1910

Figure 3 Father Edmond Maillard

Figure 4 Father W.P. O'Boyle

Figure 5 Picnic at the Booth Farm

Figure 6 Théodore Théroux

Figure 7 Émeri Paré, First Chief of Police

Figure 8 First Municipal Hall, Paré house

Figure 9 Marching band

Figure 10 Boileau pool hall

Figure 11 Johnny Dicaire, c. 1916

Figure 12 Oriental Town, Fraser Mills

Figure 13 Oriental Town, Fraser Mills

Figure 14 Entry to Fraser Mills

Figure 15 H.J. Mackin

Figure 16 Millworker, Fraser Mills

Figure 17 Millside train station

Figure 18 Fire brigade c. 1915

Figure 19 Émeri Paré, police car

Figure 20 Father E. Garon

Figure 21 General Store

Figure 22 Nuns O.L. of Lourdes Parish

Figure 23 Coquitlam Rangers

Figure 24 A. Allard

Figure 25 George Proulx

Figure 26 Arcade Paré

Figure 27 Johnny Dicaire & family

Figure 28 Father A. DeLestré

Figure 29 Hockey on church foundations

Figure 30 Arcade Paré

Figure 31 Circle F baseball

Figure 32 Pett's Meat Market

Figure 33 Maillardville Post Office

Figure 34 Fraser Mills Store

Figure 35 Wood's Hotel

Figure 36 Second church c. 1913

Figure 37 Church c. 1937

Figure 38 Municipal Hall

Figure 39 Early Pitt River Road

Figure 40 Procession

Figure 41 Procession

Figure 42 Fraser Mills strike '31   Figure 43 Fraser Mills strike '31

Figure 44 Fraser Mills strike '31   Figure 45 Fraser Mills strike '31

Figure 46 Tram at Millside

Four

The Golden Age

If ever there was a golden age in the life of Maillardville, then the dawning of it came in the mid-1940s. The great migration brought people to the west coast throughout the thirties in search of work. This trend continued into the forties as the Second World War resulted in a tremendous increase in economic activity. Military training facilities on the west coast brought others and after the war, the Veterans Land Act provided further opportunities. The dual enticements of a rural life and an established French Canadian community drew many newcomers. Many others from different cultural and religious backgrounds also came to settle here. As the decade evolved, it was characterized by the development of a dichotomy of French versus "other". This trend helped to establish Maillardville as a vibrant community but also threatened the French culture that had so far flourished unchecked. As the forties unfolded, the fears and hardships of the war years gave way to an astonishing increase in every kind of commercial and private development.

Moreover, there was a sense of urgency in the rising of civic groups, both religious and community, which leaves the impression of a sudden burst of enthusiastic and optimistic commitment to the growth of Maillardville. The French and non-French communities worked together for a better future, yet the distinction between the two remained clear. The "Frenchmen" held to their traditional way of life that centered on the Catholic Church, while "others" worked toward developing a strong economic district. While the two groups collaborated to accomplish common economic goals, French Maillardville remained a distinct entity within the Municipality of Coquitlam.

Two major themes mark the early forties. The first was the great conflagration that was World War II. The second was uncontrolled building and growth in the village brought on by an ever-increasing population.

War meant much the same for Maillardville as to any other community. Loved ones were called away to serve their country, some did not return. Rationing and coupon books and the restriction on the purchase of certain goods and materials such as tires were in effect. Maillardville had its ARP (air raid precautions) volunteers, the chief warden being Constable Jimmy McGarry. Throughout the war years, the ARP was financed solely through fund raising activities. A fully equipped ten bed emergency field hospital was set up at the church hall at Our Lady of Lourdes. Thankfully, it was never used. It is noteworthy that the ARP was responsible for bringing a volunteer fire brigade together that would later become the base for a permanent force. Gone were the hose reels. Hydrants were still scarce, but a truck was now in use and by 1946, a new station was being built next to City Hall.

The air raid siren blared for precautionary events and "blackout" would come into effect. All lights were extinguished and there was no vehicle traffic allowed except for that of ARP volunteers. Vehicles that were in use required headlight covers, a mask that allowed for a four inch by half-inch slot to allow minimal light. These precautions were taken seriously and when, during an early blackout, lights on Marmont were not immediately extinguished, protests and threats followed. Some of the men joined the Pacific Coast Rangers and went to training exercises twice a week at Hatzic Lake.

Fraser Mills went into overtime running three full shifts. Most of its product went to the U.K. The production of lumber was deemed an essential service. This meant that some men were exempt from the military. In this, Maillardville differed from some other communities. Many went to war, some stayed home and women were hired to complete the Mill's work force.

City Council also felt compelled to do their best for the war effort and so in August of 1942 the local news reported:

"Council Offers Its Blood To The Canadian Red Cross...*District of Coquitlam councilors are offering to donate to the Red Cross their blood for war purposes and believe they are the first in the Fraser Valley to do this as a complete Municipal council."*

Maillardville and Fraser Mills suffered the tribulation of the Japanese internment. In December of 1941, after the bombing of Pearl Harbour, the government required that all Japanese citizens be removed from the coastal area of BC. Consequently, properties were seized, including the entire Japanese fishing fleet of some 1337 boats. The men, women and children were taken away to internment camps in the interior of BC. Of course, Fraser Mills had their own "Japan Town". These men worked alongside the people of Maillardville. In many instances, their children played and grew up together. The sudden removal of the Japanese from Fraser Mills and Maillardville was a tragedy. Friendships were broken and there was a sense that a true injustice was being imposed upon these people. Few, if any, returned after the war.

When the war finally did end in August of 1945, there was celebrating and dancing on Brunette Avenue.

As it was during the Great Depression of the 1930s many people continued to arrive at Maillardville in search of work. Demand for increased production of goods in aid of the war effort increased the need for workers. Indeed, in a letter from Father O.A. Meunier to Archbishop Duke, dated April of 1948[13], reporting on the state of affairs at his new parish of Our Lady of Fatima, he declares that:

"You are probably well aware that French Canadians are pouring in from the prairies at an average of 1 family a week in my parish and at least 2 or 3 in Father Teck's. Many settle around in other parishes or across the river."

They came and they built! However, just as it was a decade earlier, the village's infrastructure remained overburdened. Overflowing septic systems continued to be problematic. One resident of the day had this to say:

---

[13] Archives, Roman Catholic Archdiocese of Vancouver

"raw sewage would boil over into the ditches and into the streets and the septic tanks couldn't handle the load. The kids were playing in it and such and we were quite worried about some kind of epidemic."

There were regular reports of effluent making its way into the open ditches. Council also had concerns about the large number of residents who were discharging their sink and bathwater directly into the ditches. By 1949, the problem of storm water and sewage was finally addressed;

"$81,581 Sewer Program Proposed for Maillardville
New development to serve 360 Properties in Coquitlam District.
Engineers to Make Recommendations to Council. Mr. Butler had news for the holders of 360 properties in the Maillardville area at last Monday's Municipal Council meeting. A proposal is before the board for the installation of main sewers to carry domestic waste and storm water at a cost of $81,581... A part of the cost of the development will probably be borne by the Municipality, up to one third is a possible share. The remainder of course to be borne by the holders of the proper-ties served by the service"

Probably the most visual transgression of development guidelines was the increasing number of "shacks" that were being built. Council minutes and frequent articles on the subject in the Coquitlam Herald testify to the truth of this. It is likely that during this period Maillardville acquired the unflattering nickname of "Shacktown". Usually, the "shacks" were being constructed as a temporary residence, the owners building as their re-sources allowed. On occasion, a permit was obtained for one type of development, and then something quite different would materialize. Overall, the City did not have the necessary administrative tools to deal with the sudden growth of the village. Soon councilors were calling for stricter enforcement of building permits, a zoning plan and a town plan-ning commission. By the end of the decade, much of this was accomplished.

Along with this growth came new business development. During this period, almost every commercial need was being satisfied. Gas stations and hardware stores were established in the town core. Clothing, furni-ture, appliances, groceries and more were available. There were two hotels, Bob's Burgers and eventually a theatre and bowling alley to name but a few of the entertainment offerings. This very strong commercial corridor gave rise to the founding of the Coquitlam Board of Trade, with

Maillardville's Harry Thrift as its president. A Maillardville Merchants' Association also formed and they lobbied tirelessly for improved sidewalk and lighting conditions on Brunette. Maurice Lizée, who also became involved in local politics, headed the MMA for some time.

War and building problems notwithstanding, Maillardville was becoming a more well defined and vibrant town. In 1941, H.J.Mackin of Fraser Mills was asked to consider donating the land south of Brunette for a children's playground. The secretary of the Mill proposed that the property be offered on a rental basis "*the rent being equal to the value of taxes*". Although Coquitlam rejected the proposal, they continued to improve the park with a swimming pool and concession stand. Mr. Mackin eventually pledged a personal amount to the development of the park and the land was deeded to the City of Coquitlam in 1944. The agreement stated that the land was to remain solely for the use as a playground for the children. The park now bears Mackin's name.

Other exciting developments marked the early years of the forties. For example, as early as 1941, Reeve Olivier suggested that the District should change its name to avoid confusion with that of Port Coquitlam. This example from the Herald illustrates his case:

"Stating that they are not in favour of changing the name of the City as suggested recently by the municipality, a communication from the city of Port Coquitlam was read at the last meeting of the District of Coquitlam Municipal Council...."

Eventually, through a plebiscite conducted in 1944, residents agreed that the name should be changed. A contest followed inviting citizens to enter their name suggestions. A $100 War Bond was to be the prize for the winning entry. The fruit of this effort resulted in:

*"**Coquitlam District To Pick A New Name At Polls** Representatives of Coquitlam Farmers' Institute, Meridian Heights Farmers' Institute, Burquitlam Women's Institute, Catholic Order of Foresters, French Canadian Club, Red Cross Society, Millside PTA, and the Austin Road Ratepayer's Association met in municipal hall Tuesday evening November 28 to choose a slate of suitable names for the municipality to be placed before the voters at the forthcoming election, Dec. 16. Out of the list of approximately 275 names proposed by ratepayers, each representative attending chose six and then was held on those chosen to*

determine which six names would be submitted to the voters for final determination. The six names finally chosen were Marmont, which received 6 votes, Three Rivers, 5, Austin 4, Normandy 4, Laurier 3 and Riverside 3."

When the election of 1944 took place, residents had an opportunity to vote for their choice and Riverside was the winner. It was followed closely by Normandy. Council minutes recorded the vote as "*Austin 144, Laurier 87, Marmont 184, Normandy 284, Riverside 357 and Three Rivers 50*". It was revealed at a later Council meeting that the cost of the name change would be approximately $2500. The change never took place.

Although little is reported on Our Lady of Lourdes during this early part of the forties, we know that the parish continued to grow, flourish and be a true cornerstone of Maillardville. Two noteworthy items illustrate the human journey; active and joyful youth and advancing age and life's end. In 1941 Coquitlam crowned its second May Queen, Gilberte Gamache of École Notre Dame de Lourdes.

**"Queen Gilberte Was Crowned At Coquitlam Amid Gay Scene
New Queen Delivered A Stirring Address** *Gilberte Gamache of Our Lady of Lourdes School was crowned the second May Queen of the District of Coquitlam under ideal conditions at Blue Mountain Park on May 22, before a crowd of 1000 people...heading the parade were the little flower girls Jeanette L'Heureux and Simone Grimard followed by Queen Evelyn Thacker and Reeve MacDonald, Shirley Gueho, Councilor V.Yates Queen elect Gilberte Gamache...The platform was beautifully decorated with flowers and vine maple, a large Union Jack being the background....Queen Gilberte then addressed her subjects saying:*

"My dear schoolmates of yesterday, subjects of one day only, to think of such a small and shy girl as I to have been elected Queen of the May for the district of Coquitlam. A great, great honour indeed, to be named Queen even if only for one day. Truly I would feel happier and quite more at ease to be mixed in your ranks, to take part in your drills, in your songs instead of just watching you performing them for me. All queens, true queens I mean, are far from being happy as we are today. Our Most Gracious Queen Elizabeth must feel sore at heart even if she can bestow her most sweet smile on her suffering subjects. In honour of this dear Queen of ours who rules Canada with our Glorious King

George the VI and shares his grief at this time of trial, you, my dear sub-jects will sing, perform your duties towards the little Queen of the May, who thanks you for having elected her and would be glad to hear you all shout, Long live King George and his smiling Queen; God bless them and give them victory. Long live Canada; Hail to you all Canadians as-sembled here on this lovely day."...Our Lady of Lourdes School then gave a display of physical drill followed by massed folk dancing. The seniors of Millside, Central and Mountainview performed a flag drill, then a ball drill by Our lady of Lourdes...At the banquet that followed Queen Gilberte was presented with a gold locket and chain from the May Day Committee by Councilor Yates...In the evening, the ball was opened by Queen Gilberte and the royal suite with a grand march."

Counterpointing that happy occasion is the death of Sister Marie Félicien, Principle at the convent at Our Lady of Lourdes in 1943. The Herald reported:

*"**Death of Sister Felicien** Sister Mary Felicien, Superior at Maillard-ville Convent, passed away suddenly on Tuesday July 6 1943 at 11am in the Convent. Born in Neveres France in 1874, Sister Felicien came to Canada in 1896 with three other French Sisters. Her missionary labors started at Williams Lake, Caribou, where she worked untiringly for two years for the education of the Indian children. Her next mission was North Vancouver where she worked with renewed zeal in St.Paul's Indi-an School until the opening of St. Edmund's School, North Vancouver, in 1911. Here she was a music teacher for twelve years. In 1923 she was appointed Superior of Maillardville Convent and continued there until she was replaced in 1934 for three years. During her long stay in Mail-lardville she taught music and singing, in which she especially distinguished herself. Her death has brought much sorrow to the com-munity and to her very many friends by whom her passing is deeply regretted. Requiem Mass was celebrated on Friday July 9 by Rev. Fa-ther F.X. Teck in the Roman catholic Church of Our Lady of Lourdes, Maillardville. Assisting Father Teck were Rev. Father Lacey, SM and Rev. Father Andrew O.S.B. Requiem Mass was celebrated on Thursday at 9am at the Convent of Child Jesus, North Vancouver. A large number of friends from Vancouver and the lower part of the Fraser Valley at-tended the mass. Interment was in St. Peter's Cemetery. Pallbearers were J.R.Girardi, N. Charpentier, T.Velay, E.Bohemier, N.Croteau and L.Draize."*

Parish life also included interaction with Catholics outside of Maillardville. For example, in June of 1941:

*"**Many At Mission From Maillardville**   A large number of the congregation of Our Lady of Lourdes of Maillardville attended the closing
ceremonies of the Eucharistic Congress held at St. Mary's Indian mission school at Mission..."*

As the early part of the decade came to a close, pressure on the French
community mounted. The construction of the Allard Street Baptist
Church is an example of the "encroachment" of non-French Catholic
influences in Maillardville. Nevertheless, a new wave of Frenchmen
brought to Maillardville fresh vision, excitement and energy. From the
mid-forties on, a tremendous amount of activity ushered in the stunning
growth of both Maillardville and the Catholic community. It is clear that
the French Canadians were determined to keep their language, religion
and culture alive in the face of strong pressure from Anglophone growth
in Maillardville. The short time between 1944 and 1946 saw the establishment of no fewer than three major institutions. They were Le Club
Français Canadien (soon to become a member of the FFCCB, see below), the Caisse Populaire de Notre Dame de Lourdes Credit Union and
the new Catholic Parish of Our Lady of Fatima. Each in its own way was
designed and destined to solidify and strengthen the French community
isolated as it was: a French island in an English sea.

Caisse Populaire de Notre Dame de Lourdes Credit Union: Increased
population and economic growth called for a financial institution to
serve the needs of Maillardville. Both residents and the commercial district sought to attract a bank to the village. The nearest financial
institution was in New Westminster, making banking a very inconven-
ient chore. For obscure reasons, their attempts were unsuccessful. This
article appeared in the Herald June of 1946:

*"**Credit Union Seeks Bank**   The newly formed Maillardville Credit
Union Branch is trying to have people's saving bank open in the District. Efforts to have one of the larger banks open up a branch office
have so far been unsuccessful due to unexplained reasons. The population could not be the determining factor as several smaller towns with
considerably smaller populations have bank branches operating there."*

Perhaps the reason was not so obscure to those who lived here at the time. One resident expressed his viewpoint:

"The French minority was again poorly perceived, more from ignorance than bad intentions. Moreover, the French Canadians of Maillardville had the reputation of living in "tarpaper shacks."

Whatever the true reason, the Anglophone community fared no better than the Francophone in the quest to attract a bank here. In 1946, not one but two credit unions were formed. The "District of Coquitlam Credit Union" was started primarily by the English speaking commercial and business owners of Maillardville. Reeve J. Christmas was its President. The Board of Directors included K.Olsen, E. Thirsk, F.Thirsk, Mrs. D. Philp, T. Protheroe and H. Thrift. They enjoyed a modest success. The credit union continued its quest to have a major bank open a branch in Maillardville.

At around the same time, April 6, 1946, the French Community laid the foundation for a financial institution that would not only thrive, but would become an active participant in the fostering of French culture for many decades to come. The work ahead was destined for a new generation of "pioneers". From different parts of British Columbia and Canada came Arthur Cheramy, Victor Muller, Jean Baptiste Goulet, and Arthur and Alma Fontaine. While the formation of a French credit union was the talk of the day, it fell to a few to lead and guide the community to the realization of its dreams. In the early days, this was laid largely upon the shoulders of Arthur Cheramy who was closely tied to the Fédération Canadienne-française de la CB. However, he did not carry the entire burden. In January of 1946, L'abbé Raoul Girouard of Prince Albert, Saskatchewan, was temporarily assigned as assistant at Our Lady of Lourdes to help the overworked Father Teck. He stayed for only a few months during this pivotal time in Maillardville's history. Of credit unions, he knew little, but he offered great enthusiasm for the French cause. During his short time in residence, he worked hard to see the project off. It was L'abbé Girouard who, at the fledgling institution's first public meeting, exhorted the people to support the movement and join the new Credit Union which they did in impressive numbers. The formation of the Caisse Populaire de Notre Dame de Lourdes in April of 1946 is another shining example of the commitment and solidarity of the French community.

The Caisse was formed based upon the objective of:

"consolidating the French Canadian community of Maillardville through economic solidarity"

This new financial institution was a "closed bond" credit union, requiring its members to be French Canadian Catholics. In these early days, Arthur and Alma Fontaine were an invaluable resource in setting up the new credit union. Hailing from Manitoba, the couple had experience in founding the Caisse Populaire St. Jean Baptiste in their hometown. The first meetings of the Caisse took place in their home at 405 Marmont Street. Moreover, the first manager of the Credit Union was none other than Mrs. Alma Fontaine. Its first President was Mr. H. Goulet. For the sake of posterity, here is a list of the forty-two founding members of Caisse Populaire de Notre Dame de Lourdes:

Alphonse Bernard, Mme. Aimé Caouette, U. Charpentier, Uldéric Charpentier, S. Charpentier, Arthur Cheramy, Mme. Marie Cormier, A. Coutu, J.P. Dionne, Donat Doucette, Mme. Donat Doucette, M. Filiatrault, A. Finnigan, B. Finnigan, Arthur Fontaine, Alma Fontaine, H. Fraser, Alcide Gamache, Napoléon Gareau, C. Girouard, Rev. R. Girouard, Henri Goulet, J.B. Goulet, L. Granger, Ernest Lambert, Georges Ledet, A. Lemieux, Maurice Lizée, Mme. E. Lizée, O. Marsolais, Victor Muller, E. Parent, Emmanuel Parent, Mme. E. Parent, E. Plante, M. Roberge, N. Roberge, Noël Rougeau, J.M. Schwab, D. Tremblay, G. Van Nerum, Paul Velay.

The first operating hours of the new Caisse were modest. Banking could be done at 405 Marmont on Sundays from 12 to 2pm and on Tuesdays from 7 to 9pm. Initially, the CU's resources were meager. When a particularly large loan request was considered, it became necessary to solicit extra security from members! From the beginning, Madame Fontaine took the responsibility of manager with the understanding that a permanent manager would be appointed as soon as possible. Therefore, in September of 1946, Victor Muller agreed to guide the young Caisse Populaire.

With the birth of the new Parish of Notre Dame de Fatima, some concern was expressed about the name of the credit union and the need to represent the entire community of Maillardville. To help with that goal annual general meetings were held alternately at the two parishes. In

1950, the name was officially changed to the "Caisse Populaire de Maillardville Credit Union"

As the decade ended, holding the business of the credit union at a private residence became impractical. Meetings were shifted temporarily to the O.L of Lourdes church hall. Finally, a small stucco building measuring fourteen feet by twenty-two was erected on the property of Victor Muller at the corner of Brunette Avenue and Nelson Street. It was understood that the building would be moved as soon as a permanent location could be acquired.

The Caisse Populaire would have a tremendous impact on the development of Maillardville both economically and culturally even into the twenty first century.

Paroisse Notre Dame de Fatima / Our Lady of Fatima Parish: As further evidence of the tremendous growth in Maillardville, The Parish of Our Lady of Lourdes, founded in 1909, was becoming unmanageable for the priest, Father F.X. Teck. The situation was made known to Archbishop W.M. Duke and the decision was taken to establish a new parish. The original intention was to locate north of Our Lady of Lourdes. However, it was Father Teck's opinion that few Catholic families inhabited that area and indeed, the greater part of new French families were in fact locating west of the parish. In a letter dated October 8, 1946[14], Father Teck describes the situation:

"Should the new parish be established north of Austin Road, it could not serve its purpose. It could not be located west of Blue Mountain Road, the population being insignificant on account of the Vancouver golf Court and the Cemetery. Anyway, the only population there is protestant except for 5 or 6 families. If you locate it east of Blue Mountain Rd., the same may be said on account of the Park, the lake and the mountain...Our Catholic population is grouped and lives south of Austin Rd. About two hundred families live west of Blue Mountain and Allard while the balance lives east of that boundary line."

Father Oliva Meunier was assigned the care of the new parish and took up temporary residence as assistant to Father Teck. The dividing line between the two parishes, that is the eastern boundary of O.L. of Fatima,

---

[14] Archives, Roman Catholic Archdiocese of Vancouver

would be contentious for many years to come. The original north south line ran along Blue Mountain Road, Allard and Woolridge Streets. The boundary would eventually use Lebleu Street as the dividing line but that would not become official until 1961.

It was the desire of the new priest and parishioners to dedicate the Church to Our Lady of Fatima. Although devotion to the apparitions of the Virgin Mary to three Portuguese children was already widespread, the Catholic Church had not yet formally accepted the apparitions. For this reason, Archbishop Duke was hesitant to grant the title to the parish. Disappointed, Father Meunier demonstrated that he was a very capable negotiator whose philosophy, at least on this occasion was to "catch more flies with honey than vinegar" In a letter to the Archbishop, dated November 1, 1946[15]:

"I was sorry to hear that the parish could not be dedicated to O.L. of Fatima. I thought by the fact of its approbation by the Pope who himself spoke to the pilgrims of Fatima (and who has authorized the dedication of a basilica at Fatima) was sufficient guarantee on behalf of the Church. Moreover a few precedents, I thought, could justify our petition. In New York and Montreal there are parishes under this title. The feast is established in Portugal as October 13.

However, Your Grace, these remarks want to be very respectful and submissive. Your authority and judgment will always be my rule and guide. Here are other titles I would suggest:

> *I-   In honour of Our Lady: O.L. of Victories, The Assumption, N.D. de Graces (which sounds so nice in French)*
> *II-   In honour of Our Lord: The Good Shepherd, Holy Name of Jesus, Holy Cross, Christ the Worker.*
> *III-   In honour of Saints: Saint Anne, Saint Bernadette Soubirous*

I will be glad to accept the title of Your choice and I still believe that Our Lady of Fatima may defend her cause and attract the hearts of our working class Maillardville...You will have to tell your good sisters that their prayer was unheard for I had recommended that title to their fervent prayers."

---

[15] Archives, Roman Catholic Archdiocese of Vancouver

In the face of such a diplomatic effort, Archbishop Duke relented and granted permission to dedicate the parish to Our Lady of Fatima.

On November 17, 1946, there was a meeting at O.L. of Lourdes Church hall to discuss the building of a new Parish. Mr. Donat Doucette was installed as President of this first committee. Father Ovila Meunier OMI, the founding priest, was also in attendance. In an expression of both gratitude and enthusiasm, the newly formed committee sent the Archbishop this letter dated November 17, 1946[16]:

"*Your Excellency,*

Gathered around the old parish, over 200 men of the new parish of Maillardville have attended this general meeting to discuss the interests of the new Fatima Parish. After a friendly and extensive discussion, we have directed Rev. Fr. Meunier o.m.i. to express and submit to Your Grace the following resolutions:

1. *Everyone agrees in thanking you for the erection of a much needed new parish in Maillardville*
2. *Everyone also agrees that gratefulness should be expressed for abandoning the idea of a parish site above the Austin Rd. and for the new proposed location around the Alderson St School which is the very heart of the new parish.*
3. *Before it is too late we suggest to buy without delay a property in that district and we leave it to the parish committee to pick the exact spot and to determine the amount to be paid for. Today we cannot expect to pay a low price, as all the district is booming and very few large lots remain vacant.*
4. *We have selected and elected freely our Parish Committee and give them entire freedom to proceed for the welfare of the parish which should be organized as soon as possible.*
5. *We promise to support our parish and organize it with our pastor who will have our full support.*
6. *The Maillardville population rejoices over the new parish and is pleased to be under the special protection of Our Blessed Mother. There is no dissent among us and we hope it will always be so. We also wish to express a sincere gratitude to Rev. Fr. Teck for the past.*

---

[16] Archives, Roman Catholic Archdiocese of Vancouver

Begging Your Grace to bless us all and our families, we have signed:"

At the request of Archbishop Duke, the Church would be bilingual. Initially, separate Masses were offered in French and English, but soon each Mass was said bilingually. Five acres of heavily forested land were purchased on Alderson Avenue, west of Blue Mountain Street, for $12,000.00. The deal included two small houses. A first Mass on December 8, 1946 was said in one of these. However, the small structure was completely inadequate for the needs of the people. Arrangements were made with Alderson Avenue School and for a time the congregation attended Mass there. The District of Coquitlam would haul in park benches on Saturday afternoon and then they would be replaced following Mass on Sunday.

A great new chapter in the story of Maillardville was opened. The people devoted themselves to the realization of establishing the new Parish, but of course, a tremendous amount of work lay ahead. The first order of business was to build a church! Father Meunier was an indefatigable leader for his people. From preaching upon the stump of a newly felled tree to traveling far and wide to raise funds, this citizen of the Church and of Maillardville was one of the great contributors of the community. Father Meunier also knew the value, indeed necessity, of having as many people engaged in the venture as possible. So from the beginning, there were jobs for everyone. Committees of every description were formed. People were helping out with administration, building, fund raising and music and drama projects. Mr. Jean Lambert was named as president of the first Parish Council. He was involved in the new Parish from the beginning. He was to become a leader who worked in many capacities in the Parish and in the community, and who continued to do so even as Maillardville entered its second century.

Having cleared the land, they set out to build their church, a modest one hundred by fifty foot structure. The Church was completed in late 1947 and on November 9 of that year Archbishop Duke came to bless it. But more was needed. In 1948 Mr. Fernand Filliatrault, who had built the convent school at Lourdes, was contracted to create a similar building for Fatima. This he proceeded to do, again with the volunteer work of many of the parishioners. When it was completed, the school had six classrooms and the capacity for six more. Three Sisters of the Child Jesus came to teach the children. Among the teaching staff was also the first lay teacher in the school, Mrs. Bibiane Finnegan who remained there until 1961. By the early fifties, there were some 300 children en-rolled at École Notre Dame de Fatima.

Fédération Canadienne française de Colombie-Britannique (FCFCB): On June 24, 1945, a number of French organizations gath-ered in Victoria for the first "French Language Congress" with the purpose of unifying French interests in the Province. Its mission was to:

"defend the language and religious interests of French Canadians in British Columbia."

The Congress went on to elect Arthur Cheramy of Maillardville as its first president. Member organizations became "cercles" (circles) and one was immediately established at Maillardville. A second circle quickly followed at the new Parish of O.L of Fatima. Le Club Français Canadien (the French Canadian Club as reported in the Coquitlam Herald) already had some 600 members looking out for the interests of the French com-munity in Maillardville. They were active in politics, youth activities and in the previously mentioned city name change process (Laurier, Nor-mandy, Three Rivers.)

The new Provincial French organization provided fresh energy and sup-port for the establishment of Catholic parishes and credit unions. Under its original charter, the FCFCB required that a member be French Cana-dian and Catholic. Indeed, any individual of that description had the right to automatic membership in the organization upon payment of a one dollar due. Recognition of the new organization came when Arthur Cheramy and his wife were honoured in 1946 with the following invita-tion:

"Mr. Arthur Cheramy, president of the French Canadian Federation of B.C. and Mrs. Cheramy have been invited to a banquet given Wednes-day, January 23 in Hotel Georgia, in honour of Mr. Charles Claudon, French Consul General and Mrs. Claudon."

FCFCB would have a direct impact on events in Maillardville for the next several decades.

The second half of the decade was no less eventful than the first. The village began to take on a better-defined character that was highlighted by a tremendous increase in commercial activity and civic involvement.

The Coquitlam Board of Trade, guided by Harry Thrift, and the Maillardville Merchant's Association headed by Maurice Lizée had already been formed. French businessmen were a big part of these organizations. Plans were made for new commercial development on Brunette, including a new "shopping block" and the construction of the "Cheramy building". The local media offered this headline:

*"**Modern Bowling Alleys, Theatre For Maillardville** Maillardville will have an up to the minute theatre and unexcelled bowling alley facilities if the present ideas of Joe Bouffard, Vancouver brother-in-law to Stan and Joe Parent, well known Maillardville businessmen, are carried out "according to plan". Mr. Bouffard's blueprints calling for the erection of a fifty thousand dollar building to house some 400 theatre patrons and bowling alleys were last week approved in Coquitlam Municipal Hall. The smart looking two storey building is planned to extend 85 feet along the north side of Brunette and will be 100 feet long... Graced like the bowling alley entrance by an illuminated canopy, the front of the theatre proper will consist of a foyer in modern design leading into the movie house itself. Overall measurements of the theatre side of the building will be 100x35 feet. There will be no balcony according to Mr. Bouffard. The necessary land has already been purchased..."*

The Grand Opening of the Wood's Theatre took place on Saturday, July 26. The opening program included:

"2 Features in Glorious Technicolour; Lake Placid Serenade, a gay musical comedy and Along the Navajo Trail with Roy Rogers, Gabby Hayes and Trigger, the smartest horse in movies"

On the previous evening, *"the projection machines of the new Wood's Theatre, Maillardville rolled for the first time. The workers and their families, and local business men attended this initial trial program. Reeve James Christmas addressed those present and congratulated the two owners, Sam Oustavitch and John Disdarzvich for such a welcome addition to the Municipality."*

Soon after, Mr. Oustavich became the sole owner and changed the name to the more familiar "Sam's Theatre".

By 1948/49, there were no fewer than forty-five thriving businesses in Maillardville, mostly along Brunette Avenue from Blue Mountain Street to Laval. Offerings included La Petite Dress Shoppe, Fraser Mills Taxi, Montreal Mail Order House, Maillardville Lumber Yard, Trev's Fountain Lunch, Shirley's Beauty Parlour, Bob's Burgers, Al Best Chevron…the list goes on. Furniture, appliances, clothing, hardware, beauty services and groceries could all be had on this vibrant commercial strip. With the increase in business came a strong lobby group. They were able to bring pressure upon City Hall for infrastructure improvements on Brunette Avenue.

The residents were also caught up in the enthusiasm and in 1947 formed the Maillardville Ratepayers Association. An initial meeting held at the church and chaired by A. Lanoue stressed that:

"the proposed Association would take part solely in Municipal affairs, and its politics would be non-political, free from religious and racial differences."

Perhaps that comment offers a small hint that there was indeed tension between the Francos and Anglos in Maillardville. In any case, the group met again on February 1 to elect an executive and further organize.

*"**Ratepayers Meet In Maillardville**   The Maillardville Ratepayers Association held their meeting in the Parish hall on Sunday, February 1. The following were elected: Vincent Yates, President, M. Butler, Vice President, Percy Smith, secretary and executive members A. Lanoue Mr. Rymer, R. Burgess, M. Lizée, J.B. Goulet, M. Gamache and H. Goulet. It was decided that the association would be open to ratepayers from any part of the municipality and as a result it was found unnecessary to stipulate any set boundaries. It is expected that membership will be the largest of any ratepayers association within the municipality. Membership dues were set at 50 cents a year and it was encouraging to note at this initial meeting 50 members received membership cards."*

The MRA met on the first Wednesday of each month. They became active at Council meetings, bringing forward the concerns and needs of the village. That they meant business cannot be questioned as in 1948 they put forward two of their members, Michael Butler and René Gamache to stand as candidates for Council in that year's municipal election. Both won their seats at the table.

Politics continued to be an important aspect of French Canadian life. Tom Allard remained on council until 1945. Toussaint Filliatrault served a term in 1945/46. A.D. Payer was on Council from 1943 to 1950 and René Gamache, native son of Maillardville, was to serve his community on council for twenty years beginning in 1948. This article appeared in the Herald just prior to the election:

"R. Gamache, Navy veteran and Maillardville resident, will be seeking election to the Municipal Council in Saturday's voting. Mr. Gamache has stated that he fully realizes the road, sidewalk and transportation difficulties facing the District and promises concentrated and energetic efforts if elected. He is a member of the Maillardville Ratepayers' Association."

Maurice Lizée, Maillardville businessman, twice tried for the position of Reeve, losing both times to L.J. Christmas.

Not all residents of Coquitlam were satisfied that the seat of governance was located in Maillardville. Reporting in July of 1949, the Coquitlam Herald stated

"Large Area of Coquitlam Municipality Seeks Incorporation with Port Coquitlam... *The Board of Trade has been asked to cooperate with ratepayers associations in the North and East corners of the Municipality who feel as one resident who described the point "Like an unwanted uncle in the family circle" The residents in question are of the opinion that the seat of government in municipal affairs is so remote from the particular area that they are often completely forgotten. Ratepayers are of the opinion that their natural trading area is Port Coquitlam and the services of the city would be more accessible to them than the municipal hall situated in Maillardville Members of the Trade Board expressed full agreement with the movement and have undertaken to assist the ratepayers associations in every possible way to attain their object"*

There was also a surge of concern for the youth of Maillardville. At several Council meetings in 1943, Constable Jimmy McGarry reported that vandalism was an increasing concern and that something needed to be done to engage young people in positive activity. At that time there was a popular youth movement in the lower mainland called "Teen Town". These were youth groups structured loosely upon municipal civic life and included a Teen Town "Mayor". Activities included the usual; hobbies and sports, dances and community work. Constable McGarry, not one to offer criticism without having a possible solution, was instrumental in starting a Teen Town chapter in Maillardville. Its first Mayor was Johnny Guilbeault.

There seems to have been tremendous support for this youth movement, and they were invited to speak to Council and the Board of Trade. The other thing noted by the intrepid Constable was that there really was no place for youth to meet. Drawing up his own plans, McGarry presented to Council a scheme to build a community hall in Mackin Park and no shack this! June 6, 1945:

"Original plans for the centre were drawn by Cnst. McGarry early this year and were approved by the municipal council. Blueprints for the proposed building have since been prepared by Mr. Brightwell. The centre is intended primarily as a recreation hall for the young people in the Districts of Coquitlam and Fraser Mills. The building is to contain a large auditorium fitted for basketball, lacrosse and badminton and is to be used as well for public meetings and concerts. The main floor is to contain, in addition to the auditorium, a stage with adjoining dressing rooms, and a large kitchen and dining room. Above the dining room, a similar room, suitable for committee meetings and small club meetings are planned. There is to be a large balcony on two sides of the auditorium. Estimated cost of the building is $20,000."

All parts of the community from Council to businesses, residents and the French Canadian Club heartily embraced the project. The building was to be erected at an estimated cost of $20,000. H.J. Mackin pledged 20% of the cost, the merchants kicked in with $500 while the French Canadian Club immediately raised $1000. A series of fundraisers followed including a Gun Shoot, a raffle and a Mardi Gras. But none were as popular as the "Frenchman's Frolic". This was a community Festival that took place two years in a row at Mackin Park. Brunette Avenue was blocked off for dancing and fun, a midway and the crowning of the "Frolic Queen". The Herald, August 22, 1946 reported:

*"**Hundreds Attend Big Frolic; Teen Town Queen Crowned** while thousands cheered in the traditional carnival mood, Helen Gagne, pretty 18 year old candidate from the Coquitlam Teen Town, was officially crowned as "Queen of the Frenchmen's Frolic" on Wednesday evening August 14 in front of Mackin Park, Maillardville. Celebrating its second*

annual frolic, this French Canadian centre collected more than $1500. The Community Centre fund now stands at more than $6000, which will be used to aid the Community Hall to be built in Mackin Park. One of the main features of the evening was the record breaking crowd which was estimated at above 5000. Cheers swelled from the agitated crowd as Queen Helen Gagne and her royal court were escorted by Constable Douglas Jack onto a high green lawn in front of Mackin Park. The Queen's attendants were Florette Lamoureux, Shirley Gueho, Alice Canuel and Laura Croteau. Reeve Christmas placed a floral crown on the dark haired head of Helen Gagne, daughter of Mr. and Mrs. R. Gagne, after more than 14000 votes had been cast. Formalities over the fun began in earnest as hundreds then danced and made merry beneath colored strings of lights on the Pitt River Road (Brunette) that was closed to all motor traffic. From reports from the operators of various concessions including fortune wheels, slot machines and bingo the people were ready to spend their nickels and dimes."

Sadly, both Teen Town and the dream of a community hall in Mackin Park were short lived. The youth group lasted only a few years. In an attempt to renew interest in the community centre, the foundations were laid in 1948. In the end, unable to raise sufficient funds, the project died. With all of the enthusiasm and support of every part of the community, it is difficult to understand why the Centre was not built. Perhaps this too was a portent of Maillardville's future. Nevertheless, Cnst. McGarry, the man who dreamed the dream, was to be honoured:

*"**Constable Blushes As Community Praises His Work** When a policeman is publicly proclaimed a community's "best liked and most respected citizen" that's really news. Yet that's the exact plaudit received Monday night by Constable J.D. McGarry of Coquitlam during the local Board of Trade banquet held in the Royal City. While the popular Mr. McGarry blushed and the board members and their lady guests applauded thunderously, H.J.C. Thrift, president of the Board heaped compliment on compliment in the constable's direction for the latter's efforts on behalf of the Municipality during the past three years. These efforts included the recent district-wide raffle organized by Mr. McGarry to start off a civic centre fund, his work at the head of the local ARP organization and the fire department to mention only a few, said Mr. Thrift in remembering how fortunate the District is to have a representative of the law who will also give of his time and energy to the all-round betterment of the community"*

However the village of Maillardville, bustling as it was, had plenty of other concerns with which to occupy itself. Not the least of these was the flood of 1948. Flood warnings commenced in early May. Noting similar conditions, some wondered whether the Lower Mainland was gearing up for another big flood like that suffered in 1935/36. Work began to sandbag critical areas. Children from the local schools were not exempt from the labour and were called from the classroom to help with the sandbagging. In Maillardville, the men worked hard to protect the mill. A group of women, headed by Mrs. Minnie Best, set about making pies en masse to feed the labourers. The local merchants, demonstrating once again the solidarity for which Maillardville was noted, donated most of the ingredients. In spite of the tremendous effort to bolster dyke systems, the mighty Fraser began to rise above its banks. On May 24 flooding occurred and continued until early June. The Fraser valley, Chilliwack, Maple Ridge and Pitt Meadows were all severely flooded. In the end, ten people died, there was twenty million (1948) dollars in damage and 80 bridges were washed away. Both railways and the Trans-Canada Highway were impassable and Greater Vancouver was cut off from the rest of the country for several days.

By comparison, Fraser Mills and Maillardville suffered minimally. Still, the flood did have a serious impact on the operations at the mill. It was shut down for five or six weeks. Men were called in to help raise machinery out of the water. The town site itself was also inundated as the wooden sidewalks floated upon several feet of water. One resident recalls that few houses were actually flooded, but the waters rose to their thresholds and appliances and furniture had to be put up on blocks. The threat of water borne disease was a real one, and the health department decreed that free typhoid inoculations should be given to residents. Clinics were set up at City Hall on Brunette and at Austin High School. In the aftermath of this powerful event dead cattle, parts of houses and debris could be seen floating down the Fraser River.

Human nature being resilient, the event passed into history and life went on. Maillardville of the late forties was not all about work and civic duties! Sam's Theatre was there for more than mere cinematic opportunity. In the language of the twenty first century, it was "an awesome, rocking place!", at least by the standards of the forties. The Herald declared:

"Sam's Theatre Is Hive Of Activity Sam's Theatre, Maillardville is a hive of industry these days. As well as running pictures through the week

and Sunday midnight, the management has many other attractions. Monday there is an amateur night, with local talent competing; this coming Tuesday is Ladies' night and pie contest where the best pie is bought from the winner for $10; Wednesday night there is to be a quiz show and next Thursday, November 27 a five act Vaudeville show."

Sam seems one not to have rested upon his laurels and it was announced:

"Live Gorilla Feature At Sam's Theatre *Tonight and tomorrow night, Feb 12 and 13 1947, there will be on display at Sam's Theatre, Maillardville, a large live gorilla. The monster will be in a cage in front of the Theatre and will be shown to all theatre goers on those two nights."*

In the late forties, there was also a spate of UFO sightings, mainly south of the 49th parallel, and they made their way into the papers and people's imaginations. Surely an extraterrestrial could not resist the temptation to visit le beau village! And so it was that in July of 1947, Maillardville was invaded! The Columbian July 7, 1947 reported:

"Saucers" Follow Local "Tornadoes" *The mystery of the "flying saucers" became more and more mystifying to local residents over the weekend as six persons, three of them residents of Maillardville, laid claim to having seen the flashing discs streaking through the sky at various times on Sunday Antoine Beauregard, painter, who resides at 1039 Alderson Avenue said that he was working on a house during the afternoon and suddenly saw a "shiny aluminum disc" cross the blue sky "at a height of about fifteen miles" "It was about 300 feet long" said Mr. Beauregard. "My eyesight is very good and I can judge distance and height accurately." Mrs. Beauregard said she knew little of what her husband saw. "My husband said that he saw a shiny round disc, bigger than most and sort of squared off on one side. That is all I really know about it." Two other persons, whose names are not given, were in the company of Beauregard when the "phenomenon" was witnessed."*

The great tradition of baseball continued in 1946 when Maillardville joined the Dewdney League along with Coquitlam, New Westminster, Ioco and Port Moody. Comprised mainly of Frenchmen and coached by George Messier, the team turned out to be pretty good. Referred to often in the papers as the "Frenchman" Maillardville went to the finals in 1947, only to be edged out by Haney. C'est la guerre! The Herald reported it with this headline:

"Haney Cops Dewdney Crown With 8-3 Win *Currie Twirls Four Hitter As Maillardville Fades In The Stretch   Before a capacity crowd at their home park last Friday evening a hustling Haney team came charging back to K.O. Maillardville and gain the Dewdney League championship. "*

Fraser Mills continued to be a major employer of Francophone and Anglophone alike, but modernization was encroaching upon the old ways. A 1.5 million dollar makeover to change machinery from steam to electric was started in 1946 and completed in 1948. And "Oriental Town", there from the time the pioneers first came to what would become Maillardville, was beginning to disintegrate. The Japanese internment, the modernization of the mill and the dismantling of many of the old buildings eroded what was left of the riverside community. The "Town" so long a colourful part of life at Fraser Mills and for the residents "up the hill" at Maillardville was soon to become a part of the collective memory.

The Parish of Our Lady of Lourdes did not vanish in the overwhelming wave of activity that began in the mid-forties. The original parish community continued to provide its members with a rich, vibrant life. Father Teck, who had held the reigns of the parish since 1928, gave way to his successor Father Paul Émile Vanier in 1948.

During his twenty years at Paroisse Notre Dame de Lourdes, Father Teck oversaw the building of a new church, which still stands today. He guided his parish through the difficult strike of 1931 and the Great Depression. He offered the Parish Hall as an emergency field hospital for Maillardville during the "war to end all wars". And during this hard time, he doubtless had to execute the sometimes difficult duties of a Catholic priest when families find themselves in grievous trial. He continued to advocate for the interests of the Catholic community at City Hall, and helped to bring about the birth of the new Parish of Our Lady of Fatima. Some saw him as a hard man. Perhaps he was a man for hard times. In any case, there can be no doubt that Father Francis Xavier Teck left a permanent stamp on this community.

Father Vanier arranged for the purchase of the land that would be the home of the new "high school" on Hammond Avenue for $350.00. He also encouraged the formation of a youth group that was to long remain active in the Parish; the diocesan based Catholic Youth Organization (CYO).

Card parties and fundraisers were still a part of parish life and the people found amusing new twists to old games. They had Klondike Night, the soiree being arranged by families whose last name started with the letter "F", as reported in 1948:

"Klondyke money was sold by Mrs. Filliatrault and Mrs. Finnigan. Mrs. Faucher and Mr. Finnegan were in charge of the Bingo games. The refreshments were handled by Miss Fouquette and the Misses Filliatrault."

The trend continued with the letters "I-J-K" sponsoring a card party at which the attendees were also treated to a motion picture "La Marseilles", dealing with the French Revolution. And the young folk were not forgotten with large numbers turning out for roller skating at the parish hall. Also in 1948, the size of the Parish required that Christmas Midnight Mass be said both in the main Church and the basement.

Forty years had elapsed since that first train from the east chugged into the station at Millside. What of the pioneers? They continued to honour their past; that, at least, was their intention. This article appeared in the Herald, February 1949:

*"**Maillardville Pioneers Plan Anniversary Celebration** Preparations will get underway this week for a monster celebration in Maillardville this summer for the fortieth anniversary of the arrival of the first French settlement in British Columbia....J. Dicaire will head the group until further plans are made. Tentative dates of June 27-28-29 have been set. It is estimated that there are at present about 65,000 French Canadians living in B.C. It is expected that a good percentage of these will make an effort to attend the gala three days of celebration in the District. A Pioneers of Maillardville Club will be formed to formulate and handle future plans and arrangements."*

It appears as though this celebration never took place. And inevitably, the time comes for the end of life's journey. The death of this pioneer was noted in the Herald, January 6, 1949:

*"**Maillardville Pioneer Passes** The funeral was held Monday for Mrs. Josephine Dicaire, one of Maillardville's first pioneers, who died De-*

cember 31, 1948 at her home in Laval Square. Mrs. Dicaire was 85 years of age. She came to Maillardville from Ottawa with the original group of French Canadians who settled here 40 years ago. She is survived by her three sons, John, Arthur and Wilfred all of Maillardville. One brother, N. Boyer of Ottawa, one sister, Mrs. O. Charbonneau of Los Angeles and 15 grandchildren and 12 great grandchildren. Rev. Father Vanier sang a Requiem Mass in the Our Lady of Lourdes Church Monday morning at 10am."

A final honour awaited Paroisse Notre Dame de Lourdes as the forties drew to an end. Just as Coquitlam's second May Queen in 1941 hailed from Maillardville, so it would be that the last of the decade would also come from Our Lady of Lourdes School, in June, 1949.

*" **Maillardville Crowns Queen at Impressive Ceremony**   Petite Gisele Arpin, ten year old daughter of Mr. and Mrs. J. Arpin of 413 Laval Square, was crowned Queen of the May before more than 3000 in Blue Mountain Park Friday....the little Queen welcomed thousands of her cheering subjects to B.C.'s second largest May Day celebration speaking in both French and English. Two of her classmates from Our Lady of Lourdes School, Mary Anne Maude and Richelle Beauchesne were maids of honour and Rose-Marie Manson of Millside School was record bearer."*

Once again a decade was on the wane. From depression and war, Maillardville's star waxed brilliantly in the forties. That pivotal year of 1946 brought the men and women and saw the birth of institutions that would guide the community and preserve la Francophonie for decades to come. It was also a time when other influences arose to challenge that precious cultural jewel. It should be a proud part of Maillardville's heritage that French and "other" worked together to accomplish common goals even as they respected each other's uniqueness.

Five

Growth and the Fight for Minority Rights

Main Entry: **evo·lu·tion** Pronunciation: \ˌe-və-ˈlü-shən, ˌē-və- *noun*
2 a: a process of change in a certain direction: **unfolding**

Maillardville and Coquitlam continued to grow steadily. The decade itself is a bittersweet one that saw the decline of old traditions and the beginning of a new relationship between French Maillardville and the rest of the City. In the early fifties, the realignment of the Lougheed Highway bisected the District of Fraser Mills, physically cutting the town site in two and severing the traditional link between the Mill and Maillardville. It was in 1953 that Fraser Mills merged with Crown Zellerbach and Henry Mackin stepped down as President. Mackin had been a part of the evolution of the business, from 1907 as the sales manager for the Fraser River Lumber Company, through its transition to the Canadian Western Lumber Company and on down through the decades. He was there when that first contingent of pioneers arrived and he saw the mill and its workers through depression, strikes, war and the return of the good times. The physical separation of the Mill and the Village and the breaking with the past that came with Mackin's departure is symbolic of the changes and growing pressures that continued upon the French community at Maillardville.

Another shift was also occurring. With growth in the District came new residential subdivisions at Harbour Chines and Como Lake. There was also growing dissatisfaction among residents in the east end. These and other concerns were now occupying a much greater part of Council's time and energy. Maillardville, City Hall and the French community no longer enjoyed the intimate bond that had existed since 1913.

The forties were remarkable for the cooperation displayed among local government, business and the French community to achieve common goals. Yet near the end of that decade there was, perhaps, a glimmer of the "going our own ways" that becomes apparent as the fifties unfold. But typically, death gives rise to new life. And so it was for French Maillardville. The turning inward of that community resulted in a fresh blaze of activity that saw the building of schools and a church and the continued fostering of institutions such as the Caisse Populaire and the French Canadian Club. New and important organizations like the Catholic Youth Organization (CYO) and Les Scouts et Guides Français were created to support the young people and keep them within the fold. Political activism became more important than ever and Maillardville found two champions in René Gamache and Michael J. Butler.

The fifties began much as the forties ended. Business continued to thrive and Council still grappled with the problem of inadequate infrastructure to support continued growth in Maillardville and throughout the District. Poor water supply and failing septic systems plagued the citizens of Maillardville. Another problem was also emerging. As the District grew, school facilities were inadequate to accommodate all of the children. Although a plan was in place to construct five new schools, they would not be ready to relieve the burden until September of 1952. In the meantime, schools in the District's public system operated under "double shifts" whereby half the children would be in school in the morning and the other half in the afternoon. Additionally, a battle raged between the Provincial Government and B.C. Municipalities who were demanding more funding for education. Against this backdrop, the two Catholic Parishes were also struggling to keep their own schools operational for over 800 students. The property on Hammond Avenue bought by Father Vanier in 1948 was now the site of a new school for O.L. of Lourdes, "l'école haute", bringing to three the number of schools held between the two parishes.

The Catholic School Strike of 1951 The question of the recognition of separate schools in B.C. was a long-standing one. It went back to the middle of the 19th century when the first school, St Ann's Academy was established in Victoria. The efforts of early Bishops Durieu and D'Herbomez to persuade the BC Government to recognize independent schools and thus be eligible for funding were fruitless. However, a different situation existed for the Catholic Church in Maillardville. When the Fraser River Lumber Company sent Father O'Boyle and Théodore Théroux east to recruit French Canadians to come and work at the mill, the Frenchmen had to be assured that the effort to uproot and reestablish themselves in a strange land would be worth their while. Better wages, better climate, and land and materials to build their homes were all promised. In addition, the Company guaranteed them land and lumber to build a Church and school. This is indisputable, as original receipts for materials and cash deposits exist to indicate the company fulfilled its obligations. What other promises were made to the pioneers? It seems unlikely that people such as O'Boyle or McRae, well aware of the B.C. Government's attitude toward separate schools, would assure the settlers of the same kind of government support that was to be found in Quebec at that time. (This "promise" is alluded to in a speech during the upcoming school "strike") What is known is that local government established a tax exemption on Catholic Church land and property from the beginning.

Over the years, but especially as Maillardville began to experience dramatic growth in the thirties and forties, members of the French community lobbied Reeve and Council for financial support. Not all of these requests were denied. Council minutes indicate at various times the granting of money for books, playground improvements and so on. When the new parish of Our Lady of Fatima was established in 1946, Council in October of 1947 carried a motion to grant it the same tax-free status enjoyed by Lourdes. During these same years, the Archbishop of Vancouver, W.M. Duke, unsuccessfully lobbied the Provincial government for independent school recognition.

Like the rest of Coquitlam, the sister parishes were experiencing rapid growth and the financial challenges that accompany it. The Catholic School Board at Maillardville continued to press City Council to supply relief for the school's urgent needs. In mid-1950, Joseph Haddock and J.B.Goulet put a series of requests before Council, one of which was "could Catholic children have access to the public school bus system?"

The answer was not quite a definite "no". They were told that if there was space on the bus after all public school children had been accommodated then bus drivers could pick up the Catholic children. In answer to this, a joint Catholic School Board was formed, chaired by J.B. Goulet. Far from a sudden eruption of dissatisfaction in the dramatic strike that was soon to come, it appears that the action taken by the Board was considered over the course of 1950. In January of 1951, in a letter to Archbishop Duke[17], Father Meunier expressed concern and anxiety that perhaps some in the parishes were considering more confrontational methods to achieve their goals:

"Since the blessing of the school of Lourdes, the devil must be against us, for we are threatened with municipal taxes, after a precedent of non-taxation for decades of years. Apparently R.C. MacDonald (former Reeve of Coquitlam) is behind the move. Our Catholic Councilors (3 practical and a fallen away) are fighting hard for the schools and hope to hold their ground. Our people have elected another fine Catholic last fall.

Since the fall, we have made arrangements with the Public Bus to transport some of our school children who live away from the school and now are asking the Municipality for a grant to cover the costs of transportation; we hope to succeed. I am very much of the opinion that our opponents should not be provoked by actions or speeches or writings that cannot do us any good. On the other hand, the policy of good neighbor and kindness has done us a lot of good here and had gained ground for our population. I hope we will stick to that policy."

The strategy that was subsequently developed manifested itself on April 2, 1951. Without warning the Catholic School Board removed all 840 students at the three Catholic Schools from their classes and marched to the School Board offices in protest. The Sun, April 2, 1951:

" 850 Catholic Children Quit Coquitlam Schools   Bus Issue Brings School Strike

The 850 pupils of two Roman Catholic schools in Coquitlam District closed by their authorities today, will be accommodated by the public school system as soon as it can be physically done, Education Minister W.T. Straith said today.

---

[17] Archives, Roman Catholic Archdiocese of Vancouver

Led by their teachers, the 850 pupils assembled on the grounds of Our Lady of Lourdes and our Lady of Fatima, Maillardville, this morning and marched to the district school board offices in a "strike" against the government's education policy. Catholic school officials charge that they are being discriminated against. Main complaint in Coquitlam is that the district does not supply school buses for the Catholic students. This is but one angle in the controversial separate school question that has simmered in B.C. for 41 years.

In recent months, Catholic delegations have asked government officials to provide free transport as well as text books and free medical and dental inspection which are given public school children."

Joseph Haddock, Secretary of the joint Catholic School Board emerged early as its spokesmen and he was quoted in that day's paper;

"The Catholic schools in Coquitlam will remain closed until their grievance is settled said Joseph Haddock, spokesman for the Catholic School Board. Mr. Haddock said the Catholics want equal rights with public schools, suggesting the same system in force in Quebec where public, Catholic and Jewish schools all participate in government grants regardless of religious affiliation. Only ones pleased with the spontaneous walkout today were the children themselves. They marched happily along the road from school carrying signs. One placard said "Maillardville collects taxes for Maillardville schools" Another said "We want justice." Maillardville itself is predominantly Roman Catholic. Our Lady of Lourdes was founded more than 41 years ago by Father Maillard."

Early government response to the situation was to state that the public school system would accommodate all children who presented themselves for enrollment, in spite of the fact that the teachers were already labouring under "double shifts" The provincial government was quick to assure the public that this was a "local situation" Archbishop Duke did not agree. The B.C. Catholic newspaper on April 5 offered this headline:

"Maillardville School "Strike" Affects All Catholic Schools In B.C....Commenting on the surprise "walkout", His Excellency Archbishop Duke said later, "In reference to the situation, I can only say at the present time that the Catholics of this province have received unfair treatment under the B.C. Public Schools Act, and I have reason to believe that when the claims of the people are better known there will be

much to be said in their favour. On another occasion the Archbishop also made the significant statement "All Catholic schools will be involved in this question."

A rally was held at the O.L. of Lourdes auditorium at which an estimated fifteen hundred people were present. That evening, Mr. Haddock gave an inspired speech that was later carried on radio CKNW. It was met with rousing cheers. As the speech clearly details the Catholic position of the joint school board, its entire text is included here:

"The audience here this evening believes in God. It is for the same reason that we Catholics wish and desire that all of our education be permeated with the idea of God. We are ready to go to the limits to obtain what we stand for, simply because it is a matter of conscience. The people here in Maillardville have been doing it for 41 years, at their own expense, because the Government refused all along to recognize our just claims. We have done it at the cost of untold sacrifices, but there comes a time when such a crying injustice necessitates action. Remember, 41 years ago, there was no school in Maillardville. The founders of this town came to this part of the country, not merely with the idea of providing a livelihood for themselves.

First of all they were asked, begged, to come to help the province's lumber industry. They did not come with their eyes closed. They foresaw the necessity of educating their children as Christians, in the knowledge, love and fear of God. They agreed on terms. They would not come unless they be allowed to have their schools, their Church. They promised them the same benefits as minority groups enjoy in Quebec. They promised them their own Schools, and their Church, that their schools would be tax supported as they were in Quebec.

But what happened? Once here, those same settlers were forced to build their own schools, with some assistance from the company that employed them, and for that we are grateful. But it was not enough. It was with their own sweat, their hard work, that they built the school, and have kept it going on through the years. When they built their school, there was no other school, and everybody sent their children to it, and they were mighty glad to do so. The Catholics, with their own resources, took everybody in with open arms, because they felt it was their duty to do so, because they felt it was the way a Christian should act.

What is the situation now? With our own taxes which have been levied, the local school authorities have built other schools, but it was against our convictions to send our children there. Who will deny us that privilege, a privilege that follows directly upon the principle of freedom of religion? Oh yes, they will say, we do not deny you any privileges in the practice of your religion. We even let you have your own schools. Granted. But why discriminate, why penalize us because we live up to our ideals? Why such rank injustice? You may ask what discrimination? One who discriminates is one who makes a distinction in treatment. The provincial law is quite clear in its policy of discrimination. Yes they allow us to build our schools, but they turn around, tax the buildings, tax the land, they tax us right out of existence. Now, are our children treated any differently than others? Do we pay taxes? Who gets them? Is it our children? No. Why? Because they cannot in conscience attend a school where religion is totally ignored. In other words, because they are Catholic.

But still, whose money is it? The public's money. Must we be counted with the public when it comes to paying taxes, and then when it comes to getting the benefits out of our taxes, then we are no longer the public? What then is being done with our money? They are building schools, educating free of charge those children who consent to set God aside if they believe in Him at all. They are transported to those schools free of charge, they get medical care, free of charge, and they get dental care, free of charge....with our money. I could go on and on, but what's the use, there are so many injustices demanding immediate rectification. And why, may I ask, can we expect immediate rectification? For the good reason that the School board represents the taxpayer of the district, its members are our representatives and are supposed to do what we want them to do when our demands are reasonable. And will they deny that they are? In the same way the Minister of Education represents the people of the province...It is not a bureau which dictates, but a department of a democracy which serves. Both the one and the other are supposed to respect our minority rights, and we ask for nothing more.

The question of taxes paid without getting any returns is one thing, but what money have we saved the government? What money have we saved the Municipality? It is easy to figure out. The latest statistics show that it costs approximately $209.00 to educate one child for one year, multiply that by 840 children, and you have a total of $175,560.00. That is not all; it is only for one year. If we went through the trouble of figuring out

*the amount saved in the past forty years would it not go well into the millions? Take the buildings now, how much would it take the Municipality to replace them? Well over a half million dollars. And they, that is the Department of Education, in order to continue the discrimination, to continue their programme of silent
hostility, will build those schools knowing full well that we already have them. Is that not a downright waste of public funds? Who will finance that? We will, or at least they expect us to do so.*

Tell me, why should B.C. act in this manner? Whose example is our Department of Education following? Remember that there is only this province that discriminates in this manner. But we have confidence in the fair-mindedness of the public. The people of this province wish to give us what the minorities have in the other provinces of this Dominion. From Alberta to Newfoundland, the rights of all are respected, and B.C. will follow suit, because the people of B.C. themselves are clamouring for justice. What arrangement could be better than what you have in Saskatchewan for instance, and I quote the school act for my authority;" The School Act of Saskatchewan, an example of tolerance of the religious convictions of minority groups in a democracy, contains the following provisions, regarding separate schools;

"The minority of ratepayers in any district, whether Protestant or Roman Catholic, may establish a separate school therein, and in such case the ratepayers establishing the school will be liable only to assessments of such rates as they impose upon themselves thereof"

"The persons qualified to vote for or against the erection of a separate school district shall be the ratepayers in the district of the same religious faith, Protestants or Catholics as the petitioners."

"After the establishment of a separate school district under the provisions of this Act, the district and the board thereof shall possess and exercise the rights, powers and privileges and be subject to the same liabilities and method of government as herein provided in respect of public school districts." R.S.S.1940 C.165,S.43

What do you think of that for square dealing? All we want is the same treatment as minority groups in Saskatchewan and other provinces of Canada. That is why we have led the minority's protest against the provincial educational injustices. We as Canadians recall the words of the Earl of Athlone which I will quote here; "Today there exists in the world

96

in all classes of society, a veritable revolt against the divine law, the moral law which they wish to eliminate from the education of youth and the governments of its nations....We are agreed on this point, that education without religion is like a barren land, and a country without religion, sooner or later, marches to its doom...In my opinion the formation of character is the first principle which distinguishes education from instruction, and for that there is no field so fertile for healthy humanitarian ideas than an atmosphere that is entirely Christian."

Evidently the Department of Education wishes to lead the province to the doom the Earl of Athlone warns us against, for in the Public School Act we read "The highest morality shall be inculcated but no religious dogma or creed will be taught" Now to have a morality without God is just as absurd as trying to warm a house and refusing to use any fuel whatsoever.

Some say that this is a purely local affair, others that it is only the French of Maillardville getting unruly...remember, a question of justice cannot be localized in any one place. By its very nature, justice is universal and affects all concerned. You think we are the only ones in the battle, well hear what your bishop had to say to his priests "All catholic schools will be involved in this question"

What do you think ladies and gentlemen, are we right or are we wrong? Let us stick together, we have truth, we have justice, we have Almighty God on our side."

The District made good on its promise. 840 children were presented to the Board of the School District for enrollment. As promised, albeit with some difficulty, all were placed in various schools. The Vancouver Sun reported on Monday April 9:

*"**Catholic Pupils Throng Maillardville Public Schools** Hundreds of Catholic elementary and high school pupils, many accompanied by their parents, trudged down the hilly Maillardville roads early today to enroll in the District's overcrowded public schools. Their own schools stood empty and abandoned as Catholic parents of the little community, predominantly French Canadian, took this action in an effort to force the B.C. government into providing financial relief for separate schools. Almost 200 children were lined up at Millside School in the 900 block Brunette in Maillardville by 8:50am. Smaller line ups were reported in the nine other schools."*

The situation was neither to remain local nor would the "strikers" gain the universal support for "justice" for which they had hoped. The incident was reported in major newspapers across Canada and an unconfirmed report stated that the BBC had carried about four minutes of the "walkout". On April 11th, The BC Catholic reported that:

*"**Archdiocese Approves Maillardville Action** The joint Maillardville school boards received unanimous support Wednesday night at a special meeting of the BC Catholic Education Association, who endorsed the protest action taken last week in Maillardville. The meeting was attended by pastors and lay representatives of every parish in the Archdiocese of Vancouver."*

The controversy heated up when Reeve James Christmas stated at council:

"I personally don't believe in private schools and the government doesn't recognize them either."

When a motion was put forward that arrangements should be made for a meeting between school district representatives, the Catholic School Board, Council and Education Minister Straith, the Reeve imposed special powers to veto the action. Christmas delayed the meeting several times citing his unwillingness to "go over the heads" of School Board officials. During heated debate at Council on the matter, James Christmas stated:

"a predominantly happy situation had evolved from the sudden move which placed 800 Catholic children into public schools following the closing of the schools and that it was his wish that "those children remain in our schools forever".

Christmas received a death threat blaming him "for everything" and he is pictured in a local paper holding the letter and stating that threats "*don't scare me one little bit*" When the Reeve's delaying tactics could no longer keep Council from issuing an invitation to Minister Straith to meet, Christmas stated flatly that should the minister accept, *"he would not be present for he does not wish to attend any further meeting which concerns the Catholic school question."*

Reeve Christmas was not alone in his open opposition to the Catholic school action. The Mathewson Ratepayers Association forwarded a motion to Council *"opposing the spending of public funds for religious or denominational education."* The action also drew the ire of the United Church of Canada as they passed a resolution stating that *"public education should not foster a secularistic view of life."* Baptists also *"opposed the parochial school system of the Church of Rome especially the principle of subsidizing these schools from the public treasury."*

But the parents had their supporters. In Quebec:

"Le Comité Permanent de la Survivance Française en Amérique-a group dedicated to advancement of French culture in North America-has voted $500.00 to start a drive for funds for Roman Catholics in Maillardville, B.C. The committee, with members in nearly all the provinces and in some parts of the U.S., said the money would go to maintain the school for Catholics."

And from Montréal as reported in the Coquitlam Herald:

"...the state executive of the Knights of Columbus of the province launched a drive for funds in aid of the Catholics in Maillardville. The campaign opened Saturday by Judge T.A. Fontaine, state deputy, announcing there is a "dire need" for funds in the British Columbia community"

And on the political front:

"Recognition For Catholic Schools Backed *National Young Liberal Convention Saturday swung behind B.C. Catholics efforts to gain recognition for separate schools. The convention went on record urging each province to recognize minority rights in respect to education and to preserve them if they exist....The motion pointed out that Canada is a signatory to the U.N. Declaration of Human Rights which gives parents a prior right to choose the kind of education that shall be given to their children."*

On the local scene, the Vancouver Sun reported that:

"Catholics Launch Drive For Schools *A campaign to enlist all Lower Mainland Roman Catholics in the fight for separate school rights has been launched by the B.C. Catholic Education Association. The association has scheduled meetings in every parish in the drive to win* *provincial aid grants for Catholic schools. Meanwhile, Roman Catholic Archbishop W.M. Duke today hit out at a resolution opposing separate schools passed at the recent convention of the Grand Orange Lodge of B.C. Said Archbishop Duke: "The Catholic people have known for a long time the opposition of the Orange Association to their faith and to their schools." The Orangemen said separate schools would "be an added burden to the already overburdened taxpayer and create divisions and animosities."*

The initial uproar of the "walkout" passed and the Catholic students were assimilated into the public school system. The meeting with Minister Straith never took place. In a letter to Council, the Minister said:

"I have considered the Maillardville situation as a local matter for the school board to deal with. Naturally our department has been interested in the matter and has endeavored to keep informed, but I understand that the classrooms and teachers have been provided for our children who were registered with the board on the Tuesday after Easter. Because it is a local issue I have felt, and still feel, that the department of education should not intrude itself into a purely local matter."

Perhaps a more succinct summation of the situation was offered in the Fraser News:

"Summing up the situation, Victoria says this is a purely local situation, Council says it's a problem for the school board and the school board says there is no problem."

In all of this, both children and teachers had to cope under trying circumstances. One of those students, in elementary school at that time and placed at Millside School stated:

"It was a little difficult. The teachers didn't seem too happy that we were there. It wasn't too bad, but we had to stick together."

Another who was an elementary student at Fatima recalls that there was a subtle suggestion of rebellion on the part of the Catholic students when:

"the time came to recite the Lord's prayer, those children in public school would continue the prayer with: "For thine is the Kingdom etc".

100

In Catholic school, we recited the body of the prayer only. Now we refused to recite that part in the public school and we remained silent. The teachers were not happy with that, but we continued to refuse to say it."

On the other hand, it may not have been as difficult for high school students as one of those recalled:

"It wasn't much of a problem. We had things that we didn't have at the Catholic School like sewing classes."

Teachers who were already struggling under the double shift system found a sympathetic voice in this Coquitlam Herald editorial:

*"**Pity the Teachers**   While the claims of members of the Catholic faith in relation to minority rights under the educational system may be just, and while a whole school district are disrupted from their program of development, a thought might be given to hard pressed teachers, who, already working under extreme difficulties in overcrowded classrooms, and swing shifts are suddenly faced with an avalanche of 840 students.....It is the teacher who will endeavor to gain the confidence of the new pupils, who, uprooted from their normal routine, will be faced with strange surroundings, a different system of teaching, widely apart from their familiar routine ingrained deeply within them by habit of generations. Children whatever faith or creed are invariably vigorous, boisterous young animals, injected with the temper of the present controversy, are bound to react so that an undercurrent will prevail which again the tolerance of the teacher will do much to placate."*

Faced with a stalemate, the joint Catholic School Board implemented a new strategy. On April 20th, the Board pulled the Catholic students from their classes so that they could be given one day of religious instruction. It was reported that:

"The children will return to the public schools Tuesday, but a Catholic spokesman at Maillardville said that "from time to time they will be withdrawn to supply them with religious education."...A statement from the joint committee of Our Lady of Fatima and Our Lady of Lourdes at Maillardville said today "This one day return to our schools is not an act of capitulation. The struggle to obtain a just portion of the taxes of our district will go on."

School District 43 was quick to send a letter to all parents concerned pointing out that under the law, parents were required to ensure that their children attend school under pain of a maximum fine of $10.00 per day and the possibility of having the government Family Allowance cancelled. The letter[18] also stated:

"The Board is quite aware that with the shift classes now in operation it is quite possible for the parents or guardians of the children affected to have had them receive religious instruction at a time other than the school hours. It deeply regrets that the local parochial committee has seen fit to interfere with the continued education of the children and to use them in order to exploit a situation, which the School Board itself has no authority to control other than to discharge its duty under the powers given it by The School Act. Any continued disruption can only result in the disturbance to the children and to the hindrance of their education."

The Joint School Board replied that they would continue to withdraw the children periodically and that they would risk prosecution in order to do so. Asked if they would pay any fines that were levied, the board said they had no intention of paying fines and would go to jail instead.

Although the battle lines were drawn, the standoff remained. By September of 1951, the Catholic High School students returned to Lourdes. Support and enthusiasm waned and in September of 1952, the rest of the children returned to their own schools. At the time, it appeared that the "strike" was a dismal failure. All that was gained was the supplying of free schoolbooks by the government. The struggle went on, however, and the situation had garnered such widespread attention that Archbishop Duke sought to contain it. He wanted to establish the fight for minority rights as a universal Catholic action and not one whose origins were political. Nor was it to be associated specifically with cultural minority rights. The instigation of the action, having had its roots in French Maillardville, could easily be interpreted as a movement that was culturally based and therefore a "local" issue. In fact, portraying the situation as local, and therefore more easily dismissed, was exactly what government authorities had in mind.

The Archbishop spelled out his concerns clearly to Father J. Fouquette

---

[18] Archives, Our Lady of Lourdes Roman Catholic Church

of Our Lady of Lourdes with respect to funds received from the "Comité de la Survivance" After an exchange of letters, Archbishop Duke wrote on March 13[19]1953:

"Dear Father Fouquette,

I received your kind letter of February 25 regarding any possible funds from "Le Comité de la Survivance" for which I am grateful.

It was from the Secretary of the League of the Sacred Heart that we learned that there might be some possible funds coming through that source. As you remember, when the League itself offered to help us, it was on condition that the funds would come to Catholic schools in B.C. through our office which we set up to spearhead and direct the campaign for Catholic education rights and this has always been done by the League as our records show. This was what we advised in the beginning in order to keep the thing a Catholic issue rather than a national issue. This was also the advice of the Delegate to whom the League had written concerning the matter. This was to protect everybody lest it might seem a national appeal rather than a catholic appeal. Otherwise the matter would be interpreted wrongly by our enemies and used against us to make it appear that it was only some excitable people in Maillardville who were making the claim."

Later, in 1954, the Archdiocese once again petitioned the B.C. Government, now under W.A.C. Bennett. The petition was partially successful in that medical and dental exams were granted to all children.

In 1953, the Provincial Government directed the District of Coquitlam to place Church buildings on the Municipal tax roll, thus removing the tax-exempt status enjoyed by the French Canadian Catholics since 1909. The Joint School Board, now chaired by Maurice Lizée, refused to pay the taxes. This situation went on for several years. In September of 1956, the District claimed title to the schools for nonpayment of taxes. Mr. Lizée stated that the Board:

"has no intention of paying the taxes."

---

[19] Archives, Roman Catholic Archdiocese of Vancouver

During the course of events, former Reeve R.C. MacDonald placed an offer of $15,000.before Council to buy the three school buildings. In January of 1957, a motion at Council by Michael Butler, seconded by René Gamache, sought to cancel the taxes owed by the two parishes. Reeve Christmas immediately placed a stay on the motion because he was uncertain if Council had the authority to cancel the taxes. Upon legal evaluation, it was decided that since the buildings were municipal property, the motion was void. After several meetings between government and the Archdiocese, Archbishop Duke indicated that the taxes would be paid. The government issued an order in Council, directing the Municipality to transfer title back to the Church.

The Diocese wrote a cheque to the Parish of Our Lady of Lourdes for the entire amount of the taxes of $10,790.25 accompanied by the following letter[20], directing the parish to pay the taxes immediately.

"August 22, 1957

Dear Father Frechette,

I enclose the cheque needed to pay the school tax and to release our schools in order to reopen in the new school year.
Please deposit the cheque in your account and have the committee issue a cheque of their own to the Municipality to carry out the agreement of last evening at our meeting.
The committee then should make this statement to the press, namely "after consulting with the Church Authorities, the Catholic School Board of Maillardville have agreed to cooperate in meeting the school tax in order to open their schools for the new year. This decision was reached in the interests of all and for the common good."
Please attend to this at once and advise me what has been done.
We are grateful to Our Lady on her Feast Day of the Immaculate Heart of Mary, for her continual protection in this matter of such grave importance to the Church and to the welfare of souls, and the future success of our Catholic Schools.

With kind greetings and every blessing I remain
Devotedly yours in the Sacred Heart,

---

[20] Archives, Roman Catholic Diocese of Vancouver

Most Rev. W.M. Duke
Archbishop of Vancouver"

However, on August 23, a letter of the Joint School Board was read to
Council at Coquitlam that stated:

"We refuse to accept the order in council from Victoria, in regard to
payment of $10,790.25 in arrears of unjust taxes for return of ownership
of our properties, and ask that our properties be returned to us for the
price of $1."

After this apparent reluctance to comply with the Archbishop's directive,
the taxes were finally paid on September 6 and Title for the properties
was returned to the Parishes.

The entire period is a remarkable illustration of grass roots activism. In
the opinion of some, the militant action of the French Catholics in Maillardville, particularly the school strike of 1951/52, actually set back the
cause of recognition for independent schools. Many still view it as a minor event that accomplished little. However, the struggle for recognition
that dated back to the mid nineteenth century, and the renewed drive for
"equal rights" taken up by Archbishop Duke in the forties produced no
results and there is nothing to suggest that the situation would have
changed.

It has also been stated that the Archbishop sanctioned the action taken by
the Catholic School Board in 1951. However, that approval only came
after the fact. The Catholic School Board in Maillardville acted inde-
pendently. The strike itself was truly spectacular and gained immediate
attention across the country. It provoked much discussion, and brought
the realities of dual taxation, and the larger issue of the right of parents
to educate their children in the Faith squarely to the fore. Combined with
the refusal later in the decade to pay the property taxes, the entire action
finally forced the provincial government to address the issue. By 1957,
not only did all independent schools in B.C. have access to free textbooks and medical services, but the provincial government granted tax
exemption. Father Paul Vanier and Father Joseph Fouquette fought the
good fight in the late forties and early fifties along with Father Meunier
at Fatima. Father A. Frechette arrived at O.L. of Lourdes in 1953. A very
well educated and passionate man, a resolution to the "school question"

was a goal close to his heart. When the government in 1957 granted tax exemption, he wrote[21]:

"On Monday, March 4, 1957, the Social Credit government at Victoria, British Columbia, gave first reading for tax exemption for all independent schools in B.C. This, ladies and gentlemen is a new victory for the fight for our schools in Maillardville...So on March 5, all of the newspapers proclaimed the tax exemption for all independent schools as of July, 1957 as a victory for the Catholics. Make no mistake. Everyone knows that this victory is because of the ongoing struggle in Maillardville...Maillardville was alone in this fight....Honour to all of our valiant warriors, past and present who were the craftsmen of this victory, and mainly to the joint Catholic School Board of the two parishes of Maillardville and their inflexible president. Mr. Maurice Lizée! Honour also to our municipal councilors, especially to the dynamic Mr. Michael Butler. Honour to Maillardville, wherein its little corner of the country, continues the mission of "précurseur" for the French Canadian people in a manner worthy of their ancestors."

In 1970, the B.C. Legislature received a motion by Mr. D.G. Little entitled "An Act For The Recognition of Independent Schools". In 1977, the provincial government passed legislation that allowed partial grants for the operation of independent schools. To this day, churches still must build their schools from their own resources and fund fifty percent of their operating costs while contributing, through their taxes, to the operation of the public school system.

Both parishes, though bonded through the fifties by the ongoing struggle for independent school recognition, continued their separate journeys. Changes were occurring, especially at Our Lady of Lourdes.

In 1952 the Sisters of the Child Jesus left Maillardville. The stresses of the previous year's strike played a significant role in the decision to leave, but other factors also came into play. Father Fouquette had grown increasingly concerned that there would not be enough teaching Sisters to serve the needs of the schools in the two parishes. He was also concerned that he would have to hire lay teachers; an expense he believed he could not afford. His solution was to seek the aid of another teaching order of nuns, the Ursuline Sisters from Quebec. The Superior of the

---

[21] Archives, Our Lady of Lourdes Roman Catholic Church

Sisters of the Child Jesus sent a letter dated July 28, 1952[22] to Father J. Fouquette stated that a breach of promise to be the sole teaching order for the two Catholic parishes was unacceptable.

"Reverend Father,

Before leaving for France, Mother Dorothy, under the approval of Reverend Mother General and her Council, closed St. Mary's School in order to furnish six Sisters to reinforce the teaching staff in Lourdes, Maillardville. It was understood at the time that we were the sole Congregation of Sisters teaching there.

In June, a new situation arose where three Ursuline Sisters were accepted by the Parish to teach also in Lourdes School. France objected. Orders came from our Reverend Mother to withdraw our Sisters if Ursulines were accepted. We offered to remain if the first apparent understanding with Mother Dorothy was fulfilled, that is our Sisters teaching without any other Congregation. This was not accepted. Father gave the following answer: "The Ursuline Sisters are coming."

Therefore, as directed by France, we regret to have to withdraw our Sisters from Lourdes.

Respectfully yours,

The Sisters of the Child Jesus"

In the end, the Sisters left Maillardville. They had served the village since 1909 after 41 years of continuous service. This parting of ways must have been truly painful for the community and for these good women, faithful for so many decades.

Father Leduc at Fatima brought Les Soeurs du Bon Pasteur (Sisters of the Good Shepherd) to teach at the elementary school. Les Soeurs Ursuline de Rimouski took up their teaching duties at O.L of Lourdes, where they remained until 1968.

Father Fouquette was also busy with other concerns during this early part of the decade. The Catholic community continued to grow. Our La-

---

[22] Archives, Roman Catholic Archdiocese of Vancouver

dy of Lourdes was divided in 1946 with the creation of the new parish of Our Lady of Fatima. Now, in 1953 a second division was being contemplated for the area at Dawes Hill.

An acre was purchased. Archbishop Duke approved the application of a loan to build the new church and a name was chosen. In keeping with the local tradition of honouring the Virgin Mary, and given the church was to be situated upon a hill, " Our Lady of Mount Carmel" was deemed to be an appropriate title.

Father Fouquette was not destined to see the completion of the project. As a result of his increasing stress and fatigue, it was decided to invite the Franciscan Fathers to take over the care of the parish. Correspondence between the Archbishop and the Superior of the Franciscans, Father Alphonse Claude-Laboissière, describes both the Franciscans' willingness to accept the assignment and their concern that splitting the parish (to create the new Dawes Hill congregation) might result in a diminishing of the resources required to support the new priests.

With assurances in place, Father Armand (Alberic) Frechette O.F.M. and Father John Forest Galvin O.F.M. came to Lourdes in September of 1953. They were the first in a long line of Franciscans who would serve the parish.

The anticipated birth of the new parish of Our Lady of Mount Carmel was never realised. In 1955, with fresh financial concerns burdening the parish, Father Frechette obtained permission to sell the Dawes Hill site, purchased for $2000.00. Permission was granted, and the property sold for $2500.00.

In 1951, the school on Hammond Avenue was completed. In 1959, as a Golden Jubilee project, parish plans were moving ahead to build a convent school on Rochester Avenue.

"Drive To Build New Convent In Maillardville   *Maillardville's golden jubilee year is to be marked by a new convent for the Ursuline sisters. Fund objective is $140,000.00 and the building will be erected on property owned by Our Lady of Lourdes parish at Rochester and Laval Streets. Plans call for two story and basement of reinforced concrete and concrete block with brick exterior. It will contain living quarters for five*

nuns plus 12 school classrooms, service rooms and chapel. A one canvas of the parish is to be made on Dec.6"

That building was completed in July of 1961 and in a letter to Archbishop Duke dated September 21, 1961[23], Father Fréchette describes the building:

"Your Excellency,

We have completed last July the construction of, I must say, a beautiful Convent and School, at the total cost of $194,000.00 or $7.00 a square foot. The three stories masonry construction covers an area of 27,000 square feet and comprises, besides all the Sisters quarters, 7 classrooms, recreation room, laboratory, sewing room, kindergarten, school economic kitchen, etc."

Our Lady of Fatima, meanwhile, was already outgrowing its original facilities and in 1958 the new (present day) church was completed and blessed by Archbishop Johnson. Sadly, Father Leduc, while on an errand to pick up some building supplies for the church suffered a fatal heart attack. He was 44 years old. Father Gérard Labonté succeeded him. Fatima Parish also realized a dream conceived by Father Leduc and Sister Euchariste; a convent and boarding school was completed in 1957 housing 15 Sisters and 35 boarders.

With the building of schools, convents and churches, fundraising was never very far removed from regular parish activity. Father Meunier at Fatima was said to be a true organizer and retriever of funds and did it in a big way. The Herald in May of 1950 reports:

"Maillardville Parish Will Hold Bazaar *A gala three day bazaar and carnival will be held on Saturday, Sunday and Monday, May 13,14 and 15 at our Lady of Fatima Hall, 747 Alderson Avenue, Maillardville. Doors will open daily at 10am and continue until 10pm. A galaxity of prizes including clothing, radios, refrigerators, merchandise, and also a drawing on a new Chevrolet sedan to be given away to lucky winners. Games will include billiards, pool, Wheel of Fortune, Cards, Fish Ponds, refreshment booths. Proceeds from the weekend Bazaar will be used towards completion of the school."*

---

[23] Archives, Roman Archdiocese of Vancouver

Apart from aggravating strikes, the two parish schools were also known for their choirs and their gymnastic abilities. In 1951, Fatima was singled out for its musical superiority:

"Maillardville Choir To broadcast French Canadian Folk Music *Sung by well known Lower Mainland French Canadian choirs, the broadcasts have proved to be an immediate hit with CKNW listeners. These are heard each Sunday night from 10:30 to 10:53 each night....Among the choirs to be heard will be three of the Lady of Fatima in Maillardville (senior group, young people's group and the school) the Blessed Sacrament in Vancouver, the Lady of Lourdes in Maillardville, two choirs formed by the French teachers in Vancouver Schools, and two formed by the French teachers in Haney High School."*

In 1954 and 1955, the boys' gymnastics team at O.L of Lourdes was winning championships at various competitions around B.C.and were also sought after to entertain at public functions:

"Plans Now Complete For "Largest Yet" Fall Fair *Co-operation from the weatherman is all that is needed to make the three day fall fair a success......Attractions for Saturday, September 4, the first day, include hobby, art and manufacturers exhibits, stage entertainment, games, rides and children's pet parade. Exhibition of tumbling by the Our Lady of Lourdes team of Maillardville is said by those who have seen the boys previously to be worth the price of admission alone."*

Success in the competitive arena extended far beyond the borders of the District of Coquitlam. This report c. 1954:

"At BC Open Competition Lourdes Gym team Takes Four Ti- tles *Members of the Our Lady of Lourdes gym team won two junior championships and two novice titles in the BC open gymnastic champi- onships at the University of BC at the weekend. Twelve year old Neil Godin, competing against men up to 25 years of age, won the junior mat tumbling title and Gilbert Braconnier took second place. Godin will be competing in the senior division next year when he turns 13. The Mail- lardville boys took the top three places in the flying rings, Maurice Parent finishing first, Alfie Duhamel second and Paul Painchaud third. Robert Chartier won first place in the junior free standing exercises and Gilbert Braconnier was second. Braconnier took top honours in the jun- ior long horse competition. In other competitions, 12 year old Joseph*

Marchand placed third in the novice free standing exercises. Gil Gagnon was second in the novice mat tumbling and M. Parent in the novice parallel bars. Johnny Arrowsmith was second in the novice long horse event. Team director Don Cunnings said today that he was very pleased with his boys showing and added that the squad would definitely take part in the Pacific Northwest championships at Courtney on Saturday."

The Lourdes team went on to win the BC Junior High School Championship three years running and in 1955, the District of Coquitlam set its sights on the Canadian Championship competition in Ontario. Eight were to make the trip, including three from the O.L of Lourdes team. They were Joseph Marchand, Rhéal Finnigan and Robert Chartier. Lack of funding whittled the team down to four and then two, including Joseph Marchand. In spite of this, the pair accumulated enough points to place second in the competition.

Maillardville always did enjoy its sports. Like all of the decades that preceded it, the fifties was a time for baseball. The Frenchmen from Maillardville continued to dominate the Dewdney League. From 1953 through 1958 both junior and senior teams, often referred to as the "powerful Athletics",won several league pennants and playoff series.

Another big change for the village took place in 1950 when the B.C. Provincial Police ceased to exist. Just as the switch from a municipal police force in 1926 and the departure of Émeri Paré was the end of an era, so too was the exit of the B.C.P.P. and especially of Constable Jimmy McGarry. He had been a true friend of the community, working tirelessly through the war years with the ARP.

There was a renewed effort in the early fifties to build the community centre, that dream so dear to his heart, with the establishment of the Coquitlam-Fraser Mills Community Centre Association. Its specific goal was to revive the project. The Association quickly dissolved and was replaced by the Coquitlam-Fraser Mills Youth Centre. There was consultation with H.J. Mackin but in the end the effort failed. McGarry's dream of building a "youth centre" in Mackin Park was never realized.

However, true to form, he had one last project in him; to establish a gun club. This was in answer to the growing problem of vandalism and youth crime. His project was realized with the construction of a 24 by 100 foot structure along Brunette Creek, just off North Road.

The RCMP began service in August of 1950 and, pleased with the results, Council approved a one year agreement with them commencing in January of 1951. In 1954, the Municipality purchased a new green Pontiac sporting the latest in crime fighting equipment; a two way radio! Although former BCPP officers would be accepted into the RCMP, McGarry chose to retire his star and take an executive position with Allard Cement Works. There was some discussion that a local municipal force should be organized but that did not materialize.

More significant change was on the horizon. The early fifties saw the rise of the "Shopping Centre". By 1958, there were centres located at Cariboo, Burquitlam and Maillardville.

"Maillardville Shopping Centre Opened Here   Official opening of the new $750,000 Maillardville Shopping Centre at Lougheed and Brunette took place June 25. The Centre-the buildings are finished in pink stucco-was built by Atlas Developments Ltd. Included in the U shaped structure are a supermarket, drug store, bank, hardware, beauty salon, sub-post office, dentist's office, shoe store, jewelers, bakery, dry cleaner, restaurant, community hall and service station."

A bowling centre known as B&B Recreations opened in 1954 at 933 1/2 Brunette Avenue. The ownership changed at Sam's Theatre in 1951. It was known thereafter as the "Academy" except to some of the French residents it was the "Academe". It burned to the ground in 1956. Near the end of this decade, the commercial district along Brunette and the surrounding area was still a vibrant one, looking a little different from ten years earlier. Many of the older businesses had disappeared to be replaced by new ones. The advent of easily accessible shopping centres must have added to the challenge of staying competitive in that expanding world. Yet having such a centre in Maillardville able to supply the needs of local residents provided an "anchor" that helped keep the commercial district alive. The importance of that anchor would be clearly demonstrated some decades later with its loss and the resulting devastating effect.

Nevertheless, business in Maillardville continued to thrive throughout the fifties. With a new bank at the shopping centre and the continued presence of the District of Coquitlam Credit Union, it would not be surprising if the Caisse Populaire had struggled to compete. This was not the case. In 1950, the Credit Union officially changed its name to the

Caisse Populaire de Maillardville Credit Union. With both membership and assets growing, the business of the CU could no longer be maintained in a private residence. In 1951, council approved an application to place a small commercial building on the property owned by Victor Muller at the corner of Brunette Avenue and Nelson Street. The building was indeed a modest one. With a budget of $1000.00 the building was to be 14 feet by twenty two, the interior finished in "ten-test", and the exterior in stucco. Mr. Muller was to be paid a rent for the use of his property of $1.00 per month.

The Credit Union continued on its mission of consolidation of the French community. One of the ways it accomplished this was by instituting the "school program" in 1951. A special savings program was offered to the children in the Maillardville Catholic schools. This program brought many new members to the Caisse and it continued for several decades, each successive class being marched down the hills to Brunette Avenue, led by habit-clad nuns.

Characteristic of Maillardville and seemingly of the French community, crisis was never far off. In 1955, with business booming, a serious clash of philosophies was visited upon the Caisse Populaire. Founded upon the notion of *"uniting the French community through financial solidarity"* the time had come to consider other possibilities. The dilemma was inevitable. One school of thought was that for the Caisse to remain competitive in a difficult market, the bond limiting membership to practicing French Canadian Catholics, should be opened to permit a broader membership. The opposing view, of course, was that the Caisse had to remain true to its founding principles. The crisis erupted when at the 1956 AGM and after bitter debate the membership agreed upon the former philosophy: the Credit Union would be opened to non-Catholic members. After ten years of managing the Credit Union, Victor Muller resigned his position. Some 200 members followed him diminishing the Credit Union's assets by 20%. But the immediate crisis was to find someone to take over as manager.

Mr. Léo Leblanc agreed to take the position on a part time and temporary basis. Mr. J.B. Goulet was named general manager in July of 1957. In addition, the credit union building, located on Mr. Muller's property, had to be moved as he had disassociated himself with the institution. In May of 1957, the building was moved to 1013 Brunette Avenue. In the meantime, Mr. Ernest Braconnier, the new CU president, went door to door to try to persuade those who had withdrawn over the crisis to return to the fold. The community rode out this storm, but it would take over five years for the Caisse Populaire to regain the ground lost.

While Maillardville excelled in music, gymnastics and baseball, some of the village's more mundane concerns continued to challenge. In spite of the problem with water supply and sewage disposal throughout the previous decade, these same issues remained unresolved in the fifties. Council minutes and newspaper reports tell us of residents' constant complaints that there was no water pressure. The construction of a water tower at the corner of Como Lake Avenue and Poirier Street helped to alleviate this difficulty. The problem of overloaded septic systems continued to the end of the decade and resulted in the following accusation being hurled at council as reported in May, 1957:

*"**District Denies Stalling Sewers** Charges that the District of Coquitlam is stalling the sewer development in Maillardville were denied by councilors Monday night. "We feel very little progress is being made on the project" said Harry Monk, Coquitlam Board of Trade president. "Progress is being made" retorted Councilor Mike Butler, "Sewerage is coming to the municipality 15 years too late but that is not the fault of the present Council."*

This was indeed no exaggerated concern, as at the same meeting a Simon Fraser Health Unit official told Council:

"That a breakdown of the municipality's septic tank systems had increased illness among school children. One school had an absentee rate of 43 percent, much of it due to illness attributed to "virus infection" from overflowing septic tanks, the doctor said."

By 1959, a new sewer construction by-law was in place. Brunette Avenue was also in deplorable condition and was described thus in the Fraser News;

"Brunette Street has ceased to be a road; it has become a series of potholes instead. At the foot of Lougheed Highway, which is our main shopping area in the district, is a shocking disgrace. At the bus stop lately, passengers alighting from the bus have no choice but to step into a pool of dirty water."

In 1951, a Brunette improvement project was initiated that saw the widening of Brunette from Swift's Packing House to Schoolhouse Road.

These were not the only problems facing Council. The call for secession from the District by residents of the east end was taken up once again in 1958. They were dissatisfied with the lack of services being provided by the District. They also believed that City Hall, located in Maillardville, was altogether too far removed from them for their voices to be adequately heard. Interestingly, while the rumblings of discontent were sounding from the east, the same desire for secession was being expressed in Burquitlam, which desired to join the City of New Westminster. It is not surprising then to find that Council's attention was once again drawn away from Maillardville. Council embarked upon the creation of a new zoning plan for the east end. By 1959, the plan was integrated with that of west Coquitlam. Obviously, neither the east end residents nor those of Burquitlam followed through with secession plans. Clearly, Maillardville was becoming a small fish in an ever-growing pond.

That pond also included Burke Mountain, at that time seen as a future skiing centre and endlessly promoted by Councilor Gamache. In fact he was such an ardent booster he was known as the "Burke Mountain Kid" as the Fraser News in April, 1950 reports:

"Councilor Gamache who has been dubbed the Burke Mountain Kid has been busy promoting the Burke Mountain area which is little known at this time. He has been showing colour films that were taken at various times last year...it will be but a half hour's drive from New Westminster and will be rated as one of the best ski resorts in this part of the country."

Overall, the municipality was finally acquiring the tools and skills to manage growth, and the decade included the establishment of a permanent Fire Department with its first full time Chief.

Change was also afoot on the political front. There were several notable events. The first was that M.J. Butler, friend of Maillardville, resigned his seat on Council to challenge James Christmas for the Reeveship in 1954. He lost. Mr. Butler went on to lead the Maillardville Ratepayers' Association for a time and then was reelected to Council. The MRA continued their good work in the early fifties, although a note in the Fraser News, cries:

"What is the matter with the Maillardville Ratepayers' Association? At the regular meeting for May only 14 members turned out and at previous meetings there have been less..."

The notice seemed to have made a little difference as a good crowd turned out for the following meeting. Lamentably, the MRA seems to have disappeared c.1953, resurfacing briefly in the early sixties.

René Gamache, also a tireless worker for the French community at Maillardville, threw his hat into the federal arena. In 1953, he won the Social Credit nomination for Burnaby- Coquitlam. He had the support of the party, to be sure, as the premiers of BC and Alberta W.A.C. Bennett and Ernest Manning attended a picnic and rally at Blue Mountain Park. The campaign turned ugly as the CCF candidate Ernie Regier, accused Gamache and the Socreds of dealing in dirty tactics to the detriment of Maillardville. The Herald, August 3, 1953:

*"**CCF Candidate Attacks Socred Tactics** Social Credit tactics in Burnaby-Coquitlam were branded as "unbecoming to a party aspiring to gain the confidence of Canadians" stated Ernie Regier, CCF candidate at a meeting in Agricultural Hall. Organized heckling, rowdiness, the tearing down and covering of posters and the destruction of costly billboards; and the appeal to religious feelings in such places as Maillardville will be rejected by decent citizens. The Social Credit candidate had done more to harm the reputation of the good citizens of Maillardville than had any previous election candidate, said Regier."*

One of the main issues of the election was the fight against communism. The article quoted above did not give equal airtime to Mr. Gamache, leaving us in the dark as to his response. He went on to lose to Regier by a margin of 7165 to 4172. Afterward René Gamache said:

"We did well. The odds were against us and we knew it. The cooperation of our workers was really heartwarming, something I'll never forget."

He returned to municipal politics.

Finally, a symbolic, if not significant, change took place at the polling stations. As of 1954, Maillardville was no longer polled as a distinct area, perhaps a reflection of the "lessening" of Maillardville's role in the District.

Francophone organizations thrived and contributed to the richness of life in French Maillardville. The Knights of Columbus, Council 3239, considered to be the only completely French Council in North America outside of Quebec, continued their good works. Another of her citizens, Dr. Léon Beaudoing, led the Cercle Canadien Français at Maillardville. Even those outside of le cercle had the good sense to occasionally recognize and honour pioneers and heroes of the community. In August of 1955, the Herald anticipated a celebration of pioneers:

*"**To Honour Coquitlam's Pioneers**   Sunday, August 7 is the date set for the presentation of silver trays to four of the District's pioneer residents. The four to be honoured are Mrs. L.K. Irvine, Irvine Rd., Miss Frances Atkins, North Rd., Jean Baptiste Dicaire, 1303 Laval Square, and Togo Boileau, Hammond Street...Mr. Dicaire was among the first of three groups of French Canadian settlers to come to Coquitlam September 29, 1909 to work in Fraser Mills and is believed to be the first man off the CPR train. He operates a pool hall on Brunette Street. Togo Boileau, nephew of Mr. and Mrs. Eugene Boileau was the first French Canadian baby born in Coquitlam."*

All was going swimmingly for the French community. The census of 1951 shows a French population at Maillardville of 3,768 (13000 residents in Coquitlam in 1950), double of that a decade earlier. Two parishes were prospering along with three schools. Two new convents, one including a secondary school, the other a girls' boarding facility, were constructed in this decade, much of it the work of Fernand Filliatrault. Most of the activity for young people was offered through the Church and its organizations, including school sports and social opportunities provided by the CYO.

In 1955, Mr. Jean Lambert had a dream of starting a scouting movement for French Canadian Catholic boys. At age seven, Mr. Lambert had been "louveteau" (cub scout) in Gravelbourg Saskatchewan. Working his way up through the system, he became "Éclaireur". He eventually led a troupe of cubs on a camping trip and *"enjoyed the experience very much."* So Mr. Lambert starting with the words *"We can do nothing without help"* founded Les Scouts francophones de la Colombie Britan-nique. His idea was met with skepticism, and he was strongly urged to work with the already established Boy Scouts. Eventually Mr. Lambert connected with "Les Scouts Catholique du Quebec".

Armed with the necessary program information and supported by the Knights of Columbus, Mr. Lambert, along with Napoléon Gareau, René Gamache and Lucien Ayotte formed the first "meute" comprising of 24 louveteaux. One year later a second troupe was added. The organization grew steadily and as the first louveteaux grew up, they became Éclaireurs and Pionniers. The young ladies were not forgotten. In 1957, Suzanne Lambert, Alice Gamache and Lucille Bruneau began organiz-ing. They soon had their first group of 42 girls and so the Jeannettes were born, soon to be followed by "Les guides". The establishment of these groups tied the French boys and girls of Maillardville closer still to that cultural group and it is further evidence of the distancing of the Franco and Anglo communities.

If the pioneers missed a big celebration for the fortieth anniversary of their arrival, they made up for it at the Golden Jubilee. The anniversary was celebrated with enthusiasm and panache, beginning in March with the First Mass and Ordination banquet of Father Lester Roberge, which included a concert by the parish choir. March 30 was the kick off to the three-day "Grand Bazaar". On the 23rd, the senior and junior CYO pre-sented a concert that included songs, pantomime and plays. The juniors performed *"Bobbie pulls her socks"* while the seniors presented *"The Monkey's Paw"* The day itself, September 27, was marked by the cele-bration of a Pontifical High Mass followed by a grand banquet. Among the guests of honour were three bishops, the Honourable L. Wicks repre-senting the province, Reeve James Christmas and the Consuls of France and Belgium.

The menu was served in grand style with all of the courses being named for significant people in the life of Maillardville. For example "Menu Au Banquet A La Duke" was named for Archbishop Duke. Other offerings included Lait "O'Boyle", Pain Théroux des Pionniers, Dinde a la Pelle-tier and of course Cigars du Père Teck and Cure-dents du Fraser Mills. After speeches, the evening closed with "O Canada". It was a yearlong celebration. The Federation Canadienne-française de la Colombie-Britanique held a three-day congress in Maillardville. A solemn mass for the deceased of the parish was celebrated in November. Finally, in December, the parish celebrated with a High Mass and a play following the history of French Maillardville written by Father Frechette and performed by the schoolchildren. The name of the play? *"The Little Seed Has Become A Large Tree"*. It is clear that for the French Canadians in Maillardville, language, culture and religion remained as one.

Nineteen fifty nine marked fifty years since the arrival of the first French Canadians to Coquitlam. What tremendous change occurred over five decades! From raw forest, the pioneers carved out the "French settlement" and then built Maillardville. They lived the joy of a growing French community, the trials of war, strike, Depression and the bitter disappointment of the school strike. There were victories and setbacks. Down through the decades all of it was met with laughter and tears, courage and determination.

Fifty years after Johnny Dicaire stepped off that CPR train at Millside, the Frenchmen not only survived but also lived in a time that must have seemed truly golden. Along with two French parishes, there were schools, youth clubs, men's and women's clubs, French scouts and guides, a French credit union and a provincial French association seated at Maillardville. All of these things were brought into existence for love of that unassailable triumvirate; language, culture and religion. The little seed really did produce a large tree!

But as vibrant as that community was, there were other forces and influences in Maillardville. From 1913, when the new District of Coquitlam located its council chambers in Maillardville, Anglo, Franco and others had to learn to live and grow together. Nevertheless, by the fifties, many of the old traditions were giving way to greater mobility and new social and economic opportunities. The district was growing rapidly, and there was less focus on Maillardville. Perhaps more evidence of the separation of the English and French communities can be found in what was not printed in local papers.

In examining the Coquitlam papers through all of these decades, there appears to be an ongoing "rivalry" between Port Coquitlam and the District of Coquitlam. Such a great bias in favour of Port Coquitlam exists that events in Coquitlam go unreported for long periods of time. Then, just as suddenly, news of Coquitlam once again becomes available. More subtly, the paper displays at times, a certain reluctance to print news of the French community. For example, it takes many years for the paper to mention the Lourdes parish by name, usually referring to it as the Catholic Church at Maillardville. This is in contrast to the regular naming of Our Lady of the Assumption parish in Port Coquitlam. In the late forties, the lack of reporting on Coquitlam events is very apparent. It appears the Fraser News was established in 1949 as an answer to that situation. Yet, as a "Coquitlam focused" paper, news of the French community and its activities was omitted throughout 1950.

And what of the school strike? It is clear that the action by the French Catholics did not sit well with some members of the community. Even the mention of *"the further damage of the reputation of the citizens of Maillardville"* by CCF candidate E. Regier suggests a division between Franco and Anglo. Therefore, how ironic it is that the French Canadians were brought to Fraser Mills to resolve a problem based on racism, only to find themselves the object of racist attitudes. Nevertheless, the fifties was a time of great activity and advancement for the French community and for Maillardville in general. Soon, the "Pepsi generation", the "British Invasion", the pill, and men on the moon would bring the same challenges to Maillardville as they did everywhere.

In closing the decade, and bringing to an end the first fifty years of this history of Maillardville, it is fitting to acknowledge the passing of some of its pioneers, noting the year of their arrival at Maillardville and the year of death:

M.et Mme. Rémy Boileau	1910-1955
M.et Mme. Joseph Duplin	1912-1954
M.et Mme. Napoléon Choteau	1910-1951
M.et Mme. Hector Charland	1911-1951
M.et Mme. Paul Hinchey	1911-1958
M.et Mme. Wilfred Duplin	1910-1954
M.et Mme. Ernest Gagné	1909-1957
M. Joseph Hinchey	1911-1956
M.et Mme. Stanislaus Lamoureux	1909-1957
M.et Mme. Delphis Payer	1910-1957
M. Arcade Paré	1910-1958

Six

Quantum Leap:
Change Comes to the Village

Mercury, John Glen, JFK, Bay of Pigs, "The British Invasion", mini skirts, hippies, RFK, Viet Nam, "I have a dream", long hair, Woodstock, Martin Luther King Jr., Black Power, "sock it to me", CKLG, The "Groove-yard", Ed Sullivan Show, "We're more popular than Jesus", Battle of the Bands, Be-In, Cold War, fallout shelters, CD, "this is a test of the emergency broadcast system", LSD, agent orange, 4 dead in Ohio, Walter Cronkite, "Look out! Helter Skelter", the Manson family, ratfink, the Quiet Revolution, "Vive le Quebec Libre!", "One small step for man, one giant leap for mankind."

quan-tum leap (plural quan-tum leaps) noun: **sudden change or advance**: a sudden, dramatic, and significant change or advance.

Oh what a decade it was! Maillardville, along with the rest of the world, struggled to maintain its equilibrium in the flash flood of change that engulfed it. The sexual revolution, the pill and women's rights undermined the traditional authority of religion, especially that of the Catholic Church. Mass communication brought the world, its wars, its protests and all of the rest into the homes of rich and poor alike. The spectre of nuclear holocaust and the horror of the Viet Nam war ensured that people, especially younger people, felt a profound uncertainty about their future.

In addition, Maillardville faced its own distinct challenges. Television, radio and magazines brought the English speaking world ever closer to Maillardville. Population growth in the Lower Mainland continued its dramatic rise. Where to put all the people? In the early days, Maillardville was left to grow and flourish in blessed isolation, but now the world was fully encroaching upon it, bringing a new kind of isolation that would challenge the community more than ever before.

The English population of Maillardville and the French Catholic community both had reason for high hopes at the dawn of the new decade. The robust development of the Lower Mainland of Vancouver ensured that Coquitlam and Maillardville would continue to grow and prosper. In fact, the population of Coquitlam was increasing at a rate of over 25% every five years from the mid-fifties through 1970. Yet, overall, the District was still largely undeveloped and the main commercial and residential centers continued to be Cariboo, Burquitlam and Maillardville.

But growth has its price. In 1961, Maillardville finally saw the beginning of its long awaited sewer project. The Lougheed Highway was already bringing increased traffic to Brunette. When the Port Mann Bridge and the Brunette interchange came into use, little Brunette Avenue, still functionally not much better than the original Pitt River Road, was overwhelmed. Traffic jams became a daily occurrence and by 1966, the main village thoroughfare had to be widened.

However, these were minor issues compared to the much larger problem that was now looming on the horizon. The explosive growth in population resulted in a housing shortage that was so acute it assumed almost crisis proportions. For Maillardville, it gave rise to the apartment building and the proliferation of these structures is a defining point for the village in the sixties. The shortage was complicated further by a high proportion of lower income owners in the area. The creation of "affordable housing" became a necessity. Reeve and Council set about building a zoning map to govern the development of medium and high-density projects. At the same time, they created a "plan for urban renewal and low rent public housing". Five centres were selected for such housing; Cariboo, Burquitlam, Austin, Harbour Village and Maillardville which took the lion's share of potential development with an allotment of some 95 acres. The others ranged in size from as little as eighteen acres to forty-eight for Burquitlam.

And develop they did. Starting in the early sixties, the apartments at Marathon Court were built on what had been the Booth/Bréhault dairy farm. In fact, the new building stood directly opposite the Bréhault house: the new order challenging the old. As the sixties unfolded, more and more complexes were built. Wildwood Trailer Park, Kostur's Trailer Park and the three-story walk up apartments on Brunette all blossomed in Maillardville at this time. The Canadian Mortgage and Housing Corporation, to encourage the building of low rent housing, offered up to 90% of development costs, with the provincial government and developer contributing the final 10%. Under this plan, Council considered buying up some of the large old houses on Brunette Avenue east of Marmont in order to convert them to multi-unit rentals. Unfortunately for this original core of handsome buildings, Council did not follow through with the plan. The opportunity lost, it was left to others to buy up the houses a little later on. With few, if any, improvements to the properties they were rented out on "easy" terms. The buildings were left to rot and as of 2009 only one home of the originals on Brunette remains.

There were other, more grandiose projects considered for Maillardville during this period. At least two major proposals were put forward. One was a high-rise hotel to be located in the 900 block Lougheed, just south of Brunette. Situated on a 17 acre site, the $1 million dollar structure was to be *"similar to class A hotels in the Richmond-Burnaby-Vancouver area"* according to developers. The other was for a massive $20 million development. The Herald reports in November 1969:

*"**Proposed $20 Million High Rise To Receive Another Hearing** Pending Coquitlam Council approval following a second hearing, a $20 million apartment project by Woodrise Securities Ltd. which would include three storey apartments, service stations and a number of stores will get underway. The development is located in the 600 block Alderson Avenue and bounded by Tenby Street, the Lougheed Highway and Girard Avenue...The gigantic development would involve some 1440 units, complete with town centre concept and including the Christmas Park development."*

Perhaps not surprisingly, none of these more lucrative plans ever came to fruition. As a final indignity and with a soupcon of irony, that venerable (if dilapidated) icon of early Maillardville life, the Tremblay Hall at the corner of Laval and Brunette, was demolished in 1969 to make room for the Eiffel Apartment.

The net effect of this development was twofold for Maillardville. First, it established the area as a lower income, less desirable place to be. Second, the tremendous influx of people, for the most part, did not claim French as their mother tongue. In 1955, French people comprised 23% of the total population in Coquitlam. By the end of the decade that percentage dropped to six, with most of it concentrated around Laval Square.

The French community felt the effect of that change. They were justifiably afraid that their language and culture would be overwhelmed and lost. In a 1965 CBC radio interview, concern was expressed by Councilors Filliatrault and Gamache, J.B. Goulet and Roméo Paquette that language and culture were indeed being forgotten. In Mr. Filliatrault's opinion, although some 6000 French people still resided in Coquitlam, they were not like the French Canadians of the past. Many no longer spoke French at all, or did so only in the home. The influence of television and especially radio made speaking French unpopular among the youth. It was "uncool" to speak French and one teacher from the public school system observed that: *"Maillardville youths who converse in French are considered square by their chums."* Reeve James Christmas was not worried about the young people, commenting in 1967 that:

"younger people are spreading out all over the District. This is all right. We mix with one another. There's no problem. It's the other way in fact. It's a good thing."

Nor did the rising tide of English culture seem to bother Father A. Frechette, Pastor at O.L. of Lourdes. *"Maillardville is a real fort of French culture and language. We are compact down here, very well grouped."*

Intermarriage with non-francophones also played a tremendous role in the erosion of the French community, and all in the above-mentioned interview echoed that sentiment. One also placed the blame for the young not learning the language squarely upon the shoulders of parents. However, many parents simply wanted the best for their children and feared that if they did not possess adequate English skills, they would be left behind. Nearing the end of the decade, the feeling of isolation and desolation grew. In a Vancouver Sun article c1969, a French resident of Vancouver stated that:

"some new arrivals admit that they would rather die than be seen in Maillardville."

It seems even Reeve and Council wished to abandon Maillardville. In 1966 and '67, Council tried twice to secure the support of its taxpayers to provide them with a new City Hall complex to be located on Poirier Street. The Herald, November 1966:

"One referendum will be a money by-law for a new municipal hall which is expected to cost between $750,000 and $800,000. Building plans call for modern hall to be located in the civic centre area on Poirier Street near the School Board and health unit offices."

The plebiscite was defeated both times.

It was not only the "watering down" of the French population in Maillardville that plagued its residents. No living community can perpetuate itself without the lifeblood of youth. The sixties brought fresh trials for church and state.

"Turn on, tune in, drop out" "If it feels good do it" "Sex, Drugs and Rock and Roll"

One of the three pillars of language, culture and religion, which had for so long upheld the French community, was coming under serious attack by the sociological upheaval of the sixties. From the very beginning of Maillardville's history, the Catholic Church played a seminal role in its existence. The pioneers brought the Faith with them and relied upon it through the next fifty years to bind them and to guide them. Now, in the sixties, that same Church struggled to keep her people within the fold. It was the time of the Second Vatican Council, called to examine how the Church should deal with the quantum change sweeping the world. The Quiet Revolution in Quebec cast off much of the yoke of authority that Church and clergy had held for such a long time. In the end many young people forsook their Church and faith to join the "generation of love" For a small isolated community like Maillardville, the potential for disaster was obvious. In fact, many did leave, losing that vital connection to the traditional French community. Lost faith, lost culture, lost language...three strikes.

During these turbulent times, not all of the young people abandoned culture and faith. At a youth conference in Banff, October 1967, sponsored by the FFCB a new youth organization was formed in Maillardville; the Comité des Jeunes Canadiens Français. In their quest to maintain the French language in Maillardville, and indeed by reaching out to one and all in the Lower Mainland, they conceived the idea of creating their own French discotheque. In 1968, the "Maillatheque" was born. Located in the basement of Notre Dame de Lourdes Church, the project was endorsed by Archbishop M. Johnson. The Vancouver Sun, February 23, 1968:

"New Discotheque To Dig Culture   A discotheque with a difference is the first cultural project of a new French Canadian youth group in Maillardville. Called "Maillatheque", it will be opened March 1 in the basement of Our Lady of Lourdes church, Laval Square, for teenagers of all cultural heritages. The music will be mostly French Canadian, say the promoters and the mood will be Montreal modern....Executive councilor Jean Van Houtte of Maillardville said the discotheque has two functions: It will give lower mainland teenagers, especially those in Coquitlam district an opportunity to mingle with French Canadian teens and to glimpse their culture. And its profits will be applied to the proposed French Canadian community centre which the Bicultural Society of Maillardville hopes to build...Its 15 members are decorating the discotheque in black and white, with rain barrels for tables, logs for benches and fish netting hung for atmosphere."

And from the Columbian, March 1968:

"Rock and roll music blared out of overhead speakers, tree stump chairs and wine barrel tables covered the concrete floor. Youngsters chatted in French and adults smiled good naturedly. The occasion was the opening of Maillatheque, a coffee house-discotheque operated by the French Canadian Youth Committee of Maillardville. Special guest at the opening reception was François Leduc, French Ambassador to Canada.....He told the Maillatheque group that their independent effort "does as much for the extension and perpetuation of the French culture in Canada as any formal, adult venture." Among other special guests...Georges-Henri Dagneau, Director for French Canadian Affairs outside Quebec, repre-

senting Quebec Cultural Affairs minister, Jean-Noël Tremblay; Coquit-lam Reeve L.J. Christmas and local French leaders."

The club ran for two or three seasons.

When asked in 1965, what the future of Maillardville might be, one of the previously mentioned radio interviewees stated that it was *"unlikely to survive another fifteen years."* Maillardville, having weathered many storms over its first fifty years, demonstrated that same unshakeable resolve that had characterized the community in so many past trials. The spirit of the times brought fresh ideas and opportunities. There was renewed activity from several quarters. Quebec had entered a new era in its own history and saw the rise of Quebec nationalism that spawned both separatism and a heightened interest in bilingualism and national unity. The one, separatism, received a cool reception in Maillardville and a June 23, 1963 headline in the Province newspaper proclaimed: ***"Pas de separatisme a Maillardville"*** One resident, a university student commented that: *"They (residents) support a reorientation of Confederation but reject separatism."*

But bitterness was expressed in the sentiments of one from the older generation:

"If they want to go, let them. They have done nothing for us. We don't depend on them for our survival. I don't wish the separatists any luck."

The other, bi-culturalism, encouraged renewed interest in bilingualism and offered new opportunities for French groups such as the FFCB. The mid-sixties also gave birth to the Société Bi-Culturelle de Maillardville. In close collaboration with the Caisse Populaire, its original mandate was to create a complex on Brunette Avenue that would accommodate new credit union offices, provide 142 affordable housing units and a community centre that offered space for all of the francophone groups and their many activities. Mr. Léo Comeau was its first president. The society embarked on a campaign to raise funds for the project and to acquire the necessary properties. Eventually, a large parcel in the 1000 block of Brunette Avenue was purchased that extended from Brunette north to Alderson Avenue. However, the senior citizens of Maillardville had a different vision for the property. One of Maillardville's most beloved citizens, Johnny Dicaire, headed branch 86 OAPA or Club d'Âge D'or. The Caisse Populaire made him their Citizen of the Year in 1966.

He brought forward the idea of a senior citizens' residence in Maillard-ville. With the aid of a $40,000 bequest from a Mrs. Bouchard, the Société put its original plans on hold and took on the project. Using the government's 90/5/5 funding scheme, (a loan of $506,500 for a term of 50 years at an interest of 6 and 3/8%) the first high rise building in Co-quitlam opened its doors in May 1969 and was called Le Foyer Maillard. Its first manager was Léo Comeau and soon L'Association des Dames Auxilliaires du Foyer Maillard was formed to help manage the activities there. An article appeared in the Sun, July 1969 offering this description:

"You are never too old to learn-even a second language. Senior citizens at Foyer Maillardville in Maillardville will have a chance. The residence is completely bilingual...There are 120 rooms accommodating 130 people. Ten of the rooms are doubles...Some rooms have private baths, other baths are shared by two connecting rooms. The second to sixth floors are identical, two double rooms, a great number of single rooms and a lounge on each. The seventh floor has a library and reading room which are in need of books and jig saw puzzles and the main lounge overlooks the Fraser River, Port Mann and Patullo Bridges and a flower garden in its infancy with one cluster of daisies."

The article goes on to describe all of the amenities (tour guide was Mrs. Henriette Sevigny) and the article ends with a quote from Mrs. Sevigny:

"Our people have lived full lives and have made their contribution to society. Now we are seeing that they live with dignity."

The community built on the momentum of the previous decade. Following the opening of a new church and convent in the late fifties at Fatima, Notre Dame de Lourdes responded with a new convent school of their own in 1961. Built at a cost of $195,000, the brick and concrete structure accommodated 25 nuns and classes from grades 5 to 10. Archbishop Duke blessed the building in 1961.

The Caisse Populaire had recovered from its 1955 crisis (opening the bond to non-Catholics) and was once again on an upward trend, gaining members and building assets at a steady pace. Church organizations like Knights of Columbus, Mothers' Club and Catholic Youth Organization, the schools and Scouts and Guides were flourishing.

The French Scout and Guide movement was a powerful instrument in the fight to maintain language and culture among the young. They were unique in Maillardville among groups offering services to young people: all activity took place in French. French "immersion" outside of the home (and those who communicated exclusively in French at home were, reportedly, very few) could only be had within the scout and guide activity. In 1965, according to René Gamache, there were *"14 male leaders and an equal number of female leaders and 214 members."*

It was a particularly active time for the Scouts as they joined Les Scouts Catholique du Canada in 1961. In 1962 the West Region was formed with Jean Lambert as its first president. Mr. Lambert worked hard throughout the decade to promote the French scouting movement. In 1969, 300 French Scouts from the West Region converged on Belcarra Park in Port Moody for the "Jamboree Sasquatch". The highlight was the search for that elusive creature. The Knights of Columbus put up a $1000.00 prize to anyone who could find and capture the monster; Scout leader Andre Beauregard in a gorilla suit. At the end of the camp, the "sasquatch" was lead in by some of the leaders, a rope around its neck. The boys, believing the beast to be real and lusting after loot, descended upon the beleaguered fake with knives at the ready! All ended well, but the fate of the prize money remains as mysterious as the Sasquatch itself.

The Jeanette and Guide movement was also growing under the care of les Cheftaines Henriette Sevigny, Amélie Gareau, Alice Gamache and Simone Stubbs. 1960 saw the creation of the first group of guides, "la premiere Cie St. Jean Baptiste" and in 1961, there were three "rondes" of Jeanettes.

In 1964, another significant event occurred in French Maillardville. With financial aid from the Federal Government, the Fédération Francophone de la Colombie-Britanique (FFCB) became a non-profit society, hired an executive director and opened its new provincial office in Maillardville. The Federation was a strong advocate for French language and culture both within and without Maillardville. It was also the driving force behind the push for French language education.

The parochial schools in Maillardville offered two options for students; English using the complete BC curriculum with the addition of 1/2 hour of French or the "French" option which offered a total of one hour of French including grammar and 30 minutes of religious instruction in

French. Councilor Phil Filliatrault opined that such a minimal amount of French language instruction in an otherwise totally Anglophone environment could not possibly produce functionally bilingual children. In 1965, an effort to have the public schools offer education in the French language (in other words, French immersion) was spearheaded by Roméo Paquette, liaison officer of the FFCB. Although the Provincial government under W.A.C. Bennett was lukewarm to the idea, new federal legislation dictated that French language education should be available to any who requested it. The basis for requesting this in Coquitlam, of course, was the reported 6000 French people in the area, mainly at Maillardville. The negotiations went on for some time and perseverance paid off. The plan called for the establishment of French language instruction from kindergarten through grade 3.

The Board of School District 43 at its February 1967 meeting passed the following resolution:

"1. That this Board has received a request from the French Canadian Federation to offer with the Coquitlam school system, classes in which the language of instruction will be French.
2. That the board after considerable study has determined that it should reply favorably to this request.
3. That the board wishes authority from the department to proceed with an experimental project in French language instruction in September 1968, and the acceptance of normal costs of operating classes as shareable expenses of the board.
4. That the board proposes to establish one or more kindergarten classes to be instructed through the medium of the French language, with the prospect further of establishing a similar program to carry children through the three primary years of elementary school.
5. That in the course of development of the four year program such as indicated above, directions for later development will become apparent.
6. That beyond the authorization requested in section 3 above the board would be pleased to take advantage of any assistance to curriculum and organization that could be made available through the auspices of the department and would be most happy to cooperate with the department in any way."

After receiving permission from the department, the School board issued the following release:
"The approval is granted on the following conditions:

1. That a minimum of one half hour per day at the kindergarten level and one hour per day in grade 1 and above must be spent in the study of English.
2. That the prescribed program for the public schools be followed.
3. That no textbooks or other basic printed material be introduced without prior approval of the department.
4. That a pupil be admitted to the French language class only on written request of his parents or guardians.
5. That French language classes be held in a school where there are also classes at the same grade level in which the language of instruction is English."

The following statement from the same release offers a little foreshadowing of the linguistic issues that would soon be revealed:

"We are much interested in knowing whether the child comes from an English speaking or French speaking home. Although we can see a child from either environment taking advantage of a French kindergarten program, it could be that the program itself would be quite different according to the language backgrounds of the children in the class."

Restrictions and caveats notwithstanding, Roméo Paquette proclaimed the opening of the French kindergarten at Alderson Elementary a "moral breakthrough" for Canada:

"This is a moral breakthrough for Canada. Canada is made up of people living in it and they should have all equal rights. Paquette said the accomplishment was in effect a double-barreled one. "First this is an opportunity for British Columbia citizens who want to be bilingual to actually become bilingual through the only possible process-immersion. This also reconciles the right of French speaking Canadians to have French language instruction. This move follows the principles of the BNA Act and also the recommendations of the Bi-Bi commission."

No doubt it was an exhilarating time. In spite of the muted response to the program from the government, those teachers and administrators who had "boots on the ground" in this new adventure were excited and enthusiastic. Once again, the spotlight was on Maillardville as it embarked upon a truly groundbreaking path. In September of 1968, that first kindergarten class of 47 children entered the new program, not sure of what to expect. Likely neither did the teachers. What they found was indeed a surprise. Of the 47 children enrolled in the program, (slightly over half from French families) only four were able to communicate functionally in French. What a stunning revelation. Here was proof of what undoubtedly was already known in the French community. The pioneers' children and their children's children were drifting farther and farther away from the mother tongue. After recovering from this initial shock, the teachers moved on and dug into the task at hand.

The program received much attention and praise and all were looking forward to the next year when the kindergarten class could move up and phase in grade 1. However, it became apparent that the task would be more difficult than originally thought. The children simply did not possess the linguistic tools to effectively communicate in French and thus move forward a level. Soon, focus shifted away from French immersion and the balance tipped in favour of English instruction with a few subjects taught in French. The English community failed to understand that French Canadian parents were well aware of the fact that their children had lost their French language and in some cases never had it. This was the very reason that French immersion, for English as well as French children, was asked for in the first place. The program was coming under increasing fire, and its future was in serious doubt by the early seventies. True French immersion in BC schools would not become a reality until 1978. Once again, Maillardville was at the root of systemic change in BC. It could add the birth of French language education in the province to the list of its activist successes, along with the fostering of a lumber union in 1931 and the recognition of the minority rights of private schools in the 1950s.

In 1961, the R.C.M.P. moved the Maillardville detachment into the Fraser Mills manager's house, today known as Place des Arts. The building was donated by Crown Zellerbach/Fraser Mills Division and cost the City $17,513 for the conversion to offices and jail cells.   In 1966 the RCMP were given permission by Council to use a great new device to help catch speeders; radar! Nineteen sixty eight saw the first paid, full time fire department in Coquitlam. They had come a long way from the hose reels and volunteer brigade commanded by Chief Paré in the early part of the century.

The District's name still seemed to be a problem for a certain Port Coquitlam based newspaper, as noted in the Herald editorial dated May, 1963:

*"**How About Burquitlam?** The suggestion made at last week's Board of trade meeting that Port Coquitlam changes its name is not new. Some 15 years ago, the District of Coquitlam went as far as to take a plebiscite on a number of new names-Riverside, Three Rivers, Marmont were among them....The plebiscite showed a majority in favour of Riverside, but no further action was taken, possibly because the change was more trouble than it was worth. Three years ago, the Herald received a letter to the editor advocating Marston, Galerton, or Klimerton (in honour of pioneer residents) for Port Coquitlam.....However Port Coquitlam has two major "Coquitlams"- the CPR station and the river. It has been said that one can tell a resident citizen's length of residence by the way he refers to his home town-the old timers usually drop the "Port". And, the District of Coquitlam major portion of which is west of Port Coquitlam is between Burnaby and (Port) Coquitlam. Therefore, why not change its name to the District of Burquitlam and settle the confusion. "*

Interesting logic! In 1962, presumably tired by the lack of coverage of events in the District of Coquitlam by the Herald, the District of Coquitlam United Voters Association published its first issue of "The Guardian". The publishers claimed:

"it will satisfy a long felt need for factual information concerning civic affairs in the District of Coquitlam. That this need has not been met by others...The United Voters Association was formed in 1960 with the purpose of promoting interest in Municipal affairs. "

The defunct Maillardville Ratepayers Association briefly revived as the Maillardville Taxpayers Association in 1961. They pushed for more parks in the village and following the great tradition of activism in Maillardville, considered the question of secession from Coquitlam. The reasons for dissatisfaction remain obscure and there is no mention of the issue in the City Council minutes. Only this small item from the Herald, April 10, 1961 offers evidence:

"At its meeting April 9, Maillardville Taxpayers' Association did not make any definite decision on its proposed secession from the District of Coquitlam, but did set up a committee to study industrial development possibilities in the municipality as a whole. Frank McDonald, a former councilor, will head the committee.

There was considerable discussion on secession, however, with several members from the East End ratepayers groups also present. The latter described the investigations they made into secession three years ago, explaining that the process is an involved and costly one.

Tom Filliatrault is president of the recently reorganized Maillardville group and Alphonse Roy is secretary."

Nineteen sixty four saw the beginning of what is today known as Heritage Square when the old CPR station was moved from Fraser Mills and located adjacent to the RCMP station.

"Coquitlam Historical Society To Preserve Old CPR Station *The Coquitlam Historical Society, through its secretary Frank Pobst, announces that plans for the future of the old CPR station are to preserve and retain as much as is possible the aura of the days when the building functioned as the only one serving the district. Shortly to be moved from its present site in the Fraser mill area to its new location adjoining the RCMP offices on Brunette-King Edward intersection, the building and the original slatted waiting room long seat, a pot belied stove and a guest book will be set up in the waiting room. In the telegraph office section there will be an old styled telegraph board complete with operational lights, which will flash and signal simulating actual operating conditions.....Membership fee of $1 may be directed to the Coquitlam Historical Society, 1111 Brunette Avenue."*

The great tradition of sports was also upheld in the sixties, but the new game was hockey. The Maillardville Carlings excelled in the Western Amateur Hockey League winning the Jubilee Cup in 1969 over the North Vancouver Americans 3-2. Commenting on the win, Coach Vasey stated: *"Maillardville showed by winning the Jubilee Cup that we have the talent to beat North Vancouver, Chilliwack or any team in the League."*

Politics was still an important tool for serving the needs of Maillardville, but here also influence was dwindling. In 1965, after serving on Council for four years, Philip Filliatrault was defeated in his bid to unseat Reeve James Christmas by a count of 9456 to 5921.

In early 1968, Reeve Christmas became Mayor Christmas and all councilors henceforth would be addressed as aldermen. As fate would have it,

James Christmas would spend little time as Mayor. After suffering a seizure in August of 1968, he returned to his duties in January 1969. But
the longest serving Reeve in Coquitlam's history suffered a fatal attack in
July. The Province reported his death July, 1969:

*"**Jimmy Christmas Dies After Seizure**   Coquitlam Mayor Leslie James
Christmas, 66, died Saturday at Royal Columbian hospital in New
Westminster, bringing to an end the longest service of a municipal
mayor in the history of BC....Mrs. Shirley Davies of Richmond, daughter
of the late mayor, said it was a miracle he even survived the heart attack
last August....Mayor Christmas was first elected to Council in 1943 and
reeve in 1945...The body of Mayor Christmas will lie in state Monday at
the chapel of Burquitlam Mortuary. Funeral services will be on Tuesday."*

Council chose to await the regular municipal election in November to
elect a new mayor. René Gamache threw his hat into the ring. He was
defeated by a political unknown, Jack Ballard, by a vote of 3204 to
2653. What a disappointment for Gamache and what a bitter loss for
Maillardville. He had served on Council continuously for twenty years.
Among his many achievements, he had the foresight to secure and develop the Burke Mountain lands and he was an indefatigable advocate
for Maillardville. Why was Gamache defeated? Through twenty years of
politics, he always won his seat comfortably. He was well known and
respected. He was named acting Mayor many times and his experience
and knowledge of Coquitlam was vast. One is tempted to say that his
race, language and loyalty to the French community were marks against
him and were the cause of his defeat. Perhaps that is true. If it is, then the
question arises; was he a victim of true fear driven racism, or was he defeated by prejudice? We remember that this was the time of separatism
in Quebec and the cry of "Vive le Quebec Libre" by Charles Degaulle.
Not all westerners were taken up with Trudeaumania. Perhaps René
Gamache was a victim of the times. Whatever the reason, Coquitlam and
Maillardville lost a man truly dedicated to the wellbeing of his community.

Sadly, very little information is to be found on the state of the commercial district on Brunette in the sixties. Advertisement in the Herald is
nonexistent. Snippets gleaned here and there from unrelated articles suggest that the business community continued to prosper. The Maillardville
Shopping Centre housed jewelers, hair stylists, a bank and a supermarket

among other businesses. Butchers, mechanics and insurance agents could all be found here. The Bank of Nova Scotia broke ground for their new building at the corner of Brunette and Allard in 1961.

The Caisse Populaire de Maillardville Credit Union continued to flourish, so much so that in 1963, Mr. J.B. Goulet became its first full time manager. Although the collaboration with the Bi-Cultural Society on the community centre had been put on hold, the Caisse still needed to move into larger offices. In 1967, a new building was erected at 1013 Brunette, just south of what was soon to be the site of the Foyer Maillard. Like every other French institution in Maillardville, the Caisse was struggling under the pressures brought about by a rapidly changing world.

The credit union struggled to keep pace with the larger financial institutions. Providing the same tools and financial services offered by the banks was very challenging. To create more capital to fund more options for its members, more members were needed to provide more capital! In 1968, a resolution was put forward and passed to open the bond to English speaking members. The credit union's bylaws would still require that meetings be conducted in French and that French language service must be available to any who desired it. By opening membership to all, the Caisse Populaire completed the disassociation with its original purpose *"to consolidate the French community through financial solidarity"* Philosophy aside, the credit union continued to grow and in 1969, hired its first full time staff: Marguerite Chrétien, Ghislaine Pilon and Gracia Larson.

In 1969, Maillardville celebrated its 60th Anniversary and its pioneers were honoured, as reported by the Enterprise:

*"**Maillardville Pioneers Honoured**...Early Maillardville pioneers were honoured on Sunday December 7 at the parish of Notre Dame de Lourdes, marking the sixtieth anniversary of their coming to British Columbia. In 1909 a trainload of French speaking Canadians arrived from Hull, Sherbrook and Rockland Ontario....They came to work for the Fraser Mills company who granted each family a half an acre at a price of $150.00. They were also given all the wood they needed for construction of their church, school and rectory.....Many of the people gathered for the anniversary celebration Sunday, recalled how they walked through trails and brush to get to church, some of them trekking all the way from Port Moody. Those present were honoured with a gift of the key to the*

parish, containing a removable pin inscribed "60-Pionniers N D Lourdes, Maillardville, B.C." The pioneers were honoured by a light lunch in the school following a church service, and later a dinner in Our Lady of Lourdes. Present and in charge of ceremonies were Father Paul Surette, Father Leonard Puech and Brother Cyril Morvan. Pioneers available to attend were: Mr. John Dicaire, Mr. Paulidor Gauthier, Mrs. E. Paré nee Hélène Chevalier, Hercules Lamoureux, Wilfred Croteau, Josephat Payer, Alph Payer, Mrs. A. Payer nee Charlotte Beaulieu, Louis Boileau, Rodolphe Boileau, Mrs. E. Leroux nee Irene Payer, Arthur Laverdure, Mrs. B. Proulx nee Ida Couture, Eugene Croteau, Sister Bernadette nee Alda Croteau, Miss Véronique Croteau, René Marcellin, Sister Gilberte nee Eva Marcellin, Mrs. J. Martin nee Florestine Paré, Mrs. L. Canuel nee Léontine Paré, Oméra Paré, Mrs. E. Jalbert nee Coutu, Arthur Coutu, Mrs. A. Lanoue nee Yvonne Paré, Mrs. Rompre nee Laverdure, René Hamelin, Mrs. Y. Gaudette nee Germaine Paré, Mrs. Roy nee Paré. Others unable to attend were: Wilfred Dicaire, Ludger Gauthier, Mrs. M. Sauvé, Mrs. R. Duplin nee Rose Sauvé, Mrs. J. Dicaire, Mr. Wilfred Dicaire, Mrs. W. Bouthot nee Gagné, Mrs. Boucher nee Robinson, Mrs. Vaillancourt nee Parent, Beaudoin Proulx, Pete Sauvé, Alex Coutu, Aureole Sauvé, Hervé Marcellin, Mrs. Doucette nee Simone Paré, Albert Gravelle, Mrs. J. McKimmie nee Josehine Gauthier, Paul Gauthier, Edgar Gauthier."

In spite of all the change and pressures that buffeted the community, parish life continued to be the vessel that bore the French culture through these turbulent times. At Our Lady of Fatima, with the building of the new church in 1959, the old one became the parish meeting hall. In 1962, Father Guy Michaud took over the pastoral duties. The congregation produced four vocations; Sister Anita Charpentier, Sister Claudette Ledet, Father George LaGrange and Sister Lorraine Malo.

At Paroisse Notre Dame de Lourdes, Father Frechette led his flock through those tumultuous years with the assistance of Father Antonio Dion in the first half of the decade and Father Paul Surette in the latter. The trials visited upon the French community during this decade took their toll. The number of parishioners began to decline and school enrollment fell. The loss of parishioners meant the loss of revenue and by1969, Fatima had sold its convent to the Provincial government to be used as a health facility for the mentally challenged. At both parish schools, the teaching of the higher grades was being phased out and the schools at the end of the decade would accommodate only grades 1 through 7. Our Lady of Lourdes found itself in deep financial crisis and was considering different options, all having to do with the selling of various properties held by the Parish.

At both parish schools in 1968, there was a changing of the guard. Fatima bid farewell to the Sisters of the Good Shepherd and welcomed the Sisters of Holy Cross. At Lourdes, the much-loved Ursulines de Rimouski were fêted in grand style at a banquet, which eased the pain of their departure only slightly. The silver lining behind that cloud was the return of the Sisters of the Child Jesus who resumed their work in the parish.

Indeed, what a decade it was. The world in 1969 was radically different from what it had been at the end of the fifties. From the early hope of a bright future, the world suddenly descended into a maelstrom of uncertainty and fear, the quantum leap. In Maillardville, the golden age had truly come and gone. The area had begun its downward spiral with early unchecked development, a tremendous influx of people, many of modest means, and no plan in place to arrest the decay that was beginning to settle in. The sons and daughters of Maillardville's French pioneers were in a struggle for their cultural and linguistic lives. Was the community truly interested in maintaining its culture, its way of life? Or had it, shell-shocked by those turbulent years, struggled to maintain its ground, only to find itself on the brink of dissolution? It was a death of sorts, for the Maillardville that had existed since 1909 was no more. And as if to punctuate that sad reality, at the very turning point of that decade the man for whom the village had been named passed on.

"Father Maillard dies in France   He Gave Maillardville A Name

The priest who gave his name to Maillardville died August 3, 1966. Father Edmond Maillard, OMI, 86, died in the Franco-Canadian College in Lyons, France. He was Maillardville's first priest when the uniquely French Canadian settlement was established in 1909. There was an irony in the naming of the settlement. Father Maillard spent only two years there. But it was a place that stayed close to his heart. Authority for that is Father G. Riser, OMI, his superior at the Franco-Canadian College. In a letter telling of Father Maillard's death, Father Riser mentions: "He thought often of Maillardville but didn't like to speak of it. It gave him pain." He was probably a casualty of Church growing pains in the province. His superior, Bishop Dontenwill, was promoted to Father General of the Oblates and was succeeded by Bishop Neil McNeil who came from a Newfoundland diocese. Bishop McNeil removed Father Maillard from Maillardville after only two years. Father Maillard wrote about it when the town he helped found celebrated its first half century in 1959. He wrote a letter from France describing his early experiences. It says in part: "In 1909 Archbishop McNeil arrived in Vancouver. He made many trips to the new colony (Maillardville) which interested him a great deal. "One day seeing me working with a pick and shovel, he presented me with a beautiful pair of boots. In 1911, on a certain day I was making the rounds of the village to beg for the school. They told me that a priest was looking for me. It was Father Pelletier, bearer of a letter in which Archbishop McNeil told me that this priest was named pastor of the parish. Admittedly, this was a shock. That evening, I returned to New Westminster."

Three Maillardville pastors and two years later Father Maillard was asked to return to Maillardville. Instead he took a post as the superior of the Oblate's Cariboo missions with headquarters at Mission City where he stayed for 12 years before returning to France. Archbishop McNeil moved on to become Archbishop of Toronto. A successor, Father E. Garon, is the man credited with naming Maillardville. According to Franciscan Father J. Schmidt, now at Our Lady of Lourdes parish, meeting with a committee of the pioneer families circa 1912 Father Garon heard discussion on calling the town "Cargo" because of the freight passing through or even Rosetown. He suggested Maillardville and the committee went along with the idea. Father Maillard shortly before his death: *"When I present myself before the Lord, I shall tell Him that doubtless I have committed many sins, but deep down I always sought one thing; to love Him and to make Him loved."* meditated the priest who gave Maillardville a name."

Figure 47 Father X. Teck

Figure 48 WWII poster

Figure 49 Maillardville recruits

Figure 50 First Church, Fatima

Figure 51 Preaching in the woods

Figure 52 Father Meunier

Figure 53 First church interior, Fatima

Figure 54 Our Lady of Fatima Parish

Figure 55 Brunette Avenue

Figure 56 Caisse Populaire

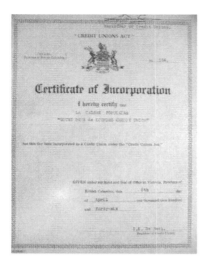

Figure 57 Credit Union charter

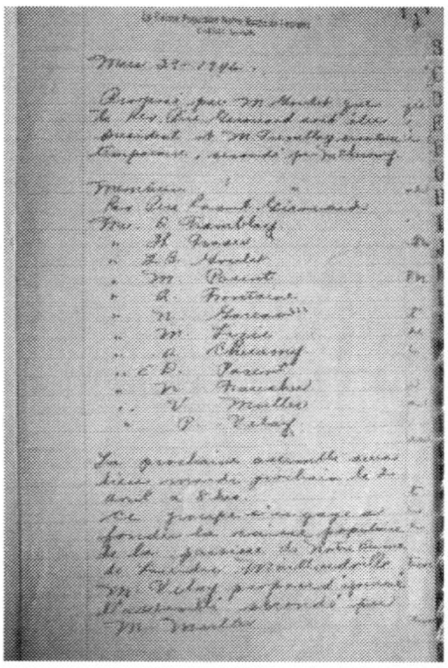

Figure 58 First Credit Union minutes

Figure 59 First neon sign, Pett's

Figure 60 Bob's Burgers

Figure 61 Quadling Bros service station

Figure 62 Al Best service station

142

Figure 63 Al Best

Figure 64 Laval St and Brunette Ave

Figure 65 Brunette commercial district

Figure 66 Brunette commercial district

Figure 67 Fundraiser for community centre

Figure 68 Opening night, Wood's Theatre

Figure 69 Fire brigade c. 1946

Figure 70 Cnst. Jimmy McGarry

Figure 71 Fraser Mills, Ryan House

Figure 72 Fraser Mills burner

Figure 73 Fraser Mills, flood 1948

Figure 74 Fraser Mills, flood 1948

Figure 75 School Strike 1951

Figure 76 R.C. MacDonald

Figure 77 James Christmas

Figure 78 Father A. Fréchette

Figure 79 Father Maillard c. 1957

Figure 80 Lourdes Gymnastics team

Figure 81 Lourdes Gymnastics team

Figure 82 Baseball 1953

Figure 83 Fire Brigade

Figure 84 Scoutes Maillardville

Figure 85 Trev's

Figure 86 Anne and Trev Protheroe

Figure 87 Sam's Theatre

Figure 88 Lourdes 50th Anniversary

Figure 89 Lourdes 50th Anniversary

Figure 90 Proposed city hall c 1966

Figure 91 Brunette Avenue c. 1960s

Figure 92 R. Gamache

Figure 93 R. Paquette

148

Figure 94 Convent c. 1960s

Figure 95 Ursuline nuns

Figure 96 Ursuline nuns leaving Lourdes

Figure 97 French Disco

Figure 98 Lourdes and mill from top of hill

Seven

The Decline of Maillardville

Just as the forties and fifties were Maillardville's zenith, so the seventies heralded its nadir. The decay that took root during the latter part of the sixties began to bear its unsavory fruit by 1970. The image of Maillardville as a "slum" was already etched in most people's minds. The "original" Maillardville, a tangible and visible French village and community, had all but disappeared. Of course, many French residents remained, but they were now very much in the minority. Language and culture seemed to vanish. An amazing trend of this decade is that good will, encouragement and help came from many quarters, some of them surprising and unexpected.

The world continued to advance as new technologies set our lives upon an inexorable journey into the digital future. It was also the time of René Levesque, the Parti Quebecois and separatism, the FLQ and the October Crisis. Pierre Trudeau led the country upon the path of multi culturalism and established a policy to create a truly bilingual Canada. The loss of the PQ in Quebec's 1970 election was met with relief in Maillardville as it was in many other parts of the nation. This headline appeared in the Columbian April, 1970:

"In Maillardville-Relief   French speaking residents of Maillardville breathed a strong sigh of relief Wednesday night after Quebec overwhelmingly voted for a united Canada. Said Jean Lambert, western regional commissioner for 1000 French speaking boy scouts, "If they'd

gone for separatism, pity us poor French Canadians here. Reaction from English speaking people would probably have been-if you want to speak French go back to Quebec." he said. Napoléon Gareau, Vancouver commissioner for the boy scouts, said people had already "slammed" him before the election. Some said maybe when the election is over you'll be sent back to Quebec. How could I do that?" Gareau protested. "I'm a westerner by birth."

The Federal Government's bilingual policy, however, did open the door to new opportunities for linguistic revitalization, resulting in a heightened interest in the preservation and building up of the French culture. Much of that interest came from the English-speaking majority. The French "immersion" program was launched at Alderson School in 1968, largely with the Francophone families at Maillardville in mind. It got off to a rocky start, and was reduced to partial French instruction when it was discovered that few children, even from Maillardville, had any functional ability to speak the language. In 1971 and '72, the program sputtered and was even threatened with closure. But with the persistence of the Anglophones and financial help from the Federal Government, new life was breathed into it. By 1978, the Provincial government announced the French "Cadre" program that would be made available to any community who could produce a minimum of ten applicants. This early program had certain eligibility requirements including:

"a student must be classified a francophone. He must have a reasonable understanding of French, no matter what his grade level and have one parent with French as his native tongue."

Coquitlam had more than enough applicants and the program continued and flourished.

Douglas College also had Maillardville in mind when it announced a new course being offered in September of 1970:

*"**New Course Tailored To Maillardville**   Douglas College, the Lower Mainland's own regional college, will be offering a course on the Social-Intellectual history of Quebec. Tailored to the needs of the community of Maillardville, the course will be taught by Charles Curmi, a French Canadian instructor whose 20 years residence in Quebec has sensitized him to the needs and aspirations of the French Canadians. The prime object of the course will be to modify some prevalent stereotypes of*

Quebec, create a better understanding of its history, culture and traditions."

No doubt Douglas College saw this as a timely offering in the light of possible Quebec separation from Canada. In 1973, that institution also considered opening a bilingual branch in Maillardville:

*"**Bilingual Arm High Priority** Establishment of a French/English arm of Douglas College in Maillardville would mean more to the area than redevelopment of any other nature." says Coquitlam Aldermanic candidate Charlie Filliatrault, "This would give young people something to start with, a reason to stay in Maillardville."*

Even the local Army Cadets considered establishing a bilingual troupe in Maillardville to be based at Millside School. Coquitlam's newest paper, the Enterprise, wanted to help. Located on Brunette Avenue, it reported regularly on events and concerns in Maillardville. For a time it allotted considerable space to French activity and printed a number of French language articles and editorials in a section called "Içi Maillardville". In its inaugural article the name of the column is explained:

"The older among us will remember that that during the years 1965 through 1967, there existed a variety show known as "Içi Maillardville ".

Les "Maillardvilliens" had three much appreciated concert evenings in the troupe's short existence. Their pianist was Anita Comeau, under the direction of Mme. Pierrette Paquette.

Clearly, there was strong support for the French language and culture at Maillardville. What a tragedy for the community that some of these initiatives, most notably the opening of a bilingual branch of Douglas College, were not realized.

However, Maillardville was already mired in its downward spiral. From within and without, the decline of that community was recognized with alarm. Was it really a slum? Certainly, the area of Brunette east of Marmont, the "old village", had reached a point of no return. Most of the houses there, available to the City a decade earlier, were now owned by several landlords. These buildings were left in an appalling state of disrepair and housed transients and "down on your luck" individuals. In 1977, three of the houses were leased to an aboriginal group for use in a "transition" program. The "Mike Rufus House" met with some opposition based on its proximity not only to Millside School, but also to two local beer parlours. Although the organizers, the Natives' Court Workers Association, denied that the project was a "half way house", project spokesman Archie MacDonald, stated that:

"Two rules are in effect; no violence and no alcohol or drugs. If anyone breaks the rules, they are not allowed back in. The only time anyone is allowed drugs is by prescription. Not even aspirin is allowed without prescription. MacDonald firmly believes people can be rehabilitated."

The project lasted approximately 18 months and terminated when it ran out of money. Deterioration of the neighbourhood was not confined to Brunette Avenue. The area of the original village centre, Laval Square west to Marmont Street, east to Schoolhouse and from Brunette north to Thomas, was in a generally shabby state. The further one moved from Laval Square, the newer and better maintained were buildings and neighborhoods. Nevertheless, anything located south of Rochester Avenue, and for some even Austin Avenue, was considered an undesirable place to live.

Who could help, what could be done? City Council seemed unable or unwilling to cope with the situation. In fact, as the decade rolled by, Council continued to foster its dreams of moving away from Maillardville altogether. The hope of relocating city hall to Poirier Street was eventually replaced by an even better scheme that anticipated a move to the new Coquitlam Town Centre. In Maillardville, the merchants had their own hopes of cleaning up the commercial zone. Notable among the businesses was the Caisse Populaire. As a cooperative institution, it gave birth to a new organization in Maillardville; the Société Coopérative Habitat de Maillardville. Habitat's purpose was to develop proposals for cooperative housing opportunities in the neighbourhood. They were also one of the key instigators in a revitalization scheme that was to become known as "Plan Maillardville". In 1972, the group in partnership with City Council applied to the CMHC for a grant of $32,700 for a study of revitalization options. This was to lead to further acquisition of government funds through their Neighbourhood Improvement Program and a plan to revitalize Maillardville and preserve its French culture and heritage. The Enterprise, March 1972 noted the birth of a new vision for Maillardville:

*"**Maillardville To Get Action, French Heritage To Be Fostered** A spe-cial committee to preserve and foster development of the French speaking community of Maillardville will be appointed by Coquitlam Council. Municipal planner D.M. Buchanan reported that the availabil-ity of federal support was "quite a dramatic step but there is no great rush" In response Alderman Jack Gilmore expressed his bewilderment: "I can't understand why we haven't had any more reaction from the Fed-eral Government. There seems to be money available for everything imaginable but not to enhance this bilingual community which is unique in British Columbia." Mr. Buchanan's report also included suggestions for the makeup of the committee: "The two parish priests should be on the committee to give voice to the Church which has holdings in the community and is a key social institution. The Coquitlam Fine Arts Council, since they are interested in a "Place des Arts" for Maillard-ville....Businessmen should be represented, both those operating businesses as well as absentee owners...The now being formed Mail-lardville Habitat Co-op Society since they will be coming forward with new types of housing for the area."*

The Maillardville Joint Committee/Comité Conjoint de Maillardville was formed of nine members, three each from the Maillardville Habitat Co-op Society, the municipality and the community at large representing community organizations. Selected from Habitat were Jean Pierre Paquette, Claude Hurtubise and Roméo Paquette. The municipality committed Alderman Jack Gilmore, municipal manager R.A. LeClair and planning director Don Buchanan. Representing community organi-zations were Jean Aussant, Caisse Populaire, Fern Bouvier, Coquitlam Fine Arts Council and Hector Viens, as President of the Knights of Co-lumbus. Mr. Viens was selected to chair the committee. The first order of business was to hire a planner. In May of 1973 a young man of 23 years, Robert Noël de Tilly from Montreal accepted the challenge. His mission was to study the Maillardville area in its entirety, from infra-structure to population demographics, and to consult with residents and business owners. The goal was to create a comprehensive plan which would include recommendations covering zoning, housing types and recreational facilities. However, before he could commence his work, Noël de Tilly and his team had to find Maillardville! In July of 1973, the Enterprise proclaimed:

*"**Maillardville Found, Project Gets Going** Maillardville isn't lost, it's just hard to say exactly where it is. That's one way of summing up the*

*dilemma that has been facing Maillardville community planner Robert
Noël de Tilly since he has started work on the Maillardville improvement
project last month. No one seems to know exactly what the boundaries of
the old sector of Coquitlam really are.....The boundaries, chosen arbi-
trarily are Austin to the north, Schoolhouse to the east, the Fraser River
to the south and the 401 highway to the west. The area is a neighbourhood where the highest concentrations of French Canadian people are
found. "But if people believe that Maillardville is a place where French
Canadians are in the majority, then Maillardville doesn't exist" de Tilly
says. Census figures reveal that there is no neighbourhood in Coquitlam
where French speaking people make up most of the population. Two
blocks around Laval Square is the area that has the highest concentra-
tion of French speaking people, 44 per cent according to census
figures."*

An office was set up at 946E Brunette Avenue. Residents and businessmen were invited to drop by to ask questions and talk about their needs
for a revitalized Maillardville. Noël de Tilly made his views on that subject known early on. The Enterprise, July 1973:

*"**Planner Says: No Cages For French**   Plan Maillardville's planner,
Robert Noël de Tilly, has squashed any ideas that the end result of the
Maillardville Neighbourhood Improvement project will be a "French
Gastown" People who expect such a result "may be disappointed" he
said. "We're not going to put French Canadians in cages for the benefit
of English speaking tourists" he promises...When rehabilitation of Coquitlam's old area was first proposed, some people put forward the idea
that Brunette could be redeveloped with sidewalk cafés such as in Paris
and French touches such as bilingual street signs. But de Tilly points out
that sidewalk cafés are not part of the French Canadian culture."*

By the end of the process, 203 people had been personally interviewed
and public meetings were held in both French and English. The Plan
Maillardville team brought their recommendations to Council in June of
1974.

There were mixed feelings on Council about the study. An unwillingness
to have any outside body (the federal government) dictate the terms of
revitalization and a statement by one alderman that the study was a
waste of time were some of the sentiments expressed. Overall, the project was received by Council, residents and business owners with some

hope for relief for Maillardville. When the study was complete, Mayor Tonn and Council gave the report its general approval, but did not accept all of the study's recommendations. Those recommendations included extending Mackin Park to Lougheed Highway, aligning King Edward Avenue with Marmont Street and making Brunette Avenue four lanes to King Edward. Another recommendation was that the City should acquire land along Brunette for the purpose of building low-income housing. Additionally, the report suggested "Mackin House" as an ideal location for a museum and that street and directional signs should be bilingual. The process itself allowed the City access to upwards of one million dollars in loans and grants for improvements to local housing and infrastructure. The Herald, June 1974:

"$1 Million Dollar Plan Unveiled for Maillardville Coquitlam municipal council Monday gave its endorsation to a scheme that could see more than $1 million dollars worth of improvement projects carried out in the poorest section of Maillardville. The aldermen agreed to begin planning to upgrade homes, streets and parks in an area roughly bounded by Thomas Avenue, Casey Street, Brunette Avenue and Begin Street under the federal government's Neighbourhood Improvement Program. Planning director D.M. Buchanan said in a report to council that the area chosen for the project has a high percentage of "poor and dilapidated housing, open ditch systems, non-engineered streets and the lowest per capita income in the municipality" Also included in the project could be the construction of low income housing, also using the NIP funding."

Some residents did take advantage of the program to upgrade their homes as did the municipality for certain infrastructure and park upgrades. However, the worst part of Maillardville, the infamous Brunette strip, remained unchanged as the owners of those rental properties apparently were not interested in taking advantage of the NIP program.

This first attempt at Maillardville "revitalization" accomplished little in terms of stimulating immediate neighborhood revitalization. Nevertheless, it was an important instrument in raising awareness of the imminent loss of a significant part of Coquitlam's heritage, and it laid the groundwork for future efforts to rebuild the village and preserve its French culture. Notable among Plan Maillardville's accomplishments was the eventual building of the Maillardville Neighbourhood House, later to be known as Place Maillardville Community Centre. The realignment of

King Edward Avenue and the identification of that area as a future "Heritage Square" was also a significant outcome.

In spite of the work of Plan Maillardville, the area continued to be known as the slum of Coquitlam throughout the seventies and usually made headlines only when problems arose. For several years the village was plagued by an infestation of rats. With local newspapers proclaiming: ***"M'ville Slums Blamed For Local Rat Menace"*** and ***"Rats Run Rampant Over Maillardville"*** and again ***"Oh rats! And right here in Coquitlam"*** the district medical officer, in 1974, cited the strip along Brunette Avenue as the worst area and expressed his frustration at both the rats and Plan Maillardville:

"Slum level conditions in Maillardville are blamed by District Medical health Officer, Dr. J.D. Munroe for a "widespread" rat infestation problem. "The trouble is that nobody can touch those buildings" stated Munroe. He was referring to the Plan Maillardville which he states prevents him from demolishing buildings when necessary. "Things are bad along Brunette Avenue" he said."

One year later, in 1975 the issue had still not been resolved when the Enterprise reported:

"Rats are rampant in certain areas of Coquitlam and Maillardville and some have even ventured up sewers landing in family toilet bowls. John Nelson, Vector Control Officer for the District says he has received twelve complaints last month including a call reporting a rat in a toilet bowl in what he terms the "near slum" area of Maillardville."

The problem continued through 1976, and the health officer cited apathy as responsible for many of the problems in Maillardville:

"When people say its Maillardville they just don't seem to care. They seem to expect rats in Maillardville and so don't bother making a fuss about it."

Problems were not just confined to Brunette Avenue's residential section. In the commercial district, a fire broke out at a building in the 900 block Brunette in 1974. The burned out structure was left to rot for a year or so. People, recognizing a dump when they saw one, disposed of their garbage, including several wrecked cars, on the site. Apathy

158

seemed to be the order of the day. Another example was the attitude toward the increasingly deteriorating pedestrian underpass at Lougheed
Highway off Gauthier Avenue. Everyone agreed that the tunnel was a
disgrace and downright dangerous, but council, not wanting to set a
"precedent" was reluctant to take responsibility for it. The Enterprise,
June, 1978:

*"**Buck Passed On Dirty Underpass** Controversy over the unsafe condition of the Lougheed underpass at Gauthier Avenue, used by school
children has resulted in a commitment by Coquitlam council to inspect
and maintain cleanliness of the structure. Council received a letter from
highways and public works minister Hugh Curtis stating his department
was prepared to assume responsibility for structural repairs but not for
cleaning the structure and footpath access. Ald. Les Garrison expressed
concern that by accepting the proposal the municipality could be setting
a precedent. "We could be asked to maintain all the underpasses in the
municipality and we could incur liability regarding cleaning" he
said...."We asked for the underpass, we should maintain it" said Ald. Len
Bewley "Conditions there are intolerable. It's filthy and dangerous." A
motion to maintain the underpass on a cost sharing basis, with the provincial government with the stipulation it not be considered a precedent,
was passed."*

Of course, this unappealing environment along with Council's apparent
inability to do anything concrete to rebuild Maillardville did not encourage new businesses to locate in the village. As late as 1979, one business
owner mused:

*"Although we understand that some properties have been zoned for
townhouse development (on Brunette) there is no indication that anyone
is gambler enough to build there."*

Yet not all was sackcloth and ashes. A modest but functional commerce
still existed in Maillardville. A new building was erected in 1970 and
fresh businesses were established there. Located at 946 Brunette and
owned by Main Home Improvements, the three-story reinforced concrete
building housed Red Rib Steak House and Delicatessen, Ted Tully's
Honey Boy Bakery, Thrift Store, Brunette One Hour Cleaners, Dennis
Hunt's Brunette Furniture and Appliances, Duncan Sales Corporation
and Titan Power. On the upper floor was the office of Coquitlam Teachers' Association, W.J. Joyce and Company Appraisals and the Credit

Bureau of Coquitlam and District Ltd. By the time of Plan Maillardville in 1974, the merchants capitalized on the renewed interest in the area and hosted a ***"Maillardville Merchants Get Acquainted Days August 23 and 24"*** Residents were asked to "*Drop by and visit with the friendly merchants of Maillardville*" Clowns performed and offered balloons. There were raffles, free bowling and a Grand Prize of a $100 food hamper. A partial list of participants included The Gift Centre, Fads and Fancy, The Drug Centre, M&C Decorator Centre, IGA, the Jubilee Hotel, Coquitlam Crafts, Holt's Banquet House, Brunette TV Rentals, Maurice's Barber Shop, Boucherie Dansereau Meats, Scotia Bank and the Caisse Populaire.

Those business men and women who had enterprises on Brunette made an effort to save their commercial district. Once again, there was frustration that City Hall was not doing enough to support their efforts. In 1974 they banded together to form the Maillardville Merchants' Association. The Enterprise, July 1974 reported:

"M'Ville Protest *Maillardville merchants are a little tired of the apathy in their area so they have taken steps to do something about it. The merchants have decided to form a merchants' association to get rid of the apathy and unite together to build a truly good shopping area. One of the major issues is the "dirt issue" The merchants want a major clean up of the area including street cleaning on a regular weekly basis. Anne Falle, an organizer for the proposed association said waste receptacles must be installed throughout the area...A three-member committee was appointed to prepare recommendations for the group. They are Maurice Beauregard, Maurice's Barber Shop, Anne Falle, Johnstone Cleaners and Lottie Charles, Fads and Fancy."*

Upgrading Brunette Street was also put on hold .Once again Council delayed the improvement because they hoped developers would come to Maillardville and do the street upgrade themselves.

When Brunette was finally upgraded in 1979 to four lanes with centre median, Council in its wisdom decreed that there would be no street parking on Brunette from Lougheed Highway to Marmont Street. One Alderman explained: *"The ultimate aim of the improvements is to ensure Brunette is functioning as an arterial street with characteristics that will not promote undue traffic."* They did give permission for merchants to build a twenty-five stall parking lot off Adair Street.

Building frustration was well expressed in this August 21 1974 Enterprise editorial:

*"**M'Ville- Really Something Special**   Maillardville, once the centre of Coquitlam, has become the most run down area of the district. Why? Some would say simply because it's the oldest section and time takes its toll. Fine reasoning, especially if you are from Ranch Park. Yet is it fine reasoning for council whose attitude it seems to reflect? How long do eyesores remain in this area before municipal action is taken? The former Flop Furniture Warehouse on Brunette Avenue burned down way back last winter. Charred remains still stand with old car wrecks added and this mess still faces Brunette only a couple of blocks from City Hall. It seems that all through last year the talk around Maillardville centered around "Plan Maillardville". Still, we have not seen any concrete proof that council took all that government funded work seriously....The merchants in the area are really making an effort this week to bring some attention to themselves and to really make Maillardville an attractive place to shop. Why can't council take up the idea wholeheartedly? Right now an office block is being constructed across the street from the Woods Hotel. It will probably make a nice addition to the business section by replacing some older dilapidated houses, but in allowing construction of the block the district also allowed one uninhabitable house with the narrow front and typical Maillardville landscaping of blackberry bushes entwined around the stately columns of the sagging porch, to remain between two new office buildings. This eyesore, right out of the depression, has a for sale sign on it. Now who is going to buy it? What on earth could anyone do with it? Fellows, where is your planning...you have left a thirty three foot lot between a new building and a fairly recently built one.....Perhaps council just doesn't care. After all, haven't council members decided instead of improving present surroundings, to leave it all behind and set up shop in the new Coquitlam Centre area? We realize that it's a little hard for some members of council to put up with the ignominy of carrying on the city business in the oldest part of the district and it must be embarrassing to take the Premier, if and when he ever comes here, to lunch at one of the local coffee houses. But is it necessary to avoid Maillardville altogether and rush, no doubt with eyes closed, right by to the Vancouver Golf Club all the time? If you really feel that way about Maillardville, why don't you just set up shop at the "club" Of course such a move is not necessary with the new town centre in sight. With a little patience our district officials can hold their heads up, drive right down from the top of the hill to city hall and never, ever have to look at Maillardville."*

The population continued to increase dramatically. City staff projected that Coquitlam would grow from 55 to 69 thousand people between 1972 and 1977. Planning allowed for almost 78 acres of apartment build-ings in Maillardville, 22 of that being in the commercial district and the remainder east along and around Brunette, for a potential of 2850 units. When developers did come forward, residents along with Société Habitat and Plan Maillardville leader Noël de Tilly protested and Maillardville saw no growth. Notable among these proposals was a 3.5 million dollar luxury hotel at Brunette and Tupper, but opposition ensured that its real-ization did not occur. Enterprise, December 1972:

"Coquitlam May get New $3.5 Million Hotel   The 15 storey, luxury hotel may be located on four acres at the north east junction of Highway 401 and the Brunette cloverleaf in the Tupper Avenue area. To be built by Contemporary Realty developers of the impressive Calgary Inn, the new hotel will have convention facilities for 500 and 200 ultra modern rooms. There will be a swimming pool, recreation facilities and a main floor shopping complex."

Apparently, Council was on board for this as the same article quotes Mayor Tonn:

"If approved, this new hotel will come as a most welcome addition to our community and most certainly be instrumental in attracting many prestige conventions to the district. Mayor Tonn said that final zoning approval by council will be contingent on approval of final plans, ac-ceptable traffic patterns and the normal by-law requirements. He said he could foresee no major obstacles."

Another high-rise was proposed for the intersection of Blue Mountain and Gauthier. Again opposition based upon the usual arguments of too much noise, traffic and too many people, ensured that the development was frustrated. A townhouse project proposed for Schoolhouse at Decaire Street was squashed and another on Rochester met the same fate. In fact, it seems that any early enthusiasm for Maillardville revitali-zation was sidelined by a quasi-moratorium on development for the three years of the Plan Maillardville process, ironically a study for the purpose of revitalizing Maillardville.

Another interesting project proposed for Maillardville was a mini For-mula 1 racetrack as reported in the Enterprise, March 1979:

*"**Mini Grand Prix Track Studied**   Coquitlam Council is studying a proposal to build a scaled down Formula 1 Grand Prix racing track on a five acre site between the Lougheed and Trans Canada Highways and west of Schoolhouse Street. The half million dollar track proposed by Malibu Grand Prix, a subsidiary of U.S. giant Warner Communications, would employ 10 full time and 15 part time employees. The race cars would be scale Formula One models worth $15,000 each. With their 28 horsepower Wankel rotary engines, they would be capable of top speed of 30 mph and would be quieter than the average family car. Included in the development would be a 72,000 square foot building housing a snack bar, a supervising arcade and car storage. Drivers would have to show a valid driver's license before setting out to race the clock on the six tenth of a mile track. They would not race against each other, only the clock."*

In spite of assurances that these tracks ran successfully with no problems, (Malibu ran 22 other similar operations) residents once again came out to challenge the group and voice their disapproval. Council went back and forth in their deliberations, eventually supporting the scheme. But the power of that decision was removed from their hands when management at Crown Zellerbach, owner of the property, decided not to lease the land to Malibu. October, 1979, the Enterprise:

*"**Race Track Plan Runs Out of Land**   There will be no Malibu Grand Prix Track in Coquitlam after all but neither Coquitlam Council nor public reaction defeated the proposal. Crown Zellerbach, owner of the land decided against leasing the property to Malibu because of public disapproval. A Crown Zellerbach spokesman told the Enterprise: "We have been carefully analyzing public reaction to the proposal and we are not able to ignore the very strong opposition of people in the area."*

A local businessman brought a proposal for warehouses on Brunette Avenue. However, Council, displaying a commendable degree of common sense, defeated the scheme. As Alderman Les Garrison put it (Enterprise May 1979):

"Warehousing for Brunette would be the last straw. It would be throwing in the sponge, giving up completely on Maillardville. Alderman Len Bewley also said the best policy would be to wait a few years before considering rezoning. He said Maillardville's "time is coming very soon."

What Maillardville did get, was further industrial development along Leeder Avenue (present day United Boulevard), the Mayfair Industrial Park and, of course directly south of the village, the Terra Nova Land Fill, an open-air dump.

Coquitlam's political world was not particularly eventful for Maillardville in the seventies. Mayor Jack Ballard lasted for one term only. He lost to Jim Tonn in the election of 1971. Mayor Tonn had some very stiff competition from that friend of Maillardville, Mike Butler. Mr. Butler lost by a relatively small margin; 3555 to 2972. Jack Ballard polled a distant 826. Perhaps Ballard's loss was some consolation for René Gamache, who had lost to Ballard in the previous election after serving on Council for twenty years. Mr. Gamache was awarded District of Coquitlam's Good Citizen of the Year award for 1970. Mike Butler was returned to council in 1976 but died suddenly in August of that year as reported by the Enterprise:

*"**Alderman Dead**   A man who served Coquitlam for twenty two years as an alderman died of a stroke in hospital Sunday morning. Alderman Mike Butler, who was first elected to council in 1949, was called a "fighter for the people" and "a great gutsy guy" by fellow council members after they learned of his death. Alderman Les Garrison called Butler someone who "had the respect of all of council" and suggested that perhaps a wing of the new Senior Citizens' Centre could be named after him."*

The political highlight of the seventies, which did have an impact on Maillardville, was the merging of Fraser Mills with Coquitlam in 1972. Negotiations had commenced in the previous decade. Crown Zellerbach was very reluctant to give up the benefits it enjoyed as its own district. Management tried to drive a hard bargain with Coquitlam, seeking various zoning, land use and tax concessions. Council, unwilling to give in and recognizing that the day of the company owned mill town was done, requested intervention from the Provincial Government. In 1972, the Province ordered Crown Zellerbach to proceed with the merger. In Council chambers, the formalities took place that saw the exchanging of keys between Mayor Jack Ballard and Mayor Harry Greenhall, the dissolution of the "ancient by-law of the Corporation of Fraser Mills" and the presentation of the Letters Patent of the new District of Coquitlam. For a short period, Coquitlam Council was comprised of fourteen members.

The Fraser Mills and the District were united. Fifty-nine years had gone by since the Canadian Western Lumber Company had seceded from New Westminster. As it had been when the pioneers first came here, there was once again unity between the Mill and Maillardville. The only other similarity was that in 1972, Crown Zellerbach, Fraser Mills division, continued to expand and remain a worldwide enterprise. Little else was left as a reminder of the "old days". The Oriental settlement, the community hall and stores had long since disappeared. Now, the mill workers' homes lining King Edward Street were slated for demolition, severing that last visible tie to Maillardville.

In the face of decay and near loss of that vibrant French community inherited from their fathers and grandfathers, the descendants of the pioneers struggled for their survival. At Our Lady of Lourdes, the erosion in numbers of their parishioners in the sixties resulted in a large and unmanageable debt. In 1970, faced with $20,000 of repairs to the school on Hammond Avenue, and laboring under the mortgage for the convent school on Rochester, Father Albéric Fréchette was forced to consider all options. In a letter to Archbishop James Carney in March of 1970[24], Father Fréchette asked for permission to sell the Hammond property, along with another parcel behind the convent. He wrote:

"Your Grace, for some time now the trustees of the parish have been talking about a project which they now wish to put up for your Grace's approval. Your Grace is aware of our financial difficulties because of our schools. We pay some $1200.00 of interest on our debt of $164,000.00 on our school-convent. We have two buildings to upkeep with only 267 students from grade 1 to 9 (grades 8 and 9 jointly with Fatima Parish, 51 students) The school on Hammond Avenue, built in 1950, is dilapidated and would require some $20,000.00 to repair adequately-trouble with the foundations even. For all these reasons, we are thinking of closing grades 8 and 9 in order to put all the children in the solid building of the convent -school on Rochester."

Father Fréchette went on to outline the financial options of leasing or selling the Hammond property. Daring to dream big, he continued in his letter to the Archbishop:

---

[24] Archives, Our Lady of Lourdes Roman Catholic Church

"We could go a step further. Seeing we would have to build a gym, we could also sell our property on Laval Square, the church property, and instead build a community centre next to the convent-school, comprising gym, church and rectory. The sale of the properties would extinguish our debt totally, we believe, and cover the cost of a new building, plus. This might meet with a bit of opposition: an historical monument!"

The Archbishop, in his response, wisely counseled further study of property values before a decision could be made. When all was said, grades 8 and 9 were terminated, and the elementary grades were moved into the convent. The Joint School Board issued a letter to the parents explaining that:

"We have been advised by Father Fréchette, of Our Lady of Lourdes parish that the Lourdes elementary school is to be sold. As a direct result of this, the elementary school children presently attending the school will be transferred to the convent as of next September. Due to lack of sufficient space at the convent, this forces the closure of the grade eight and nine classes and the whole Junior High School program. It is with much regret therefore that we advise you to place your older children elsewhere for the school year commencing in September, 1970."

The Hammond property was offered for sale to the City but they declined. The Share Society leased the building for a time as their centre of operations. School District 43 bought the property in 1973 and it is the site of present day Maillard Middle School.

The parishioners of O.L. of Lourdes still cherished and honored their past as the Enterprise noted in October of 1970:

"A pipe organ, built and paid for by the parishioners of Our Lady of Lourdes Church will be dedicated on October 11.....The organ consists of six ranks of pipes and several couplers. The console has two manuals and pedal. It was built to commemorate all past and present parishioners on the occasion of the 60th anniversary of the parish."

Nineteen seventy was a banner year for anniversaries and among them was the silver jubilee of Father Frechette's ordination to the priesthood. The occasion was marked by a Mass concelebrated by many of the area priests, followed by a banquet in the school auditorium, and a social evening. He died almost one year later in June of 1971 after serving the

Parish of O.L. of Lourdes for seventeen years. Two more priests would serve the parish in the seventies, Father Paul Surette and in 1975 Father Gerard Chabot. Although Father Frechette would not be the last pastor to serve for a lengthy commission at the parish, he was the last of that breed of priest who saw his vocation in the light of leading the community in every of aspect of its life. The Enterprise marked his passing:

*"**Pastor Dies After Illness**   Rev. Armand Frechette, OFM, retired pastor of Our Lady of Lourdes parish in Maillardville, died Saturday in Saint Mary's Hospital after a lengthy illness. He was 54 and had been pastor of Our Lady of Lourdes parish for seventeen years. Born in Lowell Mass. August 20 1916, Father Frechette studied for the priesthood in Quebec where he was ordained as a Franciscan priest in 1945. In 1953, when he was appointed pastor of Our Lady of Lourdes he was the first Franciscan to serve the parish. He worked closely with the Ursuline sisters and later with the Sisters of the Child Jesus to provide improved educational facilities for Maillardville children. Father Frechette was active in the ecumenical movement and served as secretary of the Ministerial Association of Coquitlam in 1966 and 1967. His semi-retirement had been caused by the illness that eventually took his life."*

Notre Dame de Fatima parishioners were also struggling, but perhaps not as greatly as their brothers and sisters at Lourdes. They had been forced to close their own convent school in 1969. The building became a home for the mentally and physically disabled and was celebrating its first anniversary as Alderlodge in 1970.

Fatima also had cause for celebration as they honoured their twenty-fifth anniversary in 1971. The Enterprise noted, among other things, that:

"The parish has now 500 families and 140 students attend the school. There have been three vocations to the sisterhood, Anita Charpentier and Claudette Ledet both of the Sisters of the Good Shepherd and Lorraine Malo, Sisters of St. Joseph. The first vocation to the priesthood was Georges LaGrange ordained in 1968."

It was in that same year that Father Georges Chevrier replaced Father Guy Michaud. Father Chevrier himself was replaced in 1977 by Father Alphonse Roy who would see the parish into the next decade. Anticipating future growth, a property was purchased on the north side of the existing Church to be the site of a new rectory.

The sister parishes held certain activities and organizations in common, OAP Branch 86 (Club d'Âge D'or) and the Knights of Columbus to name two. Fun and laughter was still to be found in spite of the heartache of those times. The seniors celebrated New Year 1973 with a dinner at O.L. of Fatima Hall. Guests of honour included Alderman Roy Stibbs, president of the Association Johnny Dicaire, Father Chevrier and Father Gauthier. In his address to the seniors, Alderman Stibbs commended them for their "*endeavors in giving Maillardville a French face in the community*". MC for the evening was Mrs. Roméo Paquette who offered congratulations to Mr. Dicaire on the occasion of his eighty first birthday. Entertainment was provided by the Foyer Maillard choir under the direction of Mrs. Louise Robert.

The Foyer Maillard itself continued to play an important role for the seniors of Maillardville. Social occasions, concerts and annual "teas" were all a part of life at the residence. It has to be noted that Maillardville's "first citizens" were not to be deprived of intriguing culinary adventures! In December of 1970, for example, the Foyer residents enjoyed a gala Christmas meal:

"The 132 senior citizens who live in the modern high rise built eighteen months ago under the sponsorship of the Bi Cultural Society of Maillardville were guests of the Ladies Auxiliary who donated $150 towards the gala Christmas meal....There was a grand turkey ornamented with peach slices, orange segments and grapes, a duck a l'orange, a sabot de Noël (potato salad in the form of a huge boot) a jolly old Santa head artistically formed from a leg of ham, there was Frosty the snowman fashioned from cottage cheese, trays of salads, pickles and cold meats, a decorated roast beef, a mammoth sized tray of cold salmon, lobster and crab."

What a hundred and fifty bucks bought in 1970! After dinner:

"residents were invited to the assembly room where children from Our Lady of Lourdes School performed Christmas plays and sang carols. The stage was set with a crèche scene and two bright Christmas trees heaped with Christmas gifts to each resident from the Ladies Auxiliary."

Christmas of 1972 was (only) slightly more reserved as French Chef Marcel from Paris treated residents to:

"an exquisite smorgasbord including turkey and dressing, roast beef with Yorkshire pudding, lobster, crab, shrimp and the piece de re-sistance-sugar cured ham in the shape of Santa, so realistic his eyes almost twinkled."

Invisible as the French culture at Maillardville apparently was, the pioneer spirit remained in this largest French settlement west of the Rockies. Music is an integral part of the French Canadian soul. In the early days of Maillardville, the people's music brought them together and helped to weave them into a closely bound community. Now in Maillardville's time of need, music was once again the glue that helped to bind. In 1970, the Chante Clair choir was formed and the Enterprise provides us with a little history:

"Chante-Claire was founded in 1970 by Sister Suzanne Baron, CSC to promote, preserve and take pride in our French Canadian Culture through singing. From the founding group of 18 students of Our Lady of Fatima School, the choir has grown to 55 students for the 1978/79 season. These students come from 12 different schools in the Coquitlam and Burnaby area. Thirty four of our singers are from French Canadian families, 21 of our singers are from English-speaking families who have enrolled their children in French immersion programs or just families interested in the French Canadian culture." In June of 1979, the group was busy giving concerts at Fatima and elsewhere to fundraise for a trip to a music workshop in Moncton, New Brunswick. Chante-Clair was considered to be: "the only organized French children's choir in B.C."

The adults soon followed the lead of the children. In 1973, Les Échos du Pacifique was formed. A tiny article in the Enterprise, October, 1973 heralded its birth:

*"**French Choir Being Formed** Socialized singing is the name of the game being organized by Germain Fortier and Evelyn Christie under the banner French Adult Choir. The concept is to unite singers to share choral and social enjoyment and a founding get together has been called for 8 pm Monday at Fatima Hall. People in the Maillardville area who enjoy singing are invited to join."*

From humble beginnings, the group took root quickly, becoming known as Les Échos du Pacifique.

Although there had been some division between the parishes and the Federation Canadienne française de la Colombie-Britanique (FCFCB) when the latter pushed for French instruction in the public schools, that group continued to be located at Maillardville. One of Maillardville's own, Roger Albert, was elected president of the FCFCB when they met for their twenty fifth AGM in 1971.

"The aim of the congress will be to democratize the Federation, bring it back to the people." said Mr. Roger Albert, president of the organization."

Among other decisions made at the congress, the organization changed its name to the Fédération Franco-Colombien. It also removed religious affiliation to the Catholic Church as a condition of membership and resolved to move its headquarters from Maillardville into Vancouver at the earliest possible time. The justification for the move was that statistics showed a larger number of francophones in Vancouver and the new location would be more central. The new FFC, however, also resolved to continue to support and promote the Catholic parishes as well as other francophone institutions. It also still considered the strengthening of French culture in Maillardville as part of its mandate.

La Francophonie was celebrated both early and late in the seventies. The Coquitlam Fine Arts Council chose to honour Maillardville and its French Canadian heritage as the inspirational theme for its annual festival of 1970. It was anticipated with much enthusiasm and was to provide room for:

"Maillardville folk which will include wood carving, pottery making, weaving etc with continual demonstrations."

Appearances by "local talent" in music and dancing were featured during the two-day festival. Of course, along with art, music and dance, no celebration of French Canadian culture could be complete without the smells and tastes of traditional French cooking. To accommodate this, a mammoth cooking bee was held which involved:

"many local French Canadian wives." Tables were set up to sample the fare *"a la carte or the whole menu of pea soup, tourtière, blanc mange, and maple syrup specially imported from Quebec."*

The celebration was hugely successful as reported by the Enterprise:

*"**An estimated 5000 visitors** attended the very successful two day Festival of the Arts held last weekend at the Social Recreation Centre. The festival was officially opened by Roméo Paquette. Other dignitaries participating included Port Moody Alderman S.C. Maplethorp, Port Coquitlam Alderman L.B. Scott and George Robertson, Festival chairman. Organizers of the event were extremely critical about the lack of participation in the opening ceremonies by Coquitlam council. No one was present representing the municipality. The Enterprise learned that council members were engaged in a golf tournament with civic employees in the Surrey area. Thousands of people from near and afar came to the third annual festival, this year illustrating a French Canadian Maillardville theme......Mrs. Marie Marenger was in charge of the weaving demonstrations, Soeur Suzanne of Our Lady of Fatima School directed the folk singing and dancing of pupils from the school appropriately dressed in period costume. Father Labonté and Mr. N. Gareau presented an adult folk singing group and Mr. Lebrun, of Centennial High School French department appeared with his young teen age folk singers."*

BC's own St. Jean Baptiste Day celebration took form in La Francofête. Initiated in 1974 by the FFC, it was moved to Coquitlam and Maillardville in 1977. It ran there for several years and was not only tremendously successful, but represented the pinnacle of effort, good will and respect for the French community that characterized the decade. After modest beginnings in 1977, the Francofête grew to be the "People's Festival". By 1979, the festival was no small event. Enterprise June 1979:

*"**Francofête a People's Festival**   More than 15,000 are expected to join in on the most important French Canadian Festival this side of St. Boniface, Manitoba. At 8:30pm, when the parade winds down, the opening ceremonies start at the arena, where 10 different entertainment groups are ready to entertain as many as 3,000 people. The 10 quasi-professional groups include two opera singers, a calypso drummer and local pianist, organist and singer Robert Viens of Maillardville. Many dignitaries were on hand to help out with the opening ceremonies including Mayor Tonn, MLA George Kerster and the French Consul and his wife, Mr. and Mrs. Jean Jacques Galabrux. The events were incredibly diverse. They included an Old Timers dance and a disco for the young folks. On Saturday francophone artists from all over had jewelry,*

weaving, macramé, batik and pottery on display. There were softball games, a soap box derby and a broomball match. La Troupe de la Seizième entertained the children with a play. Les Scouts et Guides organized a whole schedule of games for the children. A BBQ followed and the evening was celebrated with the Francofête Ball featuring Brick Henderson and his 13 piece band. Sunday morning saw a mass said in French by Archbishops Carney and Sabatini at the sports centre, followed by a pancake and maple syrup breakfast. Besides all of the French food to sample, the afternoon offered a variety show with some 250 participants including: "amateur singers, dancers and musicians. Two local choirs will be on hand, the Chante-Clair and Les Échos du Pacifique." The evening saw a hockey match between the Coquitlam Ambassadors old timers' hockey team and the Maillardville Canadians. A spokesman for the Canadians said: "the Ambassadors can expect the game of their lives." The article also states that: "sixty volunteers in 13 committees have laboured all year to put Francofête 79 together. Organizers said that in three or four years close to 60,000 people could be turning out for the fair and it could grow to rival the Quebec Winter Carnival."

Francofête really was a regional celebration as evidenced by the winners for best floats in the parade:

"The best overall float in the Francofête 79 parade was sponsored by Fort Langley with the Surrey centennial float a close second." But Maillardville was well represented among the winners as the Knights of Columbus 3239 won one of the marching unit awards. First prize for novelty entries went to Maillardville's Club D'age D'or and the Knights taking second for "La Famille".

Caisse Populaire took second place in the commercial category for floats. There was even a bean-counting contest won by local Edna Roset, who came closest to the true number of 8,125 beans with her guess of 5,863.

The festival spirit was so alive in 1979 that Alderson School, cradle of French immersion in B.C., decided not to wait for Francofête to rival Quebec's Carnival and had one of their own instead. The Enterprise, March 1979 reported:

***"The teachers, students and parents of Alderson Street Elementary School** brought everything from the famed Quebec Winter Carnival with*

172

the exception of the snow for the school's own version of the carni-val...participants and guests were encouraged to wear carnival colors of white, red and black complete with toques and sashes.....Then there was the Carnival Ball at which Queen Denise Caouette was crowned Queen of the Carnival....One of the highlights of the carnival was the parade that moved along Alderson, down Blue Mountain, along Gauthier, up Thrift and then back to Alderson." There was also an authentic French Canadian Banquet featuring: "tourtière, which is meat pie famed in Quebec, pea soup, beans and stews, cretons (head cheese), sugar pie and a French fudge called Sucre a la Crème. All these dishes were as they were back in La Vielle Province." "This was a creditable undertak-ing by the school and one that certainly merits becoming an annual event in Maillardville."

On Sunday, February 23, 1975, the Scouts celebrated their twentieth an-niversary with a father and son banquet at Our Lady of Lourdes Hall to which all former cubs, scouts and leaders were invited. As regional commissioner for the west, Jean Lambert, accompanied by Roger Bru-neau, Napoléon Gareau and Father Raymond Larochelle went on a promotional tour from Manitoba through Alberta and B.C. Mr. Lambert was able to report that in 1971 the organization for French Canadian Catholic Scouts numbered 32,000 louveteaux, scouts, éclaireurs and pi-onniers across Canada. Jean Lambert received the award "Croix de Jerusalem" in 1970 for his service to the Scouts. The guides celebrated their fifteenth anniversary in 1972, and the Enterprise printed a short history of the movement. It included a detailed time line and the mention of many devoted "Cheftaines" who had contributed to the movement over the years. In 1972, the French Guide movement in Canada boasted 13,000 members and grew to 16,000 by 1978. Also in 1978, on the occa-sion of Queen Elizabeth's twenty fifth anniversary, the Governor General of Canada presented Mrs. Amélie Gareau with a commemora-tive medal for her service to the Guide movement. At a time when the young people of French Maillardville continued to be disenfranchised in their language and culture, the Scout and Guide movement was a sanctu-ary where the seeds of French heritage were planted and nurtured for hundreds of young boys and girls.

There was such a heightened awareness of and desire to reinvigorate the French culture in Maillardville that in 1978, Le Conseil Central Franco Maillardville was formed. Their goal was to bring the various French organizations under one umbrella for mutual support and to coordinate the effort for cultural revitalization. Their early effort saw little success, and in 1978 they changed their name to Maillardville Uni. This new version of the association also struggled to create an identity for itself, but would steadily grow and help keep the flame alive in Maillardville throughout the next three decades.

"Community building" in Maillardville in the 1970s had taken on an urgency and the Caisse Populaire de Maillardville reaffirmed its commitment to the village. It was an extremely prosperous time for the credit union, which grew from 2200 members to 7000 and multiplied their assets from 2.2 million dollars to 27.5 million. J.B. Goulet, founding member and manager for 19 years, retired and was succeeded by Mr. Jean Aussant in 1970. Georges Perron continued to guide CPMCU as president, a position he held since 1963. The transition into modern times took place in 1974 as the building was expanded, doubling its square footage. The credit union also entered the "modern era" and became computerized. It was pretty heady times for the Credit Union and as the institution grew, the Board of Directors had to consider what long-term strategy was appropriate. Continued growth would be difficult, unless the Caisse Populaire expanded its territory, in other words, open a branch outside of Maillardville. Moving in that direction would betray a core value of the institution, namely to support and foster Maillardville. Demonstrating a true devotion to the community, the Board chose for Maillardville. Adding to their slogan "*Better in so many ways*" the Caisse now proclaimed "*Vive la Difference!*' and with a fully bilingual staff of twenty, claimed to be "*B.C.'s only bilingual credit union*"

The Société Bi-Culturelle de Maillardville, initially formed to instigate the building of a French community centre, continued to focus its attention on the operation and expansion of the Foyer Maillard. In a guest editorial to the Enterprise in November of 1970, Roméo Paquette commented:

*"**The Bi Cultural Society of Maillardville** held its annual meeting last weekend. The members approved a resolution asking the new Board of directors to focus its attention on the real aims of the Bicultural Society: the establishment of cultural facilities especially for the youth of Maillardville."*

One year later, in October of 1971, The Society struck a committee as noted in the Enterprise:

"A committee of the Bi Cultural Society of Maillardville has prepared a five point program which, it is hoped, will revive the project for a French centre in Maillardville."

At their Annual General meeting in November, it was reported (Enterprise):

"At the annual meeting of the Bi Cultural Society of Maillardville it became apparent that the majority of members were more concerned with senior citizens' recreation than the proposed cultural centre."

The dream of a French cultural centre lay dormant for some years. However, among Plan Maillardville's 1974 recommendations was a call for a community centre. At first known as the "Maillardville Neighbourhood House", Place Maillardville was opened in 1979. Acquiring the land became a contentious issue when, in a highly criticized move, Mayor Tonn and council almost lost an opportunity to buy the land on Laval Square. The Enterprise reports that Council authorized the Mayor to bargain with the owners, Micharco Western Ltd. An offer was made that was $5,000 less than the $100,000 asking price. The company did not respond to the offer and the Enterprise reported:

"Reliable sources close to Micharco Western Ltd. report that there were last minute offers on the part of Coquitlam to buy the land. They report that Micharco had another interested buyer by this point and preferred to sell rather than haggle over the $5,000 price difference."

Incredibly this all took place with the knowledge that the federal Government under their cost-sharing plan was responsible for 75% of the purchase price. The land was sold to a Surrey businessman who eventually subdivided the lot and sold a part back to the municipality. After this initial snag, the course of events included public consultation as reported in the Enterprise, March 1977:

*"**Democracy Lives In M'ville** The planning of Maillardville's community centre is becoming an exercise in true democracy as everyone from grade-schoolers to pioneers have their say. Two weeks ago, a group of about 45 senior citizens led by pioneer Johnny Dicaire attended a Neighbourhood Improvement Program meeting to let their thoughts be known. Then the grass roots of the Maillardville community took notice. A delegation of 35 children made representation to subcommittee chair-*

*man Lenore Peyton. "They were very sophisticated, very pleasant in
their speech" reports Mrs. Peyton of the meeting."*

Site preparation got underway in September of 1977 and the new hall
was to include:

*"a dance floor, requested by the senior citizens, indoor and outdoor
play areas for the children, considerations for the handicapped including special ramps, parking and washroom facilities, a games room and
library for teenagers with a special French reading room, a coffee room,
a general games room, a sunken forum for public discussions and even a
BBQ pit for summer parties."*

As is so often the case, the reality fell somewhat short of the vision. The
new Centre was operated by the Habitat Society of Maillardville.

Other physical changes in the village continued to erode its ties to the
past. Since the early part of the century, the gateway to Fraser Mills
punctuated the division between Millside and Maillardville. King Edward Avenue was lined on the east by the houses of the millworkers,
uniform in design with their distinctive green trim on white paint. Across
the road were the old Circle F Baseball field and Mackin Park. At the
head of the boulevard at Brunette was the sales manager's house on the
west side, opposite to the residence of the mill manager. The buildings
themselves had long since ceased to be used for those purposes.

With the merger of Fraser Mills and Coquitlam, mill management
founded a new company, VenDev Enterprises. Their first order of business was the demolition of those old homes along King Edward Avenue.
The city leased both managers' homes. The one, "Mackin House", was
home to a number of City services over the years. In 1974, the Kincaid
Treatment Centre was established by S.H.A.R.E. The facility took in
youth aged 5 through 14 with behavioral problems.

The other, "Ryan House", became the home of the Maillardville detachment of the R.C.M.P. in 1962. In 1972, the R.C.M.P. moved from the
house on Brunette to take up residence at the new justice building on
Christmas Way near Coquitlam "Town Centre". Another tie to the past
was lost. For the first time since 1912 when Émeri Paré was named as a
special constable and appointed chief in 1913, there were no police stationed in Maillardville.

So much of the village's history seemed to be dissolving. Even the post office located at Thrift's Store, and still bearing the Maillardville post-mark, was lost when the business was sold in 1972. The new owners did not want the responsibility of running a post office.

The original CPR train station at Fraser Mills was moved adjacent to Ryan House in 1965 and was to become a museum. It remained on cement blocks until 1970. It was suggested at that time that it be moved to Triangle Park at the corner of Lougheed Highway and Gauthier Street. The Parks and Recreation commission agreed to this. They planned to install picnic benches and shade trees and considered it an ideal location for a Chamber of Commerce information booth. This did not occur and the station was moved to Blue Mountain Park and finally opened as a museum by the Coquitlam Historical Society. Not all of Council approved. Alderman Jack Gilmore, the only member of Council to oppose the move, commented that:

"Just as Gastown has capitalized on its history, we should make people aware of the unique history of our French community. The station should be left in Maillardville where it has its roots. It's time we arrived at plans for an acceptable redevelopment of Maillardville. I don't think the station should be lifted from its natural heritage."

The loss of the CPR station notwithstanding, the future "Heritage Square" found its beginning in this early period of the seventies. In anticipation of the police vacating Ryan House, a report by John Kirk to City Council in July of 1971 was recorded by the Enterprise and suggested:

"when the present Maillardville RCMP headquarters on Brunette Avenue becomes vacant, it could be converted into a fine arts centre...The art centre could become a focal point of a reconstructed Maillardville, Kirk added. He said he envisioned an art gallery, a concert hall, boardwalks and catalpa trees."

Council tabled the motion. In the following year, however, a delegation from the Coquitlam Fine Arts Council approached City Council with the proposal for an arts and crafts centre to be established at Ryan House, a "Place des Arts". Council agreed and the new facility was an immediate hit. It was a real "people's centre". All through the decade, it offered classes in music, art, pottery and stained glass making for young and old alike. Although facing "money problems" by 1974, the Place des Arts

continued its mission to help rebuild Maillardville. With Lenore Peyton
at the helm, the Enterprise June 1974 reported:

*"As well as childrens' programs, the Place des Arts offers classes in folk
dancing, pottery and drama for teens and afternoon classes for old age
pensioners, retarded adults, exchange students, housewives and delin-
quents. Mrs. Peyton explained that the Place des Arts aims at being an
integrated part of the community and aiding in the development of the
artistic skills of community members."* The article continues: *"Generally
response to the Place des Art's program is overwhelming. Over one hundred children from Millside and Our lady of Fatima schools attend on a
regular basis."*

In 1974, on the other side of the street at 169 King Edward, the Plan
Maillardville team anticipated that the Kincaid program was soon to be
terminated. Among their recommendations was that King Edward should
be realigned to access Marmont Street directly. The space left behind
from the former King Edward would now form a plaza between the two
houses. The report further recommended that Mackin House would
make an excellent site for a museum. And so it was. King Edward was
realigned with Marmont Street and both Ryan and Mackin Houses were
purchased from Crown Zellerbach.

The nineteen seventies was a time of transition and reevaluation for
Maillardville. The body of "old Maillardville" died. Yet the heart and
soul of the community lived on, sometimes in spectacular ways, as
demonstrated by Francofête, but more so in the hearts and homes and in
the churches of the French Canadian community. Old and new organizations, the Scouts and Guides, the Caisse Populaire, the FFCB and the
newly formed Maillardville Uni stepped up and refused to let the extinction of Maillardville occur. So many different organizations and
individuals yearned for a "new Maillardville", and perhaps they are best
represented in this decade by Johnny Dicaire, always in the thick of
things. And also by Roméo Paquette who was involved in every effort to
elevate the profile of Maillardville and to foster the dream of a truly bilingual and cooperative community. It was a time when Mayor and
Council seemed to be at a loss as how to best answer the question "What
to do with Maillardville?" There was very much attention focused on the
rest of Coquitlam, not the least of which was the development of the new
Coquitlam Town Centre. It is also clear that residents contributed to the
"stalemate" in Maillardville's rebirth. They consistently opposed at-

tempts at redevelopment, particularly in the building of new housing types and of commercial opportunities for the area. They seemed to be saying: "Make it better but don't change anything." The seventies set the stage for what all hoped would become a revitalized community, but progress was slow, and Maillardville entered the eighties under a cloud of uncertainty. With the apparent "death of Maillardville", it is more than fitting to end this chapter of its history by commemorating the death of Johnny Dicaire and remembering some of the thoughts of "Mr. Maillardville"

In August of 1978, the French community had to bear the sad news of the death of the quintessential citizen of Maillardville. The Enterprise noted the event, declaring:

*"**Mr. Maillardville Passes Away** One of Maillardville's pioneers died last week at the age of eighty six. John Dicaire, born January 12, 1892 died as a result of a heart attack August 21, 1978. He, at age 17 in 1909, was among the first of the many French Canadians to move to what was then known as Fraser Mills. During the course of his life in Maillardville, John Dicaire was involved in every aspect of the community. He and his wife Regina, with her family also moved to Maillardville in 1909, were married in the Knights of Columbus hall on November 20, 1916.....John Dicaire was the father of five children. He was the grandfather of nine and the great grandfather of fourteen children. "He died the way he wanted to die and lived the way he wanted to live." said Mrs. Dicaire "He loved his friends and he loved to organize-dances, parties, fundraising schemes for charities. He loved music, and he used to call quadrilles at the Oddfellows Hall for years." His daughters met their husbands at the dances he organized. Mrs. Dicaire said her husband was active right until the last day before his heart attack. An athlete of some local note, he played hockey and lacrosse for many years and at Franco fête, two months ago, age eighty six, was right in the thick of the planning and fun. It was largely through the fund raising efforts of John Dicaire, that Foyer Maillard was built and he also had a hand in the building of two local churches. Alderman Les Garrison who was among the many people attending the funeral August 23, referred to John Dicaire as "Mr. Maillardville". He'll be missed."*

Ironically, "Mr. Maillardville" stated earlier in the decade, to a group of schoolchildren, that perhaps it might have been better to stay with the name of "French Town" instead of adopting Maillardville "because

Maillardville is slowly disappearing." The following article appeared in the Enterprise in April of 1972. It is included here in its entirety because, perhaps, it is a more fitting tribute to this man who loved Maillardville and devoted so much of himself to it.

*"**Be Proud To Be French Canadian** "Don't let Maillardville disappear" Johnny Dicaire made this poignant appeal to a group of bilingual grade seven students at Our Lady of Lourdes School. A social studies unit concerning the history of Maillardville prompted Sister Louise to invite Mr. Dicaire to speak to her class. Mr. Dicaire has resided in Maillardville for 63 years. At 80 years of age his memories of Maillardville in 1909 are as lucid as his awareness of current affairs today. "In 1909 I was 16 and selling the Ottawa Evening Journal and Citizen as well as Le Temps in Ottawa near the train station. I switched from French to English and this is what attracted the attention of Mr. Théroux from Fraser Mills and Father William O'Boyle from New Westminster." said Mr. Dicaire. "They were out to hire French Canadian saw mill workers" des bucherons de langue française" he added. "I brought them to a mill on the Ottawa River where my uncle worked. When the men there heard they could be earning two dollars a day rather than 90 cents, they became very interested." Said Mr. Dicaire. "The Bouthot and Gauthier families said yes right away." Subsequent meetings in Hull, Montreal, Sherbrooke, Rockland and Quebec attracted other families. "The names Gagnon, Valière, Boileau, Gravelle, Hammond, Labelle, Gagné, Dicaire, Leblanc, and many more are still with us today, all are descendants of the first families to arrive in this area." he stated. "My father signed up because 17 years before, in 1886, he had worked for the C.P.R. in Revelstoke for five years. With mules and oxen they used to go down to Spokane and then take the train back east to visit" explained Mr. Dicaire. "Also work in the east was seasonal but at Fraser Mills there was year round work and enough work to last 50 years. This appealed to the men." he added. "So on the morning of September 22, 1909, we left Montreal. We traveled with the Bouthot family. At the station there were tears and mixed feelings. The Gravelle family backed out but then came the following year." "On the train, on dansait" explained Mr. Dicaire "Many had violins and accordions so we had a good time." "When we got to the mountains the children became very excited. You know we have the nicest province in Canada." commented Mr. Dicaire. "Then on a Monday afternoon, we arrived at Fraser Mills. There were two white families, the Stewarts and another family. All the others were East Indian, Chinese or Japanese... Twenty four cabins had been started but they were not complete. Some moved into them anyway, many others*

stayed on board the train for a week. We ate at the company cookhouse."
added Mr. Dicaire. "My parents and myself were the only bilingual per-
sons in the group and so on October 1 when we started working I
became the interpreter. I also learned to speak East Indian, Chinese and
Japanese." "I picked up five languages in my 38 years at the mill." he
added. Later problems set in. "Skilled workers were brought in from the
U.S. and so we were no longer eligible for the higher paying jobs." ex-
plained Mr. Dicaire. Many threatened to leave. "Some did and went to
Port Moody. Mr. Chevalier eventually became manager of the mill
there." he stated. Finally, 11 months later a union was organized and
conditions improved. "I'm not propagandizing" said Mr. Dicaire "but
unions mean force. The same applies to you. Be proud to be French Ca-
nadian and never be embarrassed about speaking French."
Entertainment took the form of burning stumps and clearing the land.
"On Cartier, we would often hold parties at Dicaires or Bouthots or Boi-
leaus-we were good dancers and evenings spent together helped us to
stay together." The Americans at the mill referred to the settlement as
Pea Soup Hill and then French Town. "I believe we should have kept the
name instead of Maillardville because "Maillardville" is disappearing."
he sadly commented. "Don't let Maillardville disappear. We have per-
mission from the Post Office to use the name. Thrift's Post Office which
was set up in 1913 still uses "Maillardville" I know we're in an English
speaking part of the country, but I would like to see more French be-
cause when we were brought out here in 1909, we were hired only if we
were "de langue française" and this was partly to spread the French
language across Canada. Besides there are 9000 French Canadians in
the area now." he added. "We don't want to push French-to force it
down anyone's throat, but a person who is bilingual is better off than a
person who is not." Remarked Mr. Dicaire. "Mon Canada, je
l'aime" "But don't let Maillardville disappear!" *he concluded. "*

Eight

The Long Road Back

As the eighties unfold, "modern "Maillardville begins to emerge. In the previous decade, "Plan Maillardville" envisioned a revitalized French community within a mix of new housing types, blending the traditional and modern. Although there was little visible accomplishment as a result of the plan, much of the groundwork that would shape the new Maillardville had been laid. A revised zoning map, a realignment of King Edward with Marmont, the suggestion of a "heritage square" and the building of Place Maillardville Neighborhood House were all outcomes of that study. It was also at that time that the vision of reestablishing Maillardville as a French centre took firm root. Nevertheless, as the decade of Terry Fox, the space shuttle Challenger disaster and Expo '86 opened, the village itself continued to teeter on the brink of disaster. A November 25, 1980 article from the Columbian remarked:

"There were good old days in Maillardville. There were times, and not so long ago, when you could walk from one end of Brunette to the other and shop and eat and have your car done, stop for a couple of beers and not speak a word of English. There were dances and socials. There were clubs. And Sunday services were packed for French language mass.....Nowadays there are still dances-but the only French heard is at individual tables....The community's name is now pronounced "Ma-lard-ville" not "My-ar-ville", but no matter how they are pronouncing it, there are many people nowadays who are just saying "au revoir", Maillardville."

The degradation that Maillardville had suffered during the preceding ten years continued in the early eighties. Brunette was as bad as ever it was. City Hall focused most of its attention and energy elsewhere, specifically the Town Centre. The Lower Mainland continued to pay homage to Maillardville, laying its garbage at her feet. With no gas control in place, and virtually no drainage, the open-air dump at Terra Nova had become a stinking, rotting mess. A vivid description of the site was included in this January 1982 Herald-Enterprise article:

"Cutting Down The Stink   That putrid stench of rotting debris that permeates the air in the southwest corner of Coquitlam may be reduced in the new year if regional district takes steps to reduce the problem prove effective. The smell, which nearby residents know and hate, comes from the 70 acre Terra Nova garbage dump located west of the Fraser Mills plant site....When the wind is right, the smell can be detected in New Westminster and Port Coquitlam."

The regional district looked at various means to cope with the problem, although the dump was due to close that year. Unfortunately for Maillardville, the facility did not close until 1985. A partial solution was arrived at by the building of the Wastech recycling depot. When Terra Nova was finally terminated, a gas management plan was instituted that burned the methane accumulated from the rotting mass. Where residents on the south slope of Maillardville once could see the flames of Hindu funeral pyres, now eerie blue lights flickered on the plain below.

In some ways Maillardville of the early eighties was not so very different from that of the forties. In both eras, the village itself was in need of building up. Francos and Anglos worked together for the benefit of the community. Following the hope spawned by Plan Maillardville, the beleaguered town tried to claw its way out of the mire. After Brunette Avenue underwent upgrading in 1980, the shopping centre that housed such businesses as Johnstone Cleaners, Pant A Bode Discount Jeans, Lullaby Baby Shoppe and Zamys Supermarket, announced in the Enterprise in May, 1980:

"Whew! It's All Over! Brunette Is Now Ready   The Merchants of Maillardville would like to welcome back their old and some new customers...Come On Down To Maillardville"

The widening of Brunette resulted in a Council decision to severely restrict and eventually eliminate parking on that main commercial thoroughfare, bringing new hardship to its merchants. After their concerns were voiced, a parking lot on Adair Avenue, south of Brunette, was built. However, several merchants, appealing to Council in 1982 for at least some restricted parking to be left on Brunette, were not to be accommodated.

The Maillardville Shopping Centre, built some 22 years earlier, was itself run down and in need of a facelift. The Herald Enterprise, March of 1982 tells us:

*"**M'ville Center Deal Dies** A deal that would have seen a total renovation of the run down Maillardville Shopping Centre in Coquitlam has fallen through. Berkeley Point Development was bargaining with the owners, Jang Brothers, to buy the centre located at Brunette Avenue and Blue Mountain Street...."I was disappointed because I liked the project. We had a rendering done on the renovations and the municipality was very happy with it. The Centre's been an eyesore for years" he said"*

As is often the case, money appears to have been the final consideration and the renovation never took place. Everyone from residents and merchants to Council and City staff recognized that the state of Maillardville was intolerable. In spite of the hope that Plan Maillardville created, the planned development stalled. Many individual efforts continued to be frustrated.

In 1980, Maillardville residents turned out en masse to support a Brunette landowner who fought City Hall over the "down zoning" of his property. Woodwest Developments bought the property at the southeast corner of Brunette and Schoolhouse with the intention of building a 46-unit apartment with a street level commercial zone. After the purchase was completed, Council announced that it was proposing to rezone the land for light industrial. Company owner Murray Wood cried foul in a November 1980 article in the Enterprise, claiming that he had been working closely with City staff, with no mention of any problems. Seeing his project as a catalyst for Maillardville redevelopment, Wood stated:

"We feel like we are chasing shadows. This area needs encouragement, not discouragement."

The City went ahead with a public hearing on the rezoning, but Wood pre-empted it with a meeting of his own. Inviting residents to an information session on the site, he hoped to gain support for his position. The Enterprise, December 1983 commenting on the open house and Council's decision on the matter:

*"**Wood's Plans "Blown Away"** Council elected by a 5-1 vote to change the zoning at the property from C-2, neighbourhood commercial to M-3, light industrial. The property has been the subject of a raging controversy the last few weeks as developer Murray Wood and the residents of Maillardville have fought to keep the area residential...Council burned down his appeal and Wood took his fight to the residents of the area. He held a coffee party and open house on November 15 and endeavored to explain to the people what he was planning to do.*
Obviously he met with some success as 189 people signed letters to council stating that they did not want industry on Brunette. At the public hearing on November 17, it was standing room only as Maillardville residents turned out en masse to protest the planning department proposal."

The article goes on to report that council suggested Wood had not been totally truthful with residents in explaining the definition of "light industrial". Although a few of the residents changed their thinking, the majority remained supportive of Wood. Council disregarded the strong statement of the community and rezoned the land.

Meanwhile another modern feature of Maillardville was coming into being. Development at the new Town Centre was advancing steadily. Two trailer parks in the area, Evergreen and Parkland, stood in the way of progress and residents were given their eviction notices. The displaced had to be accommodated and Council considered Maillardville to be an ideal place to house them. Entering into a partnership with the provincial government, council sought to buy some 25 acres from Fraser Mills on which to build a park. The land just south of Brunette at King Edward (the former Fraser Mills town site that had housed many of the pioneers in 1909 and 1910) was to become Mill Creek Village. The BC government was prepared to pay Crown Zellerbach 3.3 million dollars for the land in April of 1982. But in July, Victoria pulled the plug. The July 13 Herald-Enterprise:

*"**The Biggest Let Down In 10 Years**....Ald. Les Garrison says that it is the most disappointing thing that has happened in Coquitlam in 10 years."For me it is by far the most disappointing" the veteran alderman was still shaking his head Monday over the government decision to back*

*out of a proposal on Crown Zellerbach land which would have seen
pads for 175 mobile homes. The ministry of Lands, Parks and Housing
had agreed to purchase 10 hectares of land in Fraser Mills North for 3.3
million last December......Mayor Tonn said Chabot told him the government would only pay $1.5 million for the land due to offsite costs,
development charges and the dropping value of land."*

September saw a glimmer of hope as Mayor Tonn and Alderman Len
Bewley were given the nod to negotiate a deal with CZ up to a specific
(undisclosed) amount. The Herald Enterprise quoted Ald. Bewley, September, 1982 on the pressure and challenges surrounding the
negotiations:

*"In order to keep rents between $250 and $200 a month, we've got to
negotiate a good deal. At a sale price of $3.3million, the rents would
have to be $400 which is not practical....Bewley anticipates that if the
deal goes through the government will call tenders from private contractors to build the park and when finished, the development will be taken
over by the Greater Vancouver Housing Corporation to administer as
low rent accommodation."*

A price of $1.8 million was finally agreed on in November. Although the
land was purchased and rezoned, it was not until September of 1983 that
tenders went out for a contractor. The contract was awarded in January
of 1984, but the project had shifted from a low rent development to a
"market rate" site. By early 1985, the park was finally nearing completion, but residents from the Parkland and Evergreen parks, having been
promised space at Mill Creek Village, were dismayed to find out that
pad rental would, in some cases, be doubled. After threats of picketing
the park, a deal with residents was finally reached in July, 1985.

Issues such as affordable housing, open ditches, derelict buildings and
the continued general downward spiral of Maillardville were all raised in
the early years of the decade. But it seems that Council, once again, was
unable or unwilling to respond with a definitive plan or a concerted effort to "clean up" Maillardville once and for all.

As in the seventies, Brunette Avenue east of Marmont Street retained the
distinction of being the centre of the Maillardville slum. Six of those
derelict properties were owned by a single landlord who had them painted in shades of pink, purple and green. Apparently, those bright colours
were chosen to attract the attention of Council in an attempt to have her

properties rezoned to higher residential density. While many looked with dismay on this latest humiliation heaped upon the homes of Maillard-ville's founders, at least one found a reason to celebrate those colourful structures. From the Enterprise February 1980:

*"**Valerie Morrow's gaudily painted old homes** on Brunette Avenue in Coquitlam may have failed to attract the attention of local politicians, but they have captured the interest of a local artist whose paintings of Morrow's turn of the century Maillardville homes are going on display in New West. Morrow, self-styled mayor of a slum within a slum, painted the six homes, three in the 1200 block Brunette and three in the 1400 block shockingly bright colours in an attempt to focus Coquitlam's municipal eye on urgings from her and other Maillardville property owners to rezone the area....City Hall may not have been impressed with Morrow's flamboyant use of colour, but artist Pamela Scott certainly was. She set to work transforming Morrow's bold statement onto canvas."*

As the decade progressed, a light began to shine at the end of the tunnel and there was a whisper of renewed optimism. The Caisse Populaire, the Maillardville Merchants' Association and the Société Maillardville Uni emerged as real champions for Maillardville. Mayor Jim Tonn resigned his office to take up the position of City Manager. In a close match, Alderman Lou Sekora bested Alderman Les Garrison for the Mayor's seat by a mere 219 votes. Acting quickly, Mayor Sekora put Maillardville's revitalization on the agenda, handing responsibility for the "Maillardville Project" to the existing land use committee. In his 1983 inaugural address he remarked that:

"redevelopment of once proud but now neglected Maillardville must come soon, and with $400,000 in federal funds available, I plan to appoint an Alderman to investigate this possibility."

Shortly after that, in late 1984, Mayor Sekora assigned Alderman Brian Robinson to head a new committee made up of various Maillardville stakeholders. Working with the Land Use Committee and the Merchants' Association, progress by the newly minted Maillardville Redevelopment Committee was still painfully slow.

Area residents were increasingly frustrated, and the clamor to clean up the derelict houses on Brunette grew louder as the decade progressed. In 1985, a series of suspicious fires in the commercial district of Brunette and in the residential area east of Marmont added a new layer of squalor to Maillardville. Residents took matters into their own hands and began to petition City Hall to have the burned out houses on Brunette demolished. Coquitlam Now, November 1985:

*"**Neighbours Say House Must Go*** *A group of Maillardville residents has pushed Coquitlam council into taking steps to knock down a burned out house on Brunette Avenue. Municipal manager Jim Tonn said council will probably take action next week to arrange demolition of a house at 1206 Brunette that burned September 28 and again October 11. But he said council first has to await a report from its solicitor, and then has to hear from the house owner, Valerie Morrow.....Alice Marchesseault, who lives across the street from the offending property said Wednesday the burned house is an eyesore and a safety hazard. She and her husband George have their house for sale,, but she said the neighbourhood isn't very attractive to potential buyers......She said the two decrepit houses, and others on Brunette, have ruined the Maillardville neighbourhood because of their appearance and the undesirable tenants they have attracted.....The house at 1212 Brunette, a big pink building with pictures of devils painted on the windows, now is unoccupied and neighbours say they want it demolished as well."*

The wheels of bureaucracy turned very slowly indeed. It was not until May of 1986 that the burned out hulk was finally removed from the landscape.

In April of 1985, the neighbourhood suffered another shocking blow when the Maillardville Shopping Centre was destroyed by fire. What could have been a knockout punch for the village instead brought hope that a phoenix would arise from the ashes of Maillardville. The fire did, in fact, prove to be the catalyst that kick started the rebuilding of the village. The Coquitlam Now, April 1985 offers some detail:

*"**New Hope From Ashes*** *It was the end of an era when the Maillardville Shopping Centre was destroyed by fire on Wednesday. But when the smoke cleared, a lot of people were saying the fire could mean the beginning of a new and better era for Maillardville-a beginning that could get a financial shot in the arm from the provincial government. Maillardville-Coquitlam MLA John Parks said Thursday the fire might clear the way for a downtown redevelopment grant from the ministry of municipal affairs. "Cleaning out that key component of Maillardville may well prove to be a good thing." Parks said "A grant from municipal affairs would help the redevelopment of Maillardville.....Firemen from*

Coquitlam and Burnaby fought the fire for more than five hours after it was reported at 5:37am Wednesday. It spread quickly through the 27 year old wooden structure, destroying several businesses, including the Best Value Foods supermarket. Coquitlam deputy fire chief Ralph Gildof said Friday investigators had narrowed the cause of the fire down to a couple of possibilities, but he declined to say what they were. "At this stage we believe it was an accidental fire." he said. Firefighting efforts were hampered by water supply problems and mechanical glitches that put both Coquitlam's aerial ladder trucks-including a newly purchased one-out of commission. A ladder truck from Burnaby was used instead. Gildof said inconveniently located fire hydrants, not a lack of water in the mains, contributed to water supply problems....Alderman Brian Robinson, chairman of the Maillardville Redevelopment Committee said the fire would not be detrimental to Maillardville's future as a shopping area and could actually help it develop. "The old mall was anything but a drawing card to the entrance of Maillardville. It certainly wasn't a beautiful gateway." Robinson said. Jean Aussant, manager of the Caisse Populaire de Maillardville Credit Union and vice chairman of the redevelopment committee was also optimistic about the area's future. "It's certainly not going to interfere with our plans for Maillardville." Aussant said "If they rebuild it with a nice flair any new project will be good."

With MLA Parks' encouragement, Council applied for and received a grant of $5,000 under the provincial downtown revitalization program. The money was to be used for a preliminary study and development of a proposal for revitalization. The following motion at Council July, 1986, indicates the scope of the study to be conducted:

"That council examine the opportunity to hire consultants and/or allocate appropriate staff, with the objective of preparing an official community plan for Maillardville,(the area from Rochester to south of Brunette, Schoolhouse to Blue Mountain, with possible minor boundary adjustments) involving local residential and business participation and that the process and product be carried on with the objective of enhancing existing development and triggering new development in Maillardville and that the terms of this project include (but not limited to) the following items to be addressed in the Maillardville OCP"

The items included all of the standard concerns of traffic, infrastructure and zoning, but also called for the development of a theme and style for Brunette. Twelve years after the disappointment of Plan Maillardville,

190

the community was ready for round two in the quest to rebuild. Frank Ducote of Urban Design was handed the task, assisted by Lewis Villegas. In 1974 urban planner, Robert Noël de Tilly stated that there would be no *"French Gastown"* and that *"We are not going to put French Canadians in cages for the benefit of English speaking tourists."* He also pointed out that sidewalk cafés would not be a part of the plan as these were not a part of French Canadian culture. In 1986, Mr. Ducote's vision for a renewed village contrasted sharply with de Tilly's. The Coquitlam Now reported in October of 1986:

*"**New Maillardville "more appealing"**   The new look Maillardville described by designer Frank Ducote focused on the need to make the commercial area of Brunette "more humane and appealing to pedestrians."   The changes Ducote suggested would mean the transformation of Brunette Avenue between Lougheed and Marmont into a European flavoured, pedestrian oriented zone highlighted by trees, wider sidewalks, benches and on street parking.   In his presentation, Ducote also proposed using "a redeveloped Maillardville shopping centre as a catalyst for the integrated development of this key block" with the majority of the Brunette Avenue frontage to be used for street oriented shops and restaurants.   Improved traffic circulation was another element of Ducote's presentation.   Extending Roderick and Adair Avenues would give the area a clearer separation of commercial, industrial and residential areas, Ducote said.   Finally, Ducote suggested the construction of a gateway plaza at the Lougheed end of Brunette, creating "a sense of entry" to Maillardville and a heritage square at the Marmont end."*

This latest phase of development produced new design guidelines for commercial and residential projects that would "reflect the French Canadian heritage" of Maillardville. The City, Merchants' Association and the revitalization committee worked to beautify the commercial district. A prominent "gateway" at the intersection of Brunette and Lougheed would be added. The City embarked on a major ditch elimination program for Maillardville and accepted the proposed vision for "Heritage Square" at Brunette and Marmont. A new community plan for Maillardville was created. A final outcome of this wide reaching effort was to produce an "inventory" of heritage buildings in Coquitlam, most of which were in Maillardville. They included Mackin House and Ryan House at Brunette and Marmont, the original part of Millside School and all three church buildings on Laval Square.

By 1988, the dream of a new Maillardville began to take on a physical form. The Coquitlam Now, October 1988:

*"**Maillardville Growing**   The tired face of Maillardville is finally beginning to crack a smile. The economic health spreading throughout
Coquitlam is starting to put some colour in the cheeks of Maillardville
and municipal planners want to lay down some new directions for the
historic neighbourhood. Major commercial development projects are
revitalizing the area, and a recent spurt in housing construction is adding to the area's 4,000 residents. With more than 13% of households
speaking French as a first language, Maillardville is one of the few Coquitlam neighbourhoods with a distinct cultural character. After a long
and dismal growth rate of less than one per cent, Maillardville has seen
a sudden six per cent increase in housing in the past year. Growth in
Maillardville is expected to continue at the same high rates and Coquitlam wants to revise the official community plan to guide development in
the colourful neighbourhood."*

The main commercial redevelopment was to be a sizable project on the
site of the old Maillardville Shopping Centre. The complex, built in
1988, housed office space, at grade commercial units and condomini-
ums. Two new commercial buildings were added on the Brunette
Avenue frontage between the Woods Hotel and the French Quarter Pub.
The Caisse Populaire expanded their building. They also built a sixteen
unit condominium complex for retirees that was to become known as
"Chez Nous". The demolition of many of the derelict houses on Brunette paved the way for more residential development east of Marmont.

 Mayor Sekora, in his 1988 inaugural address, declared that the work of
the committee was complete, and was forthwith dissolved. As recorded
in council minutes:

*"As far as the Maillardville redevelopment committee is concerned, all
items which were to be addressed by this committee have now been
completed and as a result this committee will not be reappointed and I
would like to extend to the members of the Maillardville Redevelopment
Committee my heartfelt thanks and congratulations on a job well done.
This committee over its years of existence has recommended and council
has put in place, design controls which can be clearly seen in the development taking place in Maillardville. As well, as the concept for the
Heritage Square and the key role they played in the Brunette Avenue
improvements and entrance to Maillardville."*

Although Maillardville did receive a major "facelift" during these years, the lack of street parking on Brunette was still very problematic. It was made worse in 1989 when, against the protest of merchants, a centre median was added from Lougheed to Allard Street. The "new" Maillardville shopping centre did support commercial activity, but the number and size of individual units was not sufficient to create a true shopping nexus. It also did not provide for a single large commercial "anchor" as did its predecessor that would act as a drawing card to the area. The outcome of this second effort at Maillardville revitalization would only be revealed in the next decade.

From the point of view of the French community, the beginning of the decade seemed to portend fresh failure. The Francofête, so successful the previous three years, was suddenly and severely downgraded. The Enterprise of May 1980:

*"**Festival Shrinks** Due to unforeseen circumstances most of the events slated for Francofête Maillardville 1980, June 22 to June 29, have been cancelled says Francofête president Germain Fortier. Fortier said that remaining events that will go on as scheduled are the Franco British Columbia artists show and the picnic and beer garden scheduled for Sunday, June 29 at Mundy Park. All other events, including the parade, teen disco, Saturday night ball and exhibitions have been cancelled due to a lack of experienced volunteers and financial limitations. The five year old French Canadian Festival attracted some 6000 people last year, the largest celebration of this type this side of Manitoba. But Fortier assured revelers that next year will see an even bigger and better Francofête."*

The same edition of that newspaper reported that the All Saints Coquitlam Community Festival would also be: *"**Bigger and Better Festival 80 All Set**"* The four-day festival ran from June 4 to 7. Taking place at the Recreation Centre and Annex, the mega event was everything Francofête had been, without the French Canadian theme. With a grand parade, giant BBQ, displays, exhibitions, games and a dance, much attention, money and volunteer time went into its success.

The downsized Francofête went ahead as planned in the wake of the All Saints event. Mass at O.L of Fatima on June 29, 1980, was followed by a pancake breakfast in the hall. In the afternoon, a picnic at Mundy Park included displays, singers, dancers and games. The day wound up with a "gala campfire and sing-along in French." 1980 was Francofête's last year. The French event and the All Saints/Coquitlam Festival were spaced less than a month apart. Utilizing many of the same venues as Francofête, and duplicating many of its events, it was clear that there was not enough room for two such similar fairs. Sadly, Francofête, an important cultural event that showed such early promise, was abandoned.

The Société Maillardville Uni, having been more or less dormant since 1978, awoke to face the challenge brought on by Francofête's demise. Léon Lebrun was its president. Jean Aussant, Edgar Ruel and Jean Riou formed the rest of the executive committee. The group began to consider new ways to support the French community at Maillardville. At a meeting in 1983, Mr. Lebrun listed some of the reasons why an initiative such as Maillardville Uni needed to become an umbrella organization for all of the community's French activity. He stated that the Catholic parishes were no longer the guardians of language and culture as they had to accommodate the ever-increasing Anglophone presence in their congregations. He declared that the era of "*living in the shadow of the bell tower*" had passed. At that "inaugural" meeting a mandate was adopted to bring together all of the francophone groups. It was further resolved that each organization would remain independent and autonomous. The goal was to work toward the common goal of preserving French language and culture at Maillardville.

Anticipating the upcoming seventy-fifth anniversary of Maillardville, the society decided to put the theory of this new "federation" to the test. The Festival du Sucre was organized and the member groups asked to participate. Put together on very short notice, the event, held in April of 1983, was a success, drawing some 400 people. So it was that Société Maillardville Uni (SMU) came into official existence, incorporating September 6, 1983. Although the birth of SMU was a humble one, it marks the beginning of yet another period of solidarity in Maillardville's history. Gathering momentum the following year with the successful organization of the seventy-fifth anniversary events, the Society embarked upon an urgent quest to preserve and enhance what remained of the cultural history the village. A newsletter "Bonjour Maillardville" was launched and committee members involved themselves in every aspect of the "Maillardville Revitalization" project that began in the middle of the decade. The importance of establishing SMU as the "new guardian" of language and culture in Maillardville should not be underestimated.

The recognition by the SMU organizers that the Church was no longer able to bear sole responsibility for the preservation of language and culture was correct and astute. Twenty five years earlier, Father Armand Fréchette energetically took on the role of prime organizer for the fiftieth anniversary. By 1984, the parish was long past its heyday, and as Maillardville declined, so did the church community. It was within this setting that SMU took on the responsibility to create a program of events for the seventy-fifth celebrations with Jean Riou as its lead organizer.

Not everything was different from 1959, when the last big celebration took place. In fact, many of the events were patterned after the fiftieth program and they were held over the entire year. Foyer Maillard hosted the official opening on January 29. Next up was the Cabane a Sucre, accompanied by log sawing, chopping and nailing contests. There were also dances, picnics and concerts. September 29 was the official tribute to the pioneers. Solemn High Mass was celebrated at N.D.de Lourdes and the Grand Banquet took place that evening. As had been done in 1959, menu items were named for some of the pioneers and various priests. Jean Riou researched and wrote a history of Maillardville: "A 75 Year Chronicle-Maillardville!" From the unveiling of a commemorative plaque at Foyer Maillard by Mayor Lou Sekora, to the blessing by Archbishop James Carney of a bas-relief depicting 75 years of Maillardville history at Our Lady of Lourdes, the goal of the celebrations was to honour the "pioneers" and their traditions.

The seventy-fifth anniversary was also an opportunity to reflect upon the future of the French community. With a cloud of uncertainty hanging over it, that future was in doubt and as a part of the official program, a conference on the "state of affairs in Maillardville" was included. One goal of that meeting was to prepare a list of resolutions to be presented to City Council. Held November 18, 1984, the participants created their wish list and noted that:

- francophones had to "sell" Maillardville, highlight its cultural heritage, and communicate to the general public that the French community had something to offer.
- promote tourism to Maillardville during Expo '86
- market and capitalize on the "heritage" of Maillardville
- preserve what exists in Maillardville before it is lost to redevelopment
- oversee development on Brunette Avenue, encourage new business, promote the building of a cultural centre and co-op housing
- prepare for the building of light rapid transit
- participate on municipal committees for development in Maillardville

With respect to community development, the goals were no less ambitious:

-Unite both parishes into one for the French language in order to pool resources
-build a centre for the Club d'age D'or (seniors)
-form a foundation to provide funding for francophone organizations
-form a business association
-create an environment where French can be spoken both social and in the workplace
-impress upon the youth the importance and advantage of retaining French language

More than ever, the francophones of Maillardville recognized the need to take serious action if language and culture were to be preserved.

That conference was followed by the first annual general meeting of SMU and, never forgetting to have fun, a BBQ organized by the Knights of Columbus.

The anniversary celebrations also helped raise awareness outside of Maillardville of the French community's existence and what a tragedy its loss would be. In January of 1984, this short but poignant editorial appeared in the Herald-Enterprise. It recognized the possibility of that loss and acknowledged Maillardville's true identity; a unique bilingual community in the far west of our vast country, the very model of the Canadian ideal:

"Vive Maillardville   Sometimes it seems like the only pocket of French culture this side of the Rockies is Maillardville. And sometimes it seems like that little pocket is quickly being eroded street by street, family by family as time takes its toll. So it is with real joy that we see the 75th anniversary of Maillardville start with a bang and have several other explosive events planned on the month. For a province so insulated from the national plan to become bilingual (how many friends do you know who are totally bilingual?) Maillardville must be treasured and nurtured. It is our country's heritage as well as our neighbourhood's."

In May, after the "Festival du Sucre", SMU president Léon Lebrun wrote a letter to the Herald-Enterprise in which he expressed the gratitude felt for the support by the non-Franco community and illustrating the remarkable financial aid given by all levels of government:

*"**Magnifique!** As we are almost in the middle of our 1984 75th anniversary celebrations of Maillardville, we would like to express our gratitude to everyone (including the press) who have helped us in the promotion of our celebrations and who have given us financial support...merci! Our last activity, le Festival du Sucre (Maple Sugar Festival) was a great success and attended by over 1200 people. The support and participation of those outside the immediate French community has been overwhelming and gratifying. Also, the presence and continuing support of our Mayor Lou Sekora and Aldermen Mae Reid, Bill LeClair and Gloria Levi along with John Parks our MLA and Pauline Jewett, our MP are deeply appreciated. We are very encouraged in our efforts to open our celebrations to the community at large. On the financial side, grants have been forthcoming from the three levels of government as well as substantial monetary contributions from companies and organizations in BC and Quebec. Through an increase in the Place Maillardville budget, the Municipality of Coquitlam granted us $5,000 and has put many of their facilities at our disposal. We received $1,000 from Crown Forest in recognition of the important role that Fraser Mills played in the lives of the French community of Maillardville. We started the year with a grant of $9,000 from the federal Secretary of State.*

The provincial secretary, the Hon. James Chabot, presented us with a grant which he announced was the largest ever given to a community organization in BC by the provincial government, $25,000. This historical year will be remembered as the beginning of another period in the struggle for the survival of a French Canadian culture in the Maillardville community. Many thanks to all for your help and support. Bravo a tous et vive Maillardville.

Leon A. Lebrun, President"

The seventy-fifth anniversary of the founding of Maillardville came and went. The celebration was characterized by the ever-present good humour of the French community, its appreciation of traditional food and music and above all, the honouring of its pioneers. However, the event itself can, as observed by Mr. Lebrun, be seen as the starting point for a new push to keep la Francophonie alive in Maillardville.

Very much like the Maillardville of the forties, residents and organizations were taken up with the desire for a rejuvenated community brought on by the effort to rebuild the commercial district. After the seventy-fifth anniversary celebrations, SMU quickly became an organizing force

within the French community and embodied that "joie de vivre", pride
and love of language and culture that refused to die. Led and fostered by
Léon Lebrun during its early life, Suzanne Tkach took the helm in 1987.
From their office at the Foyer Maillard, the Société worked hard to fulfill
its mandate. It took responsibility for the "Festival du Sucre" from the
Caisse Populaire, running that event for the remainder of the decade,
inviting young and old to *"Venez vous sucrer le bec"*. A popular event
that was run out of the new Fatima Centre, the fun included entertainment from performers such as "chanteuse extraordinaire" Joëlle Rabu in
1987. The following year, Laroche and Roy offered traditional French
music, jazz, blues, reggae, Cajun and zydeco while "Les Bûcherons"
delighted audiences in 1989 with music, dance and storytelling.

SMU also participated in the yearly Fête de la Ste. Catherine. This festival tipped its hat to the sartorial sensitivities of the community. Inviting
participants to bring a decorated chapeau, a prize was to be handed out to
the most original. Puppeteers, musicians and the making of pull taffy
provided entertainment for the children.

The Society extended its activities into the larger Coquitlam community.
In 1985, when Council established a Coquitlam Festival Committee,
SMU was asked to provide a representative. In 1986, it applied for grant
money to conduct a feasibility study to establish a cultural heritage program. And, hoping to make the French language more accessible to all,
the Coquitlam Now records in May 1989:

*"**French Collection Expands** La Société Maillardville Uni has presented Coquitlam Public Library with a cheque for $337.37. Suzanne Tkach,
coordinator of the society, presented the cheque on behalf of the four
organizations which make up the group: Dames Auxiliaires du Foyer
Maillard, Dames Catholiques de Notre Dame de Lourdes, Club D'Age
D'Or-Branch 86 and Les Échos du Pacifique. Children's coordinator
Deborah Duncan will use the money to purchase French fiction, non-
fiction and picture books."*

The establishment of Société Maillardville Uni was the single most important event for Maillardville's francophone community in the eighties.
Bringing together those diverse groups to focus on the common goal of
perpetuating la Francophonie, this grass roots, "made in Maillardville"
effort would become the rock upon which the community's aspirations
were founded. Both Catholic parishes continued to be a vital part of life

in the French community. But the role of "keeper of the flame" passed on to Société Maillardville Uni. It is worth listing here for posterity those organizations that made up SMU in 1983, and to illustrate that while the "visible" community was difficult to find, there was no lack of people and groups willing to cherish and foster the language and culture.

Member Groups, Société Maillardville Uni 1983

Société Bi-Culturelle de Maillardville
Caisse Populaire de Maillardville
Société Entraide du Pacifique
Les Chevaliers de Colomb #3239 (Maillardville)
Club de L'Age D'Or (Branch 86 Maillardville)
Les Echos du Pacifique
Les Scouts et Guides de Maillardville
Les Dames auxiliaires du Foyer Maillard
Le Comité de Sainte Anne (Maillardville)
Le Canadian Parents for French (Coquitlam-Port Moody)
Le Comité des Paroisses de Notre Dame de Lourdes et Notre Dame de Fatima
Le Foyer Maillard
Le Programme Cadre de français (Maillardville)

Association Habitat Maillardville, so involved in the seventies and eventual caretakers of Place Maillardville carried on with their mission quietly. The goals and ideals outlined in the 1977 constitution of the Society were lofty indeed. They echoed the co-operative philosophy that prevailed in Maillardville among organizers in the seventies and came with a soupçon of militancy. Among the eight items listed we find:

a) "To improve conditions of community life so that the community may prosper and develop a sense of self awareness and pride."
c)"To compile and publish statistics regarding Maillardville, in newspapers, magazines, journals pamphlets and such other publications."
e)"To provide methods and means for the members to avail themselves of the greater power of united efforts through the Association acting as an authoritative body, in demanding and securing just and honourable dealings with all levels of government."

A March 1980 document brought the society's focus closer to home. It listed as its "objects" the following:

To provide a leisure drop in centre for the community, to serve all age groups.
To determine, where possible, the community's wishes and to embody them in the operation of Place Maillardville.
To manage and programme Place Maillardville with the object of becoming as financially self-sustaining as possible, within the framework of general policy
To keep Council advised on the programming and operation of Place Maillardville.
To promote Place Maillardville so as to provide service to as great a segment of the community as possible.
To assist in the development of a community spirit

To be sure, the tone and direction had been considerably modified in the course of three years. In general, Place Maillardville was to accomplish its 1980 set of goals. Many meetings and public events were held there. The city forwarded $5000 through the society in 1984 to support Maillardville's seventy-fifth anniversary. In 1988, at the request of the seniors of Club D'Âge D'Or, Council asked the Society to provide a budget estimate for a professional study to consider expansion of the centre. But time would reveal that the objective of *"becoming as financially self-sustaining as possible"* would require increasing amount of time and space devoted to rentals from groups not attached or relevant to the community.

The Francophones of Notre Dame de Lourdes, thinning and aging in their ranks, continued the struggle to preserve the fading reality of a French community at Maillardville. Shining among their work was the "Franco café" that was organized by the Catholic Ladies of Lourdes and was a yearlong Expo '86 project. The Coquitlam Now, July 1985 reveals some of the details:

"Café Shows Off Rich Heritage "If some of these things are antiques, so am I" Coquitlam Ald. Mae Reid said last Tuesday as she examined a collection of historic artifacts at the Maillardville Coffee Shop. Many who view the display, collected over many years by long time Maillardville residents Hervé and Rose Perreault will share with Reid that bittersweet nostalgia as they recognize the glass milk bottles (1950s vintage), the bubble gum machine (used at Trev's store on Brunette Avenue in 1950) or one of the Japanese glass fishing floats that used to wash up regularly on BC shores. And some of the people on hand for Tuesday's

grand opening of the Coffee Stop/Arrêt-Café in the basement of our Lady of Lourdes Church in Laval Square could recognize many more of the 150 items on display: Rodolphe Boileau and Gertrude McClellan were in Maillardville at its birth in 1909. The heritage of Maillardville is rich and underrated and it was out of a desire to share that heritage with the world during Expo '86 that Rose Perreault and Ricky Benoit hit on the idea of a tour bus coffee stop in their church basement, to be operated by the Catholic Ladies of Lourdes. Perreault and Benoît operate Blue Mountain Charters in Coquitlam and Perreault says they were constantly frustrated by the lack of facilities in Coquitlam for bus tours; places where busses can stop for a break, have a coffee and something to eat. The women decided to meet that need and attract tours to Maillardville at the same time. For $2.50 a head, tour groups can come to the Arret Café, drink coffee, munch freshly baked maple sugar pie, buy souvenirs and examine the artifacts display. "It's a five part project" Perreault explains "First; it's a fund raiser for our Parish. It promotes the French culture of Maillardville. It promotes Coquitlam, it celebrates bilingualism and it's an Expo '86 project." Mayor Lou Sekora and Father Stan Frytec, the parish priest, officially opened the coffee shop Tuesday as pioneer Maillardville residents and representatives of the Chamber of Commerce and the federal and provincial governments looked on. Reid, chairman of the Coquitlam Expo committee lauded the coffee shop as the municipality's first Expo project. By the time you read this, the first tour group-30 Girl Guides from Prince Edward island- will have been to the coffee stop. Perreault says a senior citizen's group is booked for later in the month. Through their connections in the tour business, Perreault and Benoit have advertized the Maillardville Coffee Stop with 1500 tour agencies in 80 countries. Whoever decides to come between now and the end of Expo, the Ladies of Lourdes are determined to extend them a warm Maillardville welcome."

The Church community at Lourdes continued to be challenged through the eighties. Father Gérard Chabot left the parish and Father Stan Frytek OFM, became its twelfth pastor. As the community dwindled, it became more difficult to keep the school on Rochester open. In 1983, in a deal worked out between the two French churches and All Saints Parish, Lourdes became a fully English school.

The sons and daughters of the pioneers were also aging. One such was Roméo Couture, son of pioneer Louis Couture. He and his wife Olida celebrated their fiftieth wedding anniversary in 1980, and the Enterprise offered this tribute:

"Fifty Years and counting *Fifty years and thirteen children later, Olida and Roméo Couture are celebrating their golden wedding anniversary. Roméo, 68 and Olida, 70 still reside in the home that they built with the help of friends and relatives at 1007 Alderson Avenue. Mr. Couture was born in Maillardville in December 1911...He admits the area is pretty run down now, but in those days most of the people of Coquitlam lived in bustling Maillardville. Roméo attended Our Lady of Lourdes School from which he graduated in grade eight at the age of 14. "High School in those days was something that they just didn't have." It didn't take him long to land a job. "I quit school at 11 o'clock in the morning and went to work at 10 to 1 that afternoon." That first job was at Fraser Mills where in 17 years he worked his way from trimmer to planer feeder....Meanwhile, Olida, born in Waterloo, Quebec on January 30, 1910, kept herself busy raising the 13 children. The pair was married July 9, 1930....Besides the 13 children, 40 grandchildren and seven great grandchildren owe their existence to that union back in 1930."*

In 1989, the Knights of Columbus #3239 celebrated their forty years of service to the French community. Still the only francophone council in BC, the Knights issued this invitation:

"Les Chevaliers de Colomb de Maillardville- *le seul conseil francophone en Colombie-Britanique, vous invitent à venir célébrer avec eux une occasion très spécial...leur 40 ans d'existence à Maillardville. Lors du samedi, 17 Juin, 1989, le gentil homme débuteront cet anniversaire par la célébration de la messe à 17h00 à l'église Notre Dame de Lourdes. Ceçi sera suivi d'un 5 a 7 (aperitifs) et du banquet a 19h00, à la Salle Ste. Anne, Carré Laval. Une soirée dansante terminera les festivities."*

However, the glitziest event of the eighties, hosted by Paroisse Notre Dame de Lourdes, was the homecoming celebration of country singer Lucille Starr. The gala was one that was shared by the entire francophone community, the City of Coquitlam and many others. Among the highlights of the event were special presentations to Ms. Starr by Our Lady of Lourdes, District of Coquitlam (Mayor Sekora), Caisse Populaire de Maillardville (Jean Aussant), Provincial Government (John Cashore), CKWX radio (Terryl Rothery) and the Federal Government

(Gerry St. Germain). Opening ceremonies saw the raising of the flag by Coquitlam RCMP and the singing of O Canada by les Échos du Pacifique. A banquet, speeches and a dance rounded out the occasion. The City also dedicated a new street in the singer's honour: Lucille Starr Way. Who was Lucille Starr? From the Coquitlam Now, February, 1988:

*"**Evening Honours Starr**   A star was born the day Lucille Savoie became Lucille Starr. "When she came home and said I'm going to sing but my name will be Lucille Starr, I said what!" Starr's mother Aurore recalls. "She said 'If I flop on that name I can always come back to my own." Starr never had to go back to her own name but she is returning to Coquitlam in May for a banquet in her honour. She left Coquitlam in the fifties and became the first Canadian woman to release a million selling record, recorded a stack of gold records and recently was the first woman inducted into the Canadian Country and Western Hall of Fame.*

Born in St. Boniface Manitoba, Starr came to Maillardville as a child when her father, Gérard, found work at Fraser Mills. Starr was raised on Maillardville's Begin Street and went to Our Lady of Lourdes Catholic School. And she always sang. "She was always singing but I never thought she would become what she is" says her mother who now lives in Sapperton "Sometimes it was a little too much for us. We couldn't stop her." Starr worked as a nurse's aide at Riverview, then a paper mill in New Westminster. In the mid sixties she met a singer named Bob Regan and the two married and hit the road under the name "The Canadian Sweethearts" The Canadian Sweethearts had such hits as "Freight Train" then at the suggestion of producer Herb Alpert, Starr recorded the "French Song" as a soloist, and the tune had airplay around the world.

"I was so proud, I couldn't believe it" says Aurore recalling when the song was constantly on the radio. "As far as I'm concerned, and it's not because she's my daughter, but she's great. She sings blues, she sings pop, she sings folk and she can yodel and hillbilly and anything." The Canadian Sweethearts broke up and Starr remarried dividing her time between Nashville and Toronto. But she visits Coquitlam often and regards it as her home town. "That's her home" says Aurore "When she talks about her hometown she always says Coquitlam and Maillardville"

Meanwhile, Paroisse Notre Dame de Fatima was not only holding its own but was emerging as the "lead" parish in Maillardville. The Holy

Cross Sisters left in the early part of the decade after serving there since 1968. Father Alphonse Roy also moved on in 1981 and was replaced for a short time by Fr Robert Paradis. According to a parishioner, Father Paradis was a: *"good preacher, but a poor administrator."* The roof began to leak as did the south wall, which was made of glass block. Parishioners took matters into their own hands and, borrowing $10,000 from the Oblates, executed the appropriate repairs.

Father Paul Antoine Hudon took the reins in 1983. Father Hudon was a man of lofty plans and decisive action. When the old gym/parish hall burnt down in 1984, Father Hudon embarked upon an ambitious quest to create a new parish centre. On its completion, it was also used as a quasi-community centre housing events from a diversity of community groups outside of the Church. At a cost of $750,000, only $400,000 was covered by insurance, with parishioners making up the difference. In addition, Father Hudon, promoter that he was, managed to persuade parishioners to build the structure and provide plumbing and wiring at cost. In spite of this, the project went considerably over budget. "Build it and they will come" proved to be true, as eventually the parish centre served to help expand the school, housing ten classrooms.

Father Hudon left Fatima in 1987. He was the last of a long line of Oblate priests to serve at the French parish. His replacement was a priest of the Diocese of Vancouver, Father Craig Scott. It was that community's great good fortune to have received a pastor who was full of energy, ideas and was fully bilingual. In spite of the financial burden imposed by the construction of the parish centre, Fatima was well poised to enter the nineties on a strong footing.

Les Scouts et Guides de Maillardville continued to help young people learn new skills, build character and forge lasting friendships within a totally French environment. In 1980, twelve guides travelled to Nova Scotia on an exchange program. Coquitlam Council partially funded the trip with a $500 grant. The Enterprise August 1980:

"Local Girl Guides Nova Scotia Bound *Twelve young girls belonging to the "Guides Catholiques du Canada secteur Français, and their leaders Mrs. Louise Kidwell and Miss Evelyn Chartrand will be leaving on the 13th of August on an exchange trip to Nova Scotia. They will be participating in the celebrations of the 375th anniversary of Port Royal, the first Acadian settlement. This French association which has existed for*

22 years has now units in Victoria and is divided into three age groups: "Jeanettes" 9-11, "Guides" 12-14 and ""Kamsoks" 15-17...The young girls of Maillardville will assist in the recreation of the arrival of Samuel de Champlain. They will also take advantage of their trip to visit various sites and to be acquainted with a totally different way of life."

In 1983, the Guides celebrated their twenty-fifth anniversary. Nineteen eighty was also a big year for the Scouts who celebrated their 30th. The events included a provincial rally, a summer camp and a dance. The boys and their leaders were honoured with a visit from Jean Pelletier, then Mayor of Quebec City and president of the Association des Scouts Catholiques du Canada. In 1983, members of Troupe Maillardville joined 752 other scouts from 106 countries at a world jamboree at Kananaskis County, Alberta. Jean Lambert and Roger, Laurent and Marcel Bruneau accompanied them. Mr. Lambert also received the "Médaille Vanier" in 1980.

But just as important as the skills and lessons these young men and women were learning within their own program was the active participation of Scouts and Guides in community events such as Francofête and Maillardville's seventy fifth anniversary celebrations. It is a credit to that organization that a large percentage of the volunteer base that contributes to the life of Maillardville is comprised of former French scouts and guides.

 Sadly, in 1986, Amélie Gareau, a woman fondly remembered as a sweet and gentle person and one of the French Guides' most beloved cheftaines died. The newsletter "Bonjour Maillardville": (translated)

"It is with much regret that the community learned of the death of Mme. Amélie Gareau. Amélie Gareau, nee Ledet, died Tuesday, October 28 at her home at the age of 67. She led a very active life in our community, having been a part of many organizations. The last position she held before falling ill was that of secretary for the Société Maillardville Uni. She leaves to grieve her husband, Napoléon, 2 sons, Raymond and his wife Margaret and René, one daughter, Jeannine Neurenberg and three grandchildren, Richard and Robert Gareau and Michel Neurenberg. We will miss her very much because, with her husband, they were a living symbol of French Canadian life at Maillardville. On behalf of Société Maillardville Uni, we offer our condolences and our prayers."

"a living symbol of French Canadian life at Maillardville" This poignant tribute to a woman who worked quietly yet passionately and selflessly for the greater good of her community is one that is applicable to so many men and women who for decades have fought and continue to fight for that *"French Canadian life at Maillardville"*.

The eighties also witnessed the Caisse Populaire emerge as a true community leader. Facing the troubled economic environment that existed at the opening of the decade, the credit union arose stronger than ever. The building was expanded twice. The 1984 effort was a reshuffling of space and refurbishing of the existing facility. In 1987, the structure itself was expanded under the new architectural design guidelines for Maillardville. Georges Perron, President and Chairman of the Board since 1963, announced his resignation in 1982. Fern Bouvier took the helm and helped lead the credit union through the remainder of the decade. In 1986, it celebrated its fortieth anniversary, dedicating its special annual report to:

"The spirit of co-operation demonstrated by those who worked together over the past 40 years to make our progress possible."

The credit union also unveiled a new logo to honour the occasion.

Caisse Populaire was an active participant of Société Maillardville Uni from the beginning. After the initial success of the Cabane à Sucre, they organized this popular activity for Maillardville's seventy fifth anniversary celebrations. Although SMU took over responsibility for the Festival du Sucre for the remainder of the decade, the "Caisse Pop" continued to support it and many other events. Reaching out to the larger community, management and staff entered into "competition" with other credit unions in Coquitlam to gather the most food and money for the local food bank run by the SHARE society.

That challenge was renewed annually for many years. Among the participants, Vancity Credit Union, Westminster Savings, IWA and Community Credit Union it was, as reported by the Coquitlam Now in November of 1988, Caisse Populaire setting the trend:

*"**Last year the credit unions succeeded** in raising over $4000 cash and a large pile of food items for needy Coquitlam families. Traditionally, Caisse Populaire members have been the most generous. Last year,*

Caisse Populaire alone raised over $1500 of the total cash donations. "This year the goal is to raise over $5000 not including food donations" says Heidi Parks of Caisse Populaire which initiated the food drive four years ago."

They also created the coveted "Univercité de Maillardville" sweatshirts and, as sole distributors, donated the proceeds to local charities.

The credit union's most visible legacy of that era and of the drive to "re-vitalize" Maillardville was the creation of the "Chez Nous" housing complex situated between the Caisse Populaire and Foyer Maillard. The concept belonged to the Société Bi-Culturelle de Maillardville. Manager Jean Aussant declared in the Coquitlam Now that with this project:

"we have taken a major step towards the beautification of Maillardville."

The complex comprised 16 "heritage" condominium units, a central courtyard and a common amenities building and was built as a facility for retirees. Its sixteen units sold quickly.

Of the 1987 credit union building expansion, Mr. Aussant commented in the Now:

"First we want a more efficiently laid out office and second we want a more attractive building that will set the pace for the rest of the Mail-lardville revitalization project."

Founding member of Société Maillardville Uni, active with the Mail-lardville Merchants Association and a member of the Maillardville Revitalization Committee, Jean Aussant was a most visible Maillardville booster throughout the eighties. He received the Knights of Columbus "Certificate of Patriotic Service" in 1985, the Coquitlam Chamber of Commerce Service Award for outstanding community service in 1986, and in 1988 the federal government honoured him with a Certificate of Merit for outstanding volunteer contribution to the community.

However, with the rise of a new "pioneer" for Maillardville, the community lost another. J.B. Goulet, one of Maillardville's most ardent citizens from that second wave of pioneers in the forties, died. His passing was recorded in Le Soleil, May 16, 1986:

*"**Jean-Baptiste Goulet Est Mort** Jean Baptiste Goulet est mort à l'hôpital jeudi 7 juin. Avec lui, la communauté francophone perd un combattant. Après des années d'enseignement à la Saskatchewan, à l'époque où les écoles françaises y étaient encore interdites, il est arrivé en Maillardville, plate forme de son désir de lutte. Co-fondateur de la Caisse Populaire de Maillardville, et du foyer Maillard, militant, de la première heure d'un organisme regroupant tous les francophones (l'actuelle F.F.C.) il a passé la dernière parti de sa vie à essayer d'imposer l'idée des Caisse Populaire francophone en dehors de Maillard ville."*

Its activities as a good corporate citizen aside, monumental change was in the offing for Caisse Populaire de Maillardville. The same question that followed the credit union through most of its history once again came to the fore. How to compete and survive in an ever more complex financial environment? How to grow and attract new members? In 1946, the Caisse Populaire Notre Dame de Lourdes was a "closed bond" institution, accepting only those who were French Canadian and practicing Catholics. Its mission was to *"consolidate the French community through financial solidarity."* In 1955, in an effort to build up the fledgling institution, the bond was opened to include non-Catholics. That proved to be a critical move as the manager of ten years, Victor Muller, resigned taking 200 members with him.

Caisse Populaire survived of course, recovering lost ground and emerging stronger than ever. Again in 1968, facing that same dilemma, the bond was completely opened, accepting all as members. Full service in French was to be continued for French members and board meetings were still conducted in that language. The seventies saw tremendous growth, and the credit union capitalized on its position as the *"only fully bilingual credit union in BC"*

Now, Board and management found themselves struggling once again with those same issues. The solution contemplated however, was very different from action taken in previous decades. A multifaceted strategy included a change of name that *"would be meaningful in either French or English."* A revamping of the mission statement clearly broadened the credit union's mandate in anticipation of a new direction: the opening of branches outside of Maillardville. The new mission statement adopted in 1985 read:

"To improve the financial and social well-being of our members by be-ing a progressive and dynamic financially sound institution effectively serving the members and communities according to the co-operative philosophy."

Although the actual change of name and first "extra Maillardville" branch would only be accomplished in the nineties, the storm clouds of controversy were already brewing by 1989.

It is not the author's intent to dissect the motivation or challenges that management and Board faced in coming to their decision. We need only recognize the fact that from this point forward, the credit union would no longer be an institution dedicated solely to the growth and well-being of the French community and of Maillardville.

The credit union's dramatic shift in strategic direction was not the only fundamental change for Maillardville conceived in the eighties and brought to fruition in the nineties. Council, having dreamed of a new city hall outside of Maillardville since 1964, now finally put the plan to move to the new "town centre" in motion. The Coquitlam Now, August 1988 reported:

*"**Planning Funds Okayed For New Municipal Hall** Coquitlam's long awaited municipal hall is one step closer to reality. Council gave munic-ipal staff $50,000 last week to begin planning the complex to be located in Coquitlam's new town centre."*

At least one councilor voiced disapproval. The same article went on to report:

*"**But Alderman Walter Ohirko opposed the planning dollars** saying the move will hurt the district's revitalization plans for Maillardville. "I think it's crucial that municipal hall stay in Maillardville" Ohirko told Council on Monday. "While we are going to make a very pretty place of Maillardville with all of the beautification projects planned, relocation of the hall would be a mistake."*

The removal of City Hall from Maillardville was now inevitable. How-ever, Mayor Sekora, offering some consolation to the community, vowed that the old hall at the corner of Brunette and Marmont was to become a centre housing a multitude of local organizations and their activities. The Coquitlam Now, May, 1989:

*"**Sekora looks at hall for arts**......A wave of cultural and community group support is gaining momentum in Coquitlam. And the major push is Mayor Lou Sekora who says the existing municipal hall on Brunette Street will be dedicated to both cultural and community groups for their use as soon as a new municipal hall is built, probably in mid-1991..."I am making this a promise. I talked to my council members (about the proposal) and there's no negative feedback, so there's no problem" he (Sekora) said. "I'm not guaranteeing we'll fit everybody in there, but we'd like to hear from anyone, interested like the ones I have already heard from like the Coquitlam Volunteer Bureau, the Maillardville Boy Scouts, the SHARE Society and Stage 43."*

Council was generally supportive of the plan, with some reservation. The Coquitlam Now conducted its own council poll in its May 30, 1989 issue:

*"**Coquitlam Now's May 25 poll of council members** regarding Mayor Lou Sekora's proposal indicates mild chagrin, an element of caution and firm agreement in principle. "He's moving pretty fast on this isn't he?" said Eunice Parker when asked to cast her vote. "It sticks in my craw that the fire halls won't be saved, but I was pleased to hear him come up with the idea."....Ald. Walter Ohirko agreed that comments were favourable among council members and that there appears to be consensus. "But we agreed that before we make any commitment, we'd get an outside inspector to check on the health of the building." And at least acknowledging that moving city hall away from Maillardville was a valid concern, the same article quotes Ald. David White: "I see a significant benefit to Maillardville in turning the existing hall over to community groups...we're going to fill the vacuum created by moving the municipal hall to the Town Centre. There are economic spin offs for the area with this proposed use." he said."*

The eighties was another challenging decade for the village, its general population and the French community specifically. Rising up ever so slowly and painfully from the desolation of the previous decade, the community once again rallied. By the mid-eighties, momentum for a rebuilding effort was gathering strength and a new optimism was born. Perhaps this decade best exemplifies the strength of purpose and deep resolve of the French community to sustain its culture and presence in Maillardville. With its ranks decimated and most visible evidence of the original settlement gone, les Francophones invented new ways and means to preserve their heritage, most notably in the creation of Société Maillardville Uni. The desire of the larger community to support that effort once again underscores the cooperative spirit that had existed between Anglo and Franco since the thirties and forties. Thus, modern Maillardville began to emerge. East of Marmont, the wrecks of the original pioneer's homes were being demolished and townhouse and condominium development according to the new design guidelines was beginning. King Edward and Marmont had been aligned to allow for the creation the future "Heritage Square" between Ryan and Mackin Houses. The commercial district along Brunette had embarked upon the path of beautification and revitalization led by the Caisse Populaire and its two development projects. Indeed, there was cause for renewed optimism. But, with the continued focus on the new Town Centre and the anticipated move of City Hall, would the momentum be enough to carry Maillardville forward?

Nine

Rebirth

The changing face of Maillardville continued to reveal itself throughout the nineties. The beautification of the commercial district was completed with the addition of the Tower Plaza at the west end of Brunette Avenue at Lougheed Highway. Maillardvillians could now soon expect a pedestrian friendly shopping experience with a "European flair". Modern day Heritage Square was yet a dream as the decade opened, it would be finished in 1999. The deconstruction of the pioneers' homes along Brunette, around Laval Square and through Cartier Avenue erased most visible signs of "Old Maillardville". The new village would be a string of condominium and town house developments with "French character". Typically, this meant the use of mansard roofs, tall thin profile dormers, the occasional turret and widow's walk. Most of the projects fulfilled the letter of the law, a few the spirit. The great bog south of Brunette, once considered undevelopable did, in fact, see much commercial building. The move of City Hall from Maillardville in 1998 completed the transformation.

Once again, great hope and enthusiasm was alive in Maillardville during the early decade and the reasons were twofold. First, there was real excitement that the village was finally being cleaned up and tangible progress was being made. Second, the French community embraced this injection of new life wholeheartedly and with renewed vigour in reclaiming their heritage. Additionally, in Maillardville and Coquitlam and indeed throughout greater Vancouver, there was renewed interest in the French language and culture. French immersion and Programme Cadre flourished. Festivals, concerts, films and activities of all kinds abounded to celebrate la Francophonie.

Coquitlam's approaching centennial celebrations also sparked rekindled interest in heritage. One of the projects was the completion of a book, *"Coquitlam 100 Years-Reflections of Our Past"* in which many from the older generation were interviewed and their stories told. Naturally, Maillardville pioneers had the opportunity to share their memories and experiences, as much of the first half of Coquitlam's history was intimately tied to that of Maillardville's. One of those pioneers, Lambert Leroux, was on hand for the official cake cutting ceremony with Mayor Lou Sekora. Daughter of Maillardville, country singer Lucille Starr, was also there as an honoured guest and gave a concert as part of the festivities.

For some however, there was fear that a significant part of Coquitlam's heritage was on the verge of being lost forever. George Porges, a member of the Coquitlam Historical Society, a passionate historian and advocate for the preservation of "Old Maillardville" had this to say in a Coquitlam Now article of July 1990:

*"**Our Past Is Part Of Our Present** Coquitlam is a growing community whose history stretches back one century. Unlike its neighbours, it has failed to establish any official memories of bygone days. One of the reasons for that omission may be the fact that Coquitlam has developed without a core but rather as an agglomeration of pleasant neighbourhoods.*

However, Coquitlam possesses a splendid historical treasure, unequaled in its way by anything west of the Rocky Mountains: the settlement of Maillardville which deserves our attention, respect and care. Many of the visible reminders of Maillardville's unique past are gone; it will be our eternal shame if we do not use the occasion of the Centennial Year to preserve what is left"

The article goes on to describe a brief history of Maillardville and then concludes:

"Yet, to this day, its French Canadian roots are discernable to the attentive observer, and francophone life continues to exist in many ways. It is a symbol of the unity between Canada's "two founding peoples" Thus, in

*the words of a contemporary commentator "Maillardville is a precious
resource and deserves our attention and respect" It must be the task of
the Centennial Year to ensure that we do not lose this heritage."*

History would show that most of the "visible reminders" did, in fact, disappear. The homes of Paquette, Allard, Proulx, Croteau, Dicaire, Frank
Thrift's store and so many others all were demolished in the years between 1989 and 1993. Most of those homes were built between 1909 and
1912, truly a part of Maillardville's heritage, were lost. Today, only one
pioneer's house remains on Brunette. However, the homes of those two
early dairy farmers, Bréhault and Booth did survive. The Booth house
was completely restored in the early nineties. The Bréhault house at 310
Marathon Court has also been preserved by its owners. But the city did
miss an opportunity to secure the future of the Bréhault farm house,
when it refused the donation of that building in March of 1990, as the
Now reports:

"Thanks But No Thanks   *After sending a "signal" it wants to protect
the district's oldest house for posterity, Coquitlam council has rejected
the owner's offer to donate it to the municipality. Two weeks ago at an
in-camera executive meeting, council rejected the donation of the
house....Since then the owners have all but closed the sale of their property and their realtor believes there may be a party interested in
acquiring the 92 year old house for a restaurant site....*

*The district has provided three possible relocation sites for the house:
Laval Square, Mackin Park and a site at Brunette Avenue and Begin
Street. Land use committee chairman Ald. Bill LeClair said the district's
goal is to preserve the house, not necessarily to own it. LeClair said the
donation had a down side "The problem is the timing" he said "They
want to move on selling their property-if we want the house we have to
take it now. Rather than going through that hassle we suggested they
find an alternate."*

*However, Mayor Lou Sekora said this week that the problem is the pub-
lic purse "I'm not going to ask the taxpayer to pay for the move and the
maintenance on that old building. What would we use it for? Let a private developer take it and set it up as a restaurant or store. You never
get something for nothing. And you always look a gift horse in the
mouth."*

The loss of opportunities to rescue and preserve heritage buildings not-withstanding, a spirit dedicated to honouring Maillardville's history manifested itself in 1990 with the proposal of a "Heritage Square". In truth, the proposal was nothing new. "Plan Maillardville", that study of Maillardville renewal in the mid-seventies, had already identified the land and buildings adjacent to Place des Arts as a natural location for a museum and plaza. In August of 1990 the Now reports:

*"**Heritage Square Proposed** Mayor Lou Sekora has recommended the formation of a task force to explore the possible transformation of Place des Arts in Maillardville into a "Heritage Square" area...Place des Arts executive director Gillian Elliot outlined an "overall vision" that would include the present Place des Arts building on Brunette Avenue across from the municipal hall, a new dance and recital space designed as a complement to the heritage nature of the area and Mackin House and the possible relocation of other heritage buildings to the site. "We would welcome the inclusion of other heritage buildings in the concept." Elliott said, referring to 310 Marathon Court (Bréhault house) a heritage home for which a more "public" location is needed."*

Once again, results were slow to materialize. The project received a kick-start when Council determined that the anticipated move of City Hall to the new town centre would have to be delayed. To relieve the growing problem of space, the new plan saw some municipal services moved into a renovated Mackin House. The building would ultimately house a museum when the city was finished with it. In the meantime, the Historical Society was given the basement to store and display some of its artifacts. By 1992, architect's drawings for the square were in the making and council allocated $350,000 to the renovation of Mackin House. Work began in October of that year, and City staff moved in up-on its completion. Further development of the "Heritage Square" project stalled for some time after that. Eventually, in the summer of 1996, the phase 2 building of an "education centre" was completed behind Ryan House. In September of that same year, a frustrated delegation presented itself before council to plead for the completion of the project and the Now offers these details:

*"**Council Defers Decision On Heritage Square Funds** A request that council come up with the money to finish the Heritage Square project turned into an argument between Mayor and councilors at Monday's meeting. Fern Bouvier, a member of Place des Arts board and Bob Ma-*

son of Intracorp Development asked council for an immediate commitment (money) to proceed with phase 3 and 4 of the development. No exact figure was requested but it is believed the rest of the renovations will cost about $1.4million.

The city has set aside $110,000 in the 1996 budget for planning, but the building was to take place in a few years when pledges that have been made to the trust have been paid out. However, in asking council to release the planning money for construction, Bouvier said it's important to "keep the faith of donors" who expect to see their names engraved.

If renovations don't proceed, Bouvier said, Place des Arts will be running programs in an unsafe building."

The article reports that a heated debate followed with Sekora promising the money, and aldermen putting on the brakes, arguing that funds could not simply be committed without an accounting of money spent to date. The article continues:

"In the end the rest of council voted to defer a decision on releasing the planning money for two weeks until an accounting to date is complete."

In 1997, with the move of City Hall now imminent, the process began to accelerate. December saw Denis Desautels, new CEO of Village Credit Union, presenting a cheque for $5000 to the Heritage Square committee as a part of its pledge of $25,000 to the completion of the project. The Coquitlam Now, December 1997:

*"**Another Boost for Heritage Square** Village Credit Union will give Heritage Square a $5,000 boost Thursday. Denis Desautels, Village Credit Union's chief executive officer noted the credit union has now contributed $15,000 toward the square and plans to give another $10,000 over the next two years to fulfill its pledge of $25,000. Desautels said Village supports the project because "we think the restoration of this square will bring tourists to Coquitlam and increase business for everyone."*

More help came in May of 1998 when the city received $1.1 million in grant money to build phase 3 and 4 of the project. Phase 3 was a link constructed between the new education building and Ryan House. Phase 4 completed the project, finishing the plaza between Ryan and Mackin

Houses. An amphitheatre, landscaping, lighting and moving the original CPR station from Blue Mountain Park to the square were all a part of this phase. And so it was that on September 18, 1999, Maillardville had a complete Heritage Square just in time for its 90th birthday celebration.

From its first mention in the Plan Maillardville recommendations to its official ribbon cutting ceremony in September of 1999, almost a quarter of a century had elapsed. Truly, Maillardville's rebirth was indeed a work in progress. Throughout this long process, it was Place des Arts that continued to anchor interest in the area and to advocate for the completion of the Square. It fulfilled its original mandate of providing opportunities for artistic development tailored to the needs of the community. It also was an active supporter of the drive to foster the preservation of French culture. It offered shows by French artists, history displays in conjunction with Festival du Bois and even French language acting classes. Aside from the expansion of the facility itself, Place des Arts celebrated two other milestones in the nineties. In 1992, founding member Fern Bouvier was honoured for his contribution to Canadian culture, and the Coquitlam Now of June 1992 records that event:

"Commitment To Culture Earns Bouvier Honours   A Coquitlam teacher is being honoured for his outstanding contribution to the cultural needs of his community. Fernand Bouvier will be presented with the Lescarbot Award by Ian Waddell, MP for Port Moody-Coquitlam, at Place des Arts. Waddell says the Federal communications Canada award is being presented to Bouvier for his extensive contribution to Canadian culture and heritage in this community......"This award is but a small token of our appreciation to Mr. Bouvier for his outstanding and continued volunteer commitment to the cultural needs of our community and we sincerely thank him."

The other event was Place des Arts' 25th anniversary in 1997. Through the ravages of the seventies and the early eighties, Place des Arts helped preserve that glimmer of hope for a renewed Maillardville. Its contribution during the dark times of the village cannot be underestimated as it helped to "hold the line" against the disintegration of Maillardville. As much as Mr. Bouvier was instrumental in the founding of Place des Arts in 1972, so Lenore Peyton, executive director from the beginning through to 1989 was the "craftsman" who built it. The Now, December 1997 records a few of her memories on the occasion of Place des Arts' 25th birthday:

*"**Place des Arts Turns 25**   Variety The Secret To Success   Lenore Peyton remembers the afternoon more than two decades ago when federal representatives were coming to inspect Place des Arts. Still in its early days, the Coquitlam arts centre was running on a shoestring and offering classes only at night. Anxious to keep the federal dollars coming, Peyton quickly phoned some teachers. By the time the bureaucrats arrived, the quiet centre was a hub of activity.*

"There was something going on in every room. They were deeply impressed and we had a grant for another year." recalls Peyton, Place des Arts executive director from 1972 to 1989. Things have changed considerably since the centre opened in an old house on Brunette in Maillardville. Built in 1908, the house was originally occupied by a Fraser Mills manager named Ryan, and later by the RCMP.

Around 1970, some community arts members came up with the idea to open an arts centre. The project was taken up by a committee, including Peyton, and the house was leased from the municipality for a dollar.... This Friday, exactly 25 years later, staff and students will gather at Place des Arts for a 25th birthday party....When it opened, Place des Arts offered only weaving, spinning, drawing, painting and hand built pottery. Music and dance were added the second year and drama classes soon after....

Place des Arts now has an annual budget of $800,000, close to 70 teachers and support staff and, as of November, more than 1,100 students.....Peyton, who is retired, has visited art centres in the U.S. and Europe and says she hasn't seen anything quite, like Place des Arts. "It's the variety and the feeling you listen to the public. You produce what the people want." she says.....For her the evolution of Place des Arts has been more than a dream come true. "I'm very satisfied. I wouldn't have dared to dream as luxurious as it has become."

The heightened interest in heritage during the nineties also fostered another project that today remains a valuable legacy for Maillardville and Coquitlam. Antonio (Tony) Paré, native son of Maillardville and grandson of Émeri Paré was also a member of the Coquitlam Heritage Society. After having done extensive research on his own family history, Mr. Paré felt compelled to share what he had discovered. He wrote several books including "*My Memories of le vieux (old) Maillardville*" about some of Maillardville's pioneer families and the homes they built and

"*Mansions on the Hill*", the story of the two Fraser Mills homes at Heritage Square, Ryan House and Mackin House. In addition, he created a large scale map of the early village of Maillardville and donated an extensive collection of photographs, all now preserved in the Antonio G. Paré room at Mackin House Museum.

There is no doubt that the crown jewel of the nineties for the French Community at Maillardville was the advent of Le Festival du Bois. Société Maillardville-Uni had, through the latter half of the eighties, maintained the connection with the earlier Francofête and with Maillardville's 75th anniversary celebration by the continuation of the Cabane a Sucre. Now in 1990, the organization was ready to take on an event of a much broader scope. Designed as a festival to remember the pioneers who came to Maillardville, it incorporated elements of B.C.'s forest industry of which they and the village were so much a part. In fact, the inaugural festival coincided with the 100th anniversary of Fraser Mills. That first festival was a grand event with advertising in local newspapers calling everyone to:

 "Come join the party" and "1st Annual French Canadian Winter Festival (Le Festival du Bois) Come experience the sights and sounds of the French Canadian culture in a rollicking and colourful revue..."

Taking place at a number of venues, the festival ran from March 2 to 4, 1990. And what an amazing variety of events! The Now, February 1990 offers us a few details:

"Maillardville Will Make Merry *Maillardville, B.C.'s historical French Canadian community will hold a traditional winter festival, March 2-4. Le Festival du Bois (Festival of Wood) is a rollicking toast to the songs, dances and good spirits of the French Canadian culture blended with B.C.'s forestry heritage. The fun will include sporting events, evening concerts, children's' entertainment, traditional food and fun for the whole family.*

Though the festival will take place in a variety of Maillardville locations, the focal point will be the circus sized, heated festival tent that will envelop an area of Mackin Park. From the parking lot of Real Canadian Superstore, families may ride a free horse drawn shuttle to the festival tent complete with a sing-a-long or old time fiddler. On Saturday March 3 from 10am to 1pm, entertainment will include the Beaver Lumber Lit-

tle Logger's Show. This will feature top children's' entertainment such as three time Juno award winning singer-songwriter Carmen Campagne and the energetic "Les Bûcherons."

At 1pm Saturday March 3, the Caisse Populaire Loggers' Sports Show will open. The first loggers' competition this year, the show has attracted loggers from as far as Washington. Beginning 9am Sunday March 4, is a new loggers' event, the Caisse Populaire's Loggers' Triathlon which begins at Como Lake and ends at Mackin Park. Competitors will have to portage their canoe 50 metres to the Como Lake and then paddle 200 metres across the lake, followed by a run of 2.5 kms to Mackin Park where they must bucksaw through an 18 inch log. Teams can have two canoeists, one runner and two buckers. Other logging events include Jack and Jill bucking, power saw event, axe throw, chokerman's race, obstacle pole and the underhand chop."

Another sporting event took place Sunday March 4 from 11am to 2:30pm on the 1.5km loop surrounding Mackin Park. The "Maillardville Criterium" was a bicycle race. In fact there were two races, a 40 km for "category 3" women and veterans and a 56km race for pros. White Rock's Damon Jones took the $200 prize in this inaugural race. The article goes on to describe even more fun with the Cajun music of Hadley Castille, the Swamp Fiddler and harmonica master Gerald Laroche. There were all the traditional food offerings:

"tourtières, baked beans and pork, pea soup, sugar pies and grandpères (dumpling cooked in maple sugar) ...and festival goers can roll a popsicle stick into snow and pure maple syrup to create a traditional toffee treat."

Fraser Mills offered tours of the mill. Les Échoes and Les Danseurs du Pacifique performed. There was a Beard and Moustache grooming contest, a lacrosse tournament and an "old-timers'' hockey game. The event was tremendously successful, attracting some 6000 visitors, and it was uniquely Maillardville. Not only were the French culture and the lumber heritage blended wonderfully, but Maillardville's other great tradition, a love of games and sports was also honoured. But most important of all was that Société Maillardville-Uni succeeded in rallying the community to create and build what would become a signature event for the village and strengthened the bonds among Maillardville's francophone community.

The following year, festival organizers represented by Léon Lebrun, and looking to build on the success of 1990, went to Council with a request for $60,000. In stating their case, Mr. Lebrun informed Mayor and Council that the anticipated cost for running the festival would be $200,000. The Now of November 1990 further records:

*"**The province's French Federation** last week endorsed Le Festival du Bois as the "festival of the province." The celebration will be affiliated with other French Canadian winter festivals, he said, including Quebec's Le Carnaval, Ottawa's Winterlude and Winnipeg's Festival du Voyageur. "What it will mean is that Coquitlam and Maillardville will be a focal point in Canada" Lebrun said. Festival coordinator Diane Dupuis also thanked council for helping this year's first festival over some rough spots. Without the district's assistance, she said, the festival would not have been possible."*

Apparently, Council was not wholly convinced of the broader implications the festival might have for Coquitlam. Council minutes indicate that they would contribute a $15,000 grant and an additional $13,000 in services, pending a review of an audited financial statement. The 1991 version of the festival went ahead and added such events as the Lumberman's Ball, the Coca-Cola Teenage Dance at Place Maillardville, arts and crafts by the Club bel Âge, a wine cellar and French historical display. The weather was unusually cold and snowy that year, resulting in the collapse of the unheated logging tent. Fortunately, there were no injuries and the logging event took place at a later date. The festival also enjoyed an increase in attendance over the previous year, welcoming 7700 people.

The inclement weather did highlight a problem with the festival other than collapsing tents. The sub terrain at Mackin Park is a poorly drained bog. With characteristic rain aplenty, it did not take long to saturate the land and turn the park into a mucky mess. In fact some affectionately dubbed the annual event Le Festival du Boue (Festival of Mud.) The following year, 1993, organizers abandoned the Mackin Park site and moved most of the events to the Parish Centre at Our Lady of Fatima Church. This resulted in a scaled down version of the festival. The main losses were the logging events and the Criterium bicycle race. But the triathlon and most other activities remained. There was one delightful addition and that was a special presentation by the Program Cadre students from Millside: "Maillardville Hier et Aujourd'hui"

Things remained more or less the same for the next couple of years, but in 1996, the entire event found a new home at Blue Mountain Park. There was some concern that moving the festival outside of Maillardville would result in diminished attendance. The loss of numbers did not materialize and the Festival continued at that venue for many years. Still, it was a loss for the village itself, as it drew the spotlight away from Maillardville at a time when it would have greatly benefited from continued attention. In spite of the move away from Maillardville, the festival remained focused on French Canadian culture and specifically that of Maillardville. The Coquitlam Now of March 1996 offered this explanation of the festival and its events to those new to Le Festival du Bois:

"Triathlon Recalls Pioneer Days When Loggers Welcomed Spring *The first settlers arriving in Maillardville from all over Canada brought with them customs that today remain an integral part of Festival du Bois. Tradition had it that during winter the men left their homes for months at a time, heading off to forested regions. There, the loggers would work through the long cold months to provide for the families they had left behind. Come March, workers would return knowing they would soon be reunited with their loved ones for "le temps des sucres", a time for celebrating and enjoying maple syrup.*

But in 1909, when the pioneers arrived in Maillardville, there were no maple trees from which came the sweet sap used to make maple syrup. Consequently, they had to improvise on the traditions heralding the arrival of spring, and commemorated the end of their labour with a village wide celebration. Today at the Festival Du Bois, the triathlon serves as a reminder of the hard work of the pioneers, which helped make the community what it is now."

By 1997, the festival was attracting in excess of 13,000 visitors and in 1998, a weeklong educational component was added to bring an appreciation of French art, culture and music to young students. Suzanne Tkach, SMU's first executive director from 1987 handed the responsibility to Ginette Denis in 1993. Ms. Denis held that position until c1998 when Ms. Johanne Dumas took over.

Clearly, the creation of Festival du Bois was a defining moment in the life of the French Canadian community at Maillardville. Bringing together all of its francophone organizations, a truly Maillardville experience was created. The festival served to galvanize the community, bring attention to Maillardville and helped foster a better understanding of French culture among non-Francophones. The event, successful year after year, also helped to keep alive that dream of bilingual existence on the west coast of British Columbia.

However, not everyone was convinced that la Francophonie could survive, or even really existed in Maillardville. Writing in the Vancouver Sun in March of 1991, columnist Nicole Parton voiced her skepticism on the future of "French" Maillardville:

*"**Maillardville's French Roots Fading Into Obscurity** The map in Coquitlam's municipal hall describes it as C19, a district within a district. No one quite agrees on its boundaries. It is not as French as I expect, nor as large. The 1986 census records 505 people here whose mother tongue is French, but more than 3700 whose mother tongue is English.*

Change is coming to Maillardville. They don't speak French in the French Quarter Pub. Along the main drag, Brunette Avenue, Gary's Custom Autobody vies for space beside Paradise Travel, Digger O'Reily's and the Maillardville Market, where a clerk stares blankly in response to simple French...Maillardville is a memory. It is a state of mind. It is a culture sliding into obscurity, despite the efforts of the Société Maillardville-Uni and the annual Festival du Bois which earlier this year drew more than 7000 people to celebrate things Francophone-spoon dancing, fiddling contests, maple sugar twirling-as they once were, not as they are today....

Occasional street names in this section of Coquitlam reflect the area's heritage: Laval, Therrien, Boileau. New developments honour the area's Francophone roots with names such as Place Fontainebleau, but at Place des Arts cultural centre, the clerk on duty speaks no French. At the Caisse Populaire, manager Jean Aussant shrugs off the changes he has seen in the past twenty years: "I'm a realist. Sure there is assimilation through evolution."...Aussant takes heart as younger, French speaking families move to Maillardville: "I'm convinced we can live in French here if we want to, within certain restrictions. We can't expect everything to be French because we are in British Columbia...I strongly believe it is not government that should help us save something, but people should help us save something." But as English speaking Coquitlam presses in

*on small Maillardville, one can't help but wonder if good intentions can
ever be enough."*

A commentary in June of 1992, also in the Sun, examined Francophone
culture in BC and noted that Maillardville could no longer be considered
the seat of French language and culture in an article headlined:

"French Fact Now Being Found Far From Maillardville Centre" The
article highlights Vancouver's Maison de la Francophonie, Studio 16 and
Le Théatre La Seizième as the new pillars of the French community. Of
beleaguered Maillardville, the author had this to say:

*"But for most of this century the soul of the French Canadian community
in BC was Maillardville. Founded in 1909 by French Canadian sawmill
workers, Maillardville was once touted as the largest French speaking
town west of the Rockies. But the years have not been kind to Maillardville. Swallowed up by suburban Coquitlam and gussied up into a tourist
area, the community has fulfilled the nightmare scenario of assimilation
predicted by Quebec nationalists. You're more likely to hear Punjabi
spoken around Main and 49th than French on the sidewalks of Maillardville. These days, being French in B.C. is no longer synonymous
with being confined to Maillardville. It means living in cities such as
Vancouver, Victoria and Kelowna."*

These interesting perceptions of Maillardville can, of course, be interpreted in different ways. In the first instance, the community is
discounted as being almost mythical and its "francophoness" is described
as "a state of mind". That the "visible" community had all but disappeared was not new information, the progress of its demise tracing back
almost two decades. That the culture remained alive against all odds in
the hearts and minds of those residing in Maillardville was truly remarkable and it was a fact to be celebrated.

The second article bewails Maillardville's demise, describing it as the
now dying origin of la Francophonie in B.C. Again, while acknowledging the truth of that notion, the article does confirm Maillardville as "the
origin". What a testament to the pioneers of Maillardville down through
the decades that they indeed spearheaded the growth of the francophone
movement in B.C. French parishes, a credit union, Fédération des Fran-
co-Colombiens, French immersion, Programme Cadre and the French
scout and guide movement, to name only a few, all found their origins,

were nurtured and strengthened there. Building on all of that, interest in French language and culture in B.C. flourished in the nineties both by Francos and perhaps even more so by Anglos. As testament to this, we can highlight some of the many francophone programs and events that were taking place in Maillardville/Coquitlam as well as in Vancouver and the Lower Mainland.

They included La Fête Colombienne des Enfants, a 7-day festival at Fort Langley aimed at students in French immersion from all over B.C. Of 25,000 students enrolled in French programs, 17,000 visited this 1990 event that centered on music, theatre and cooking. La Maison de la Francophonie celebrated "Le Saint Jean Baptiste", blocking off West 7th Avenue for a street festival. The Canadian Parents for French, supporters of many activities throughout the eighties, sponsored French film festivals at Coquitlam Theatres offering such films as "Les Jetsons", "Bye Bye Chaperon Rouge" and "La Gloire de Mon Père" There were exchange programs with students from Quebec. Even Maillard Middle School got in on the act, offering an annual "pétanque" tournament (French version of the Italian bocce) for French immersion students from 1994 through the rest of the decade.

Along with French immersion programs, the Programme Cadre was also enjoying continued success. This program offered education totally in French for children who had at least one parent of French Canadian origin. By 1990, with the program located at Millside School, the student body had grown to 43 and leapt to 75 the following year. Parents formed the Société Cheramy, named for Arthur Cheramy, that early Maillardville champion of la Francophonie. The group's goal was to establish a French community school in Maillardville. Aside from providing French language education, another aspect of the group's vision was that such a school could attract new francophones to the area. They got as far as purchasing land behind Millside School. Plans for the building did not materialize, however, when serious environmental concerns for the nearby watershed became known. The group also sponsored a French youth drop-in at Place Maillardville. The Millside Program Cadre students were treated to "walks" around historic Maillardville. This letter to the editor, by Millside teacher Marie Laure Chevrier, appeared in the Coquitlam Now, December 1990:

*"**Walking History**   On a rainy November morning, a group of young pupils from Millside Elementary School's program cadre left on a short*

walking tour of the Maillardville village. Mr. Rodolphe Boileau, 91, was waiting for them with Mrs. Henriette Sévigny in front of Notre Dame de Lourdes Church to guide them inside the historical church and answer their questions. Mrs. Sévigny was also proud to show the children a magnificent bronze high relief sculptured by the artist Roy Lewis which highlights what made Maillardville history.

Then, Mrs. Sévigny accompanied the young group to the Foyer Maillard, stopping here and there to point out some vestiges of the time when Maillardville was mostly inhabited by French Canadian workers at the saw mill. At the Foyer Maillard, the group was welcomed by Alexandre Spagnolo, well-known author of "Regards sur Maillardville" who introduced two other respected French Canadian citizens, Mr. Napoléon Gareau and Mr. Georges Ledet, who have spent their lives working and raising their children in Maillardville. All of them were happy to learn that the program cadre clientele has increased substantially this year. Who knows, one day those young pupils might wish to return in the pioneers' steps..."

Eventually, the dream to build a school where education was offered in the French language was realized. École des Pionniers de Maillardville was finally built. However, the joy of that success was tempered somewhat by the fact that the school was located not only outside of Maillardville, but also out of the City of Coquitlam. By 2005, the school was well established in the City of Port Coquitlam. It offered French language education from kindergarten through grade 12 and enrolled 320 students.

That Maillardville was the "origin" for francophone culture cannot be overemphasized. Its own community may have diminished over the years, but the contributions made by Maillardville to the greater B.C. francophone community are considerable. Not the least of these was its groundbreaking foray into French immersion in schools. The Tri Cities News of September 1993 offers us this reminder of history:

"25 Years Of French Success *It all started in a kindergarten classroom with 33 youngsters greeting their teacher with a hearty "Bonjour". That was September 5, 1968 and those students had just learned their first lesson in French while at the same time participating in a turning point in B.C. educational history. It was the first day of a bilingual class* *at Alderson Elementary-an innovation in the province and in Western Canada.*

What was momentous about this occasion is what has emerged from it in 25 years-the extensive French immersion program that exists today in elementary schools and high schools throughout the province. "The first class came about at the request of francophone parents in Coquitlam who wanted French education for their children in the public school system" said Lionel Daneault, coordinator of language programs in the Coquitlam school district...Today French immersion has grown in B.C. from a small class into a program that will draw close to 30,000 students this year. In Coquitlam alone over 2,500 elementary and high school students will be reading, writing and speaking in classes mostly in French."

Of course, those "Francophone parents in Coquitlam" were none other than Maillardville's own citizens, led by Roméo Paquette.

But the times they were a changin'! That was especially true of one venerable Maillardville institution: La Caisse Populaire de Maillardville. Having set a new course in 1989, the credit union was determined to garner a greater market share for itself. The strategy included a change of name that would be meaningful in both official languages and, perhaps more significantly, an expansion to markets outside of Maillardville. As one might expect, the change of name elicited a much stronger emotional response from the French community than did the opening of new territories for the credit union. Although there were many who opposed or were uncomfortable with the prospect of changing the name from Caisse Populaire de Maillardville, it was founding member Napoléon Gareau whose vociferous opposition gained most of the media attention. The Toronto Globe and Mail reported in early 1990 under the banner The Nation, Maillardville, B.C.:

"A Caisse By Any Other Name Will Soon Change To English   After Napoléon Gareau helped found the Caisse Populaire de Maillardville in 1946, it became the hub of commercial life in Canada's westernmost French speaking community. Now, as the last few hundred elderly pioneers who moved from Quebec and the prairies after 1909 struggle to keep their language and culture alive in what has become a densely populated eastern suburb of Vancouver, the Caisse Populaire is offering

$1,000 to the person who can come up with the best English name for the company.

"They want more clients and they think they can't get them with a French name, but I don't think the English are scared by the present title," said Mr. Gareau..."I can tell you they don't have my vote," the amiable 74 year old pensioner said in an interview in his home, which is filled with memorabilia of Maillardville's French history. "I can't see what they are worried about because most of their clients are English now anyway."...

The Caisse's executive assistant, Lise Martel, a recently transplanted Quebecer, said the name change is necessary because "there is a perception with our name that we only serve French Canadians. We are looking for a name that will give us access to all communities, but we will not change our philosophy of serving French Canadians. We've always offered French services and we always will, but since this year we've had some English employees."

The Vancouver Province also reported on the controversy and quoted others in its January 26, 1990 edition:

"Lucien Racine, 80, is also outraged by the proposed change. "It will take away from efforts to make Maillardville a truly French area" said Racine. It's the community's heart and soul" said Suzanne Tkach of Société Maillardville Uni representing 15 French groups... "Bilingual banking services and our responsibility to the community will not change one bit but in fact may be enhanced with new business" said Jean Riou who sits on the board."

In the end, the Caisse received over 600 submissions in the contest and the Board selected ***"Village Credit Union"*** as the institution's new name. Throughout the process, management and board pledged that their commitment to Maillardville and the French community would be undiminished. They held true to their word. They added a line underneath the name of Village Credit Union that read "Notre Caisse Populaire a Maillardville" The credit union was a strong supporter of the Société Maillardville-Uni and Festival du Bois throughout the nineties. It was very active in the renewal of the Brunette commercial district and pledged $25,000 to the Heritage Square project in 1995.

Nineteen ninety brought a change on the Board when Daniel Roberge took over as Chairman from Fern Bouvier. Mr. Roberge oversaw the second part of the new strategy, the opening of a branch outside of Maillardville. Port Moody was the location and the 2000 square foot office opened in March of 1992. For good or bad, Maillardville had lost something that was uniquely its own.

The early part of the decade was a profitable one for Village CU. Gilles Lizée took over as Chairman in 1993. Assets and profits increased year over year, the new strategy seemed to be paying off. By the middle of the decade, they had surpassed $50million in assets and were targeting $100million. To support this plan, the board made the decision to increase the credit union's commercial portfolio. By 1996, Fern Bouvier was named once again as Chairman of the Board. That year Village recorded a loss of assets, delinquent commercial loans being the cause. The losses continued in 1997, and Village was put under supervision by system watchdog, Stabilization Central Credit Union.

It was also in 1997 that after 26 years at the helm, Jean Aussant announced his retirement for reasons of health. Mr. Aussant, as had J.B.Goulet before him, guided the Caisse Populaire through some turbulent times and tough decisions. He was an indefatigable supporter of the community throughout his tenure. Mr. Jean Aussant can certainly be considered an outstanding citizen of Maillardville.

Village Credit Union moved on. The board embarked upon the process to replace the CEO and hired Mr. Denis Desautels. By 1998, the institution was back in the black and released from supervision.

Maillardville's commercial district had most of its renewal completed by 1991, including the gateway plaza and tower. Combined with the ongoing residential development on Brunette and surrounding areas, there was much hope that this would finally mark a new beginning for Maillardville. The Province reported in January of 1990:

"Les Temps, Ils Changent   While Canada is in an uproar over the Meech Lake accord, some Francophones are quietly creating their own distinct society in a small B.C. suburb. Coquitlam citizens and cultural organizations are transforming the 81 year old community of Maillardville into French quarters-with the blessing of municipal hall. "Our objective is a French district that is bilingual where everyone's rights

are respected." said Suzanne Tkach, executive director of La Société Maillardville-Uni....

Two major developments are already underway: Le Château, a 150 unit apartment complex and a mixed commercial and residential building. Last Monday, council Ok'd plans for the Gateway Plaza, a $121,000 tower to mark the entrance to the French village. Private businesses in the 4,000 resident community are helping pave the way with funding for cobblestone walkways, widened roads, French style street lighting, shops with bilingual signs and French facades."

In the meantime, the Great Canadian Superstore had paved the way for further large-scale development on the flat between Brunette Avenue and Lougheed Highway. First, Famous Players proposed a 20-screen complex for that area. They were met with considerable opposition from local residents, who feared that there would be an increase in traffic and crime and that it would become a hangout for delinquent kids. Environmental concerns were also raised, as they would be later in the decade when land was purchased behind Millside School to build a French community school. Arguments went back and forth, and when the dust had settled, Silver City was built. Another proposal for 18 screens was put forward by Cineplex Odeon for the land at Woolridge Street and Lougheed. The plan for this complex was to build in the style of a French château. Although Council gave it the green light, the project was never built.

Perhaps the most significant development of the day, along with the building of the Superstore, was approval by Council for the building of a commercial centre at the north west corner of Schoolhouse and Lougheed. Not all were comfortable with this move and the Now of April 1991 offers us this interesting insight:

*"**Parker Opposes Maillardville Plan**   Coquitlam council approved first reading of a zoning amendment bylaw April 2 which permits a commercial centre including banking facilities and a restaurant at the northwest corner of Schoolhouse and Lougheed. Ald. Eunice Parker opposed the amendment saying council had made a commitment to Maillardville not to approve anything which could work against Maillardville redevelopment plans.*

"Council spent over $1.5million in the area and convinced businesses to share costs of the streetscape and so on in the hope of attracting new customers." she said. "The Maillardville Official Community Plan is less than two years old...if we hold true to what is considered good planning, redevelopment will come and we won't have to reap the sorrow of sacrificing the redevelopment of Maillardville." Land Use Committee chairman Ald. Dave White said Maillardville is meant to be a community centre for people to walk and cycle to. He said the proposed development would attract highway commuters and thus won't compete."

Development did go forward and it is arguable that Ald. Parker's concerns were justified. Without an "anchor" to draw people into the Maillardville commercial centre on Brunette, the temptation for shoppers to go to the new development a few blocks away, where many more goods and services were becoming available was overwhelming.

What of Alderman White's vision of a Maillardville "community centre" to which people could walk or cycle? Part of the answer is to have a look at a plan, accepted by Council in 1994. It saw a major bicycle and pedestrian route built from Woolridge, through Mackin Park and Heritage Square all the way to Millside School. Quoting from the introduction of that document illustrates the concept envisioned for the commercial area:

*"**The Maillardville Area Streetscape & Pedestrian/Bicycle Corridor Design Guideline** has evolved from the Maillardville Official Community Plan, March 1990. Policy 7.2 "Pedestrian Circulation" which states Council will consider the implementation of a pedestrian/bicycle corridor to strengthen accessibility between the neighbourhood centre area and the residential areas to the west and to lessen the need for vehicular trips within the neighbourhood. Streetscape Design Guidelines have been prepared for Adair Avenue, Woolridge and Nelson streets.*

This is inclusive of the area extending from the existing parking lot near the Maillardville Village Tower and Gateway Plaza, through to Mackin Park. A 15.0-metre wide parkland acquisition is planned for the area between Adair Avenue and Nelson Street. This area is proposed as an open space linkage between Mackin Park and Adair Avenue. Improvements to the west side of Mackin Park at the east end of the parkland acquisition will be designed to establish a visual terminus and orientation area between Adair Avenue and Mackin Park.

Pedestrian/Bicycle Corridor Design Guidelines have been prepared for the 4.9 metre wide linear corridor or lane easement between the residential developments that connect Heritage square to Millside School. This corridor is an existing GVRD water easement. Since Mackin Park is a major open space component linking the two study areas we anticipate the need to integrate the pedestrian/bicycle corridor through the park to allow access to and from Adair Avenue."

The vision saw a 4-metre wide, paved corridor running from Millside, behind the ongoing condominium development south of Brunette that included landscaping, lighting and benches. Where the path crossed roadways such as Laval and Begin, the use of pavers, bollards and land-scaping elements would highlight and define the corridor. The connector would continue on the west side of Mackin Park with a Adair Avenue as a "grand boulevard" as it went west from Mackin Park and joined with Woolridge Street. That intersection itself was to become a quasi-plaza with brick pavers, heritage lighting, stamped concrete and benches.

Alas, that grand vision never materialized and the new "Euro Maillard-ville" was left with little enticement for pedestrians or cyclists to enter the area: another dream unfulfilled.

The final significant loss occurred in 1998, with the move of Coquitlam's seat of governance from Maillardville to the new Town Centre. The drive to move City Hall away from Maillardville began in the mid-sixties when Mayor and Council were twice defeated in their attempts to create a new City complex on Poirier Street. That plan was abandoned when the much more exciting development at "Town Centre" got underway in the seventies. The move there was anticipated for the early part of the nineties, but was frustrated by more pressing needs. However, the inevitable came to pass. Maillardville, with its long and proud history of political agitation, ensured the move was not without controversy.

When final plans were being drawn up for the new hall in the latter part of the eighties, then Mayor Lou Sekora had promised that the old City Hall building in Maillardville would be given over for community use. Many groups immediately expressed interest in obtaining space there. But the old building which had "supplemented" with several portable units, was deemed to be unsatisfactory for any further use as a public facility. What to do with the land?

There certainly was an outcry from the public to create a community facility there. Somewhere along the line, the notion of building "social housing" jelled and became the proposition to oppose. A group, the Concerned Citizens of Maillardville headed by lawyer Dennis Howarth, came forward to challenge the process by which City Hall rezoned the land to accommodate the construction of the housing complex. There were court challenges, public hearings and many speeches and presentations before City Council. In fact, the final public hearing saw over sixty people speak on the subject and the meeting was finally adjourned after midnight. Most who spoke that night were opposed to the social housing proposal and in favour of some type of community amenity. Despite promises and council resolutions to create a community centre, and the manifest opposition of its citizens to the housing project, Council sold the land to Carrera Developments who, with substantial grant money from the B.C. government, proceeded to build the affordable rental-housing complex that now exists at the corner of Marmont and Brunette known as Château de Ville.

In 1997, the final council meeting was held at 1111 Brunette Avenue and it was modest in its ceremony. And so it ended. The District of Coquitlam, incorporated in its new form after the secession of Port Coquitlam and Westminster Junction in 1913, had established its seat of governance in Maillardville. It remained there for over 80 years. The original City Hall was located in the home of Émeri Paré. He was to become the new district's first police chief. The hall location at 1111 Brunette was an integral part of the history of Coquitlam and, in a very intimate way, of Maillardville. It had shared in and contributed to the growth of the village. But somewhere along the line, the determination to move away from Maillardville took hold. The need for increased space and the more central location of the town centre were undoubtedly valid arguments in favour of moving from Maillardville.

The notion found its origin in the days preceding the development of the land that was to become the town centre. The plan to build a new complex on Poirier Street, not so very far removed from Maillardville, demonstrates an early desire to relocate away from the village. It's all history. City Hall at the town centre was built, and with it came the loss of another pillar that supported the life and growth of Maillardville that had existed from almost the earliest days of "Frenchtown".

In 1998, Lou Sekora resigned as Mayor upon his election as Coquitlam's Federal Member of Parliament for the Liberal party. Councilor Jon Kingsbury was elected to lead the City, besting several challengers including Dennis Howarth of the Concerned Citizens of Maillardville. In 1999, one of Maillardville's own, Richard Stewart, announced his intention to seek the Liberal nomination for the upcoming provincial election. The Now, December, 1999:

"Coquitlam/Maillardville", Stewart says, "is an evolving community, one that is coming to grips with its heritage and growth. I've lived here all my life and I want to work with the community in facing that challenge."

For every season there is a time. Maillardville weathered the changing seasons of the nineties with patience, humour, enthusiasm and resignation. Whatever the changing times, however the vagaries of Council decisions uplifted or undermined the village, life had to continue and it did. One of those uplifting moments came early in 1991, when Council created a new honour for its citizens: Freeman of the City. Among the first to be honoured were none other than two who had made significant contributions to the life and development of Maillardville. At a council meeting on July 2, 1991, René Gamache and Lenore Peyton received this highest of honours from the city. Mr. Gamache, native son of Maillardville, had spent twenty years serving the city on council. Through all of that time, he fulfilled his duties to all of Coquitlam's citizens, yet kept the interests of Maillardville close to his heart. Lenore Peyton was honoured for her dedication to the founding and building of Place des Arts.

Another of Maillardville's venerable institutions ended in the nineties. Trev's (it could not be known by any other name) closed its doors for the last time in July of 1995. One of the few early businesses to survive into the present era, Trev's and Anne Protheroe were a part of the village's landscape and touched the lives in one way or another of almost every family in the community.

Opened in 1936 after she purchased the building from part time barber Toussaint Filliatrault, Anne (who also could not be known by any other name) became a veritable icon of Maillardville. Starting her business as a beauty salon, she tended to the coiffures of generations of Maillardville brides, mothers of the bride, mothers in law and so on. She married Trevor Protheroe and in the early 40s, added a grocery store and coffee shop. The building was expanded and over the years a kindergarten and a "men's' club" both found their homes at Trev's.

Trevor Protheroe himself was an eminently social creature and many of the workers from Fraser Mills who lived in Maillardville found themselves engaged in late night conversation and other enjoyable indulgences at Trev's club. Anne served coffee and doughnuts to a long line of reeves, mayors, aldermen and councilors. She offered hearty nourishment to Coquitlam's firefighters when the main station was attached to City Hall. The closing of Trev's was just another in a long line of losses for "old Maillardville". Le village would continue, diminished by the loss of a business and a citizen who contributed so much colour to the history of Maillardville.

A soupçon of culture from France flickered briefly for Maillardville in the late part of the decade. The philosopher's cafe, the tradition of engaging in philosophical or political discussion in the surroundings of charming coffee shops, found a niche at the Planet Restaurant, 932 Brunette Avenue. Moderated by former school principal and Coquitlam councilor Bill Melville, the first topic for discussion was "Government, the most dangerous institution known to man." with guest speaker Paul Geddes, Libertarian Party member. The Now of February, 1999 offers us a little glimpse inside the Planet:

"They came, they ate and they talked philosophy at the Planet   They quoted economists, historians and philosophers. They discussed anarchy, communism, social contracts and governments in general, wondering why we allow them to decide what we smoke and drink and who gets to live here-and what would happen if there were no elected controls.

During the exchange at Coquitlam's first Philosophers Café Tuesday at Maillardville, Planet restaurant, people made notes on their paper place mats and alternated between nodding their heads in agreement or shaking them in dismay, reaching often for the travelling microphones to express their opinions. With dishes clanking, servers wandering around with wine, water, dinner and dessert and the espresso machine hissing in the background, the cafe was filled with people of all ages...

Former Centennial Secondary school principal Bill Melville acted as moderator, linking people and their ideas. No stranger to provocation,

236

Melville threw in religion when it looked like the discussion on anarchy vs. government might be going nowhere. Still, the atmosphere was always civil, often enlightening and sometimes amusing. A little surprised at the turnout, Melville said, "I think this is a watershed for Coquitlam."

The finer things would not last long and the Philosopher's Café on Brunette was short lived.

While council was busy making decisions on the fate of Maillardville and some Coquitlam citizens were busy philosophizing, what was our "invisible" French community up to? The Festival du Bois brought attention to it once a year, but Sun columnist Nicole Parton stated nonetheless that the French community was not to be found in Maillardville. But they were alive and well. Notre Dame de Lourdes, Notre Dame de Fatima, Les Scouts et Guides, Foyer Maillard and all the rest carried on with their varied activities quietly and almost anonymously in a village that was no longer their own. Petit Maillardville had indeed been overwhelmed by the growth of Coquitlam. Amazingly, the life of the French community at Maillardville found a way. The establishment of Société Maillardville-Uni held them together and brought a collective strength to individual groups. But each one carried on in its own right.

The French Scouts and Guides continued to flourish in the nineties, with old leaders showing the way and those upcoming preparing to receive the torch. A participant in the Festival du Bois from the beginning, the group continued their tradition of sharing in the life of the community and conducting all of their activities exclusively in French. In 1990, Napoléon Gareau was honoured for his years of labour. He was presented with the Vanier medal at Rideau Hall in Ottawa. He also received the medal "Service Émerite" from the Federation des Scouts de l'Ouest. Jean Lambert, founder of the movement, received the "Louis Riel" trophy from the Federation. Messrs. Gareau and Lambert were not the only ones in the movement to be recognized for their achievements. While the movement owed its beginning to those two gentlemen (and many others) its continued life depended upon new leaders. Three of those were Daniel Roy, Diane Johnston and Suzanne Tkach, all three receiving the "Service Scout" award for service in leadership in 1991.

The movement suffered another grievous loss with the death of Napoléon Gareau in 1991. The TriCities News recorded the death of this much loved and respected Maillardville citizen:

*"**Soul of Maillardville mourned by hundreds**   Napoléon Gareau, hailed as the nucleus of Coquitlam's Maillardville and the local French Canadian scouting movement, died Monday of a massive heart attack. Gareau, who died a week before his 77th birthday, "will be remembered for his involvement in the community-he spent his whole life at that," his son Raymond Gareau said on Wednesday.*

Gareau's funeral Thursday at Our Lady of Lourdes Church was attended by at least 400 friends and family members, many from the numerous groups he had been involved in. He was buried in Burquitlam cemetery in his scouting uniform...His enthusiasm for scouting was born in 1955, when he, friend Jean Lambert and relative René Gamache started the first French scouts in B.C. Gareau's French heritage was always very important to him his son René said. "He wasn't a radical, that wasn't his style. But he felt very strongly about maintaining his French heritage and culture." he said.

Gareau's wife Amélie, who died of cancer in 1986, was involved in the French girl guides, which evolved after the boys' version. Scouts combined everything Gareau loved-outdoor activity, working with young people and the french community. He was involved in every aspect of Scouts from being scout master to national commissioner. "He was always very active" Jean Lambert said Wednesday "He was a composer and singer. He always had a song and he was always full of jokes. He was very jovial and very considerate and a man of his word."

Gareau's contribution to Scouts earned him two governor general awards, including the Vanier Award, Canada's highest Scouting honour....Suzanne Tkach, executive director of Société Maillardville-Uni, knew Gareau for about 11 years. "He was the foothold of Maillardville, and somehow or other, he was the person recognized in the province. When you spoke of Monsieur Gareau, you spoke of Maillardville. If he had something to say, he'd say it in a tactful way without hurting anyone. Communities always have one person they look up to and we were very fortunate to have him."

Although he is best remembered for his work with Scouts, Mr. Gareau was involved with every aspect of Maillardville. He was a founding member of Caisse Populaire Notre Dame de Lourdes. He worked with the Société Bi Culturelle, the Foyer Maillard and the Knights of Columbus. As a final honour to both Napoléon Gareau and his wife Amélie, the

Francophone community created two volunteer service awards: the Prix Napoléon Gareau for service to the Francophone community in B.C. and la Médaille Amélie Gareau for service in the French Scouting movement.

In 1992, les Scouts et Guides francophone de la Colombie-Britanique opened an office at the Maison de la francophonie in Vancouver.

They celebrated their fortieth anniversary in 1995. What a remarkable achievement for a small organization and what a testament to the devotion of the movement's founders and its leaders. It was noted in a newspaper in September, 1995, source unknown:

*"**French Scouts Mark 40th**   Some Coquitlam Scouts are celebrating their 40th anniversary of their special program-it's all in French. Boys and girls, ages 7 to 17 are celebrating the movement, started by the determination of a few local fathers. They included Jean Lambert and the late Napoléon Gareau and later, Amélie Gareau, also deceased, and other friends. Many of the early scouts went on to become leaders, keeping the tradition alive. Today there are French scout troupes located in Coquitlam and Victoria."*

Celebration activities included a historical display at Place des Arts, a souvenir history album and a banquet in November of that year. An article in the Now of 1998 reported that the French Scout movement had more than 100 boys and girls enrolled.

The Foyer Maillard was also going quietly about its business of helping to give Maillardville's seniors a measure of dignity in their later years. In 1992, the Foyer received a two million dollar grant from the B.C. government for a building expansion project. In reporting on the grant, the TriCities News described the Foyer as:

*"**Foyer Maillard is unique in B.C.** and is the only such facility providing service in French and English. The grant will allow renovations including a new dining room, new washrooms, new bathing facilities, improved wheelchair access and upgraded fire and safety features."*

The Foyer continued to participate in the life of the French community at Maillardville, providing a venue for concerts and teas. That the care received at the Foyer was outstanding can be illustrated by two centenary birthdays celebrated there in the nineties. They were Albertine Bedel and Marie-Ange Boivin. The Now, January 1996 reported that Mrs. Bedel could:

"bundle grain at breakneck speed, is renowned for her home-style cook-ing, and still plays a mean game of euchre." Born Albertine Pilon in Quebec in 1895, she married Alfred Bedel in 1917 and spent the next 35 years farming in Saskatchewan before moving to Maillardville in the early 50s. She celebrated her birthday at her home, the Foyer Maillard."

Nineteen ninety-seven was the year Marie-Ange Boivin reached that 100-year milestone. Madame was a relative newcomer to Maillardville, arriving here with her husband, Alfred in 1964. Madame Boivin would later, at age 102, see in the new millennium, having lived in three sepa-rate centuries.

However, the elders of the community, one by one, were passing away. Three of those were Jim Allard Sr., Aurèle Boileau and Anthony Finne-gan.

James Allard was a native son of Maillardville, son of Amédé Allard, an early Coquitlam councilor. His father died in a logging accident, and James quit school to work and help his mother raise the family. He founded Allard Contractors. Allard Street in Maillardville is named for his brother Tom who also served as a councilor.

Aurèle was also a native "Maillardvillois", born August 4, 1911. The Now, September 1992:

"Aurele Boileau, the first French Canadian baby born in Maillardville died suddenly September 2. Born Aug.4, 1911 Mr. Boileau went to work at Fraser Mills when he was 17 and was nicknamed Togo by the fore-man after the Japanese worker he replaced in the plywood plant. His parents were among 75 families recruited from the east by Fraser Mills..."

The Finnigan family is a well-known one in Maillardville. Mr. Anthony Finnigan died at the age of 100 years. The Now, October 1991 records:

"Coquitlam Pioneer Dies at Age 100 *Coquitlam pioneer Anthony Fin-nigan died Friday in a New Westminster nursing home. Mr. Finnigan*

celebrated his 100th birthday on August 27 surrounded by five genera-
tions of his family. Born and raised in New Brunswick, Mr. Finnigan
married Elvina Doucet in 1915 and the couple had nine children. After
spending five years farming in New Brunswick, they moved to Ontario
and in 1929, rode the Canadian Pacific Railway to B.C. settling in Co-
quitlam.

Mr. Finnigan found work at Fraser Mills and built a family home on
Begin Street. He continued to work at Fraser Mills until the end of WWII
when he quit to operate a grocery store on Laval Square. He subse-
quently sold it and bought a small planer mill at the corner of North
Road and Lougheed highway but sold that after two years and went to
work for the District of Coquitlam.

He helped clear Mackin Park and built cement culvert pipes which be-
came known as Finnigan pipes...A devout Roman Catholic, the church
was central in Mr. Finnigan's life."

An earlier article on his 100th birthday stated that Anthony Finnigan had
37 grandchildren, 68 great grandchildren and 20 great great grandchildren!

Place Maillardville, the community centre on Laval Square saw some
ups and downs during this decade. In 1990, the building was expanded
to accommodate the seniors' club, Branch 86/Club Bel Âge, and so Centre Bel Age came into existence. Place Maillardville continued to
provide a venue for a variety of activities in the community, including
events associated with the Festival du Bois. Overall though, the Centre's
management seemed to be losing their direction. More and more, space
and time at Place Maillardville was taken up by rentals for weddings,
social functions and programs that had little to do with the community.
By the end of the decade, the City entered into discussion with the Société Habitat Maillardville with the aim of helping them to refocus the
purpose and function of the community centre. The result of this process
would only be revealed in the new millennium.

The sister parishes continued on their respective paths and like the rest
of the French organizations, kept their activities quietly in the background of life in the broader Maillardville/Coquitlam area. Very rarely is
either church mentioned in the local papers. The two congregations were
not as closely tied as they once were.

At Fatima, the school with its immersion program continued to flourish. An increasing percentage of the English speaking population induced them to include a full English curriculum at the school in 1994. Father Craig Scott was moved from the parish in 1998. They were once again favoured by the Archbishop of Vancouver, sending another French-speaking priest to guide them. Father Patrick Tepoorten arrived there in 1998. Our Lady of Fatima Parish celebrated its 50th anniversary in 1996. The TriCities News did report on this special occasion on December 11, 1996:

*"**Archbishop visits to launch 50th Maillardville:** Historic Catholic parish celebrating its 50th anniversary as church, centre of community life On December 8, 1946, the parishioners of Our Lady of Fatima parish in Coquitlam held their first mass in the school across the street at Alderson and Walker. "Starting a church, you always start with a mass," said Jean Lambert, one of the founding members of the church. "We're Catholics so that's the way we do it."*

On Sunday, Fatima parishioners celebrated 50 years of masses with Archbishop Adam Exner saying mass with four other priests, assistance from church groups and one original altar boy, now in his late 50s. Lambert remembers trucking benches to Alderson School to seat the parishioners for the first mass and he remembers helping to build the church fifty years ago.

Father Ovila Meunier said the first mass and Father Gérard Leduc presided over plans for a new church in 1958, eventually built by Maillardville pioneer Fernand Filliatrault....This Sunday's anniversary mass turned out well. Said Diane Johnston, Lambert's daughter and organizer of the 50 year anniversary celebration. "The music was absolutely wonderful," said Johnston, who said the church was painted, waxed, cleaned and shining for the big day." There was also a new mural of clouds and an angel behind the altar, framing the archbishop as he said mass. After mass, the church hosted lunch for 500, also attended by Coquitlam Mayor Lou Sekora and Port Moody-Coquitlam MP Sharon Hayes."

It could no longer be said that the church permeated every aspect of community life as it once had. But the original threesome of religion, language and culture upon which Maillardville was founded continued to thrive at Fatima after the first 50 years of its existence. A great support of this was the health of the Catholic school there, bringing the same values cherished by the pioneers to a new generation of young Francophones.

Looking to the east, Paroisse Notre Dame de Lourdes, the "soul" of old Maillardville, (that venerable institution upon which the pioneers had built their village) was meeting the challenges of the nineties in its own way. While the revitalization on Brunette was well underway, the church and parish buildings received their own facelift. All the buildings were resided in vinyl (to the dismay of some) and some structural work was done on the rectory and at Saint Anne's Hall.

The crowning event was the addition of the steeple. The bell tower, of course, was a part of the 1938 construction, but diminishing funds prevented the completion of the steeple. The church at Fatima, built in 1958 with all the bells and whistles of the day, did add a steeple, though of a somewhat unconventional design. It was affectionately known by some as the "witch's hat". Now in 1991, Notre Dame de Lourdes was finally receiving her crowning glory. Sitting atop the original 60-foot tower, the 30-foot steeple was traditional and stately and emphasized the position this historical Maillardville institution so rightly deserved.

The nineties saw no fewer than two significant anniversaries for Maillardville. First was the Sisters of the Child Jesus' 100th anniversary of service to the Archdiocese of Vancouver and 87 years of ministering to the needs of Maillardville at both parishes. Sister Berthe Pellerin was asked to speak on the Sisters' behalf after the commemorative Mass at Our Lady of Lourdes. A more appropriate representative for the good Sisters could not be imagined. Soeur Berthe epitomized the humble, dedicated servant of the community that was the hallmark of the Order's service for so many decades in Maillardville. The B.C. Catholic recorded the event:

"Sisters of Child Jesus celebrate centenary Parishioners packed Our Lady of Lourdes church in Coquitlam July 7 for a mass marking a century of service to the Vancouver Archdiocese and 87 years of service to the francophone community in Coquitlam by the Sisters of the Child Jesus. The Mass was concelebrated by Father James Comey, rector of Holy Rosary Cathedral, vicar general Monsignor David Monroe, pastor of St. John the Apostle parish and Father Stan Frytek OFM, pastor of Our Lady of Lourdes and a number of other priests.*

*The Sisters of the Child Jesus worked in Our Lady of Lourdes parish
1909-1951 and from 1968 to the present. After Our Lady of Lourdes was
divided, they also worked in Our Lady of Fatima parish from 1946-1951.
"In my efforts to prepare a short resume of the presence of the Sisters of
the Child Jesus in Maillardville's two parishes, I was struck by the principle of divine providence." said Sister Berthe Pellerin SCJ after the
Mass.*

*"The right people came together at the right place at the right time."
when the sisters came to Maillardville she said. She praised the "devoted
priests" who have pastored the two parishes-Oblates and Franciscans as
well as diocesan clergy-singling out Father Frytec and Father Craig
Scott, pastor of our Lady of Fatima. "Both Our Lady of Fatima and Our
Lady of Lourdes Elementary Schools have been left in the capable hands
of lay persons." Sister Berthe noted. "Also as time progressed, both parishes welcomed many different nationalities. Today they are filled with
generous and capable people.*

*She remarked on the number of vocations produced by the two parishes:
Sisters Rose Théroux SA, Yvonne Duplin SP, Madeleine Duplin SCJ,
Agnes Duplin SCJ, Bernadette Croteau SCJ, Charlotte Girard SCJ,
Marguerite Girard SCJ, Georgette Jacquiard SCJ, and Jeanine
Marchand SCJ from Our Lady of Lourdes and Sisters Anita Charpentier
RGS and Claudette Ledet RGS from Our Lady of Fatima."*

A brief history of the founding of Maillardville followed and then the
article continued:

*"In September 1909, school classes began under a lay woman. On De-
cember 1, two Sisters of the Child Jesus, Sister Amélie and Sister Alix,
made the 5-kilometre journey from their convent in New Westminster to
what came to be known as the Maillardville School. The following year
Sister Stephanus joined them. Until the convent and Our Lady of
Lourdes School were built in 1911, the three sisters continued to live at
St. Louis College in New Westminster, making the daily journey by
tramway to Sapperton and then walking the rest of the way. In 1911, a
few more sisters joined the teaching staff. In all, 62 Sisters of the Child
Jesus have served in Maillardville since 1909."*

This history of Maillardville has highlighted the contributions of many
citizens, French and English, and of pastors and politicians down

through the decades. It can be said without falsity, theatrics or hyperbole that without the Sisters' humble devotion to the education and well-being of the children of the pioneers, Maillardville might not have survived the challenges it faced. They were, in a very real sense, the glue that bound the community. Along with all of the teaching orders of Sisters who served at both schools, Maillardville owes the Sisters of the Child Jesus a great and un-repayable debt of gratitude.

The second significant milestone of the decade came in 1999. It was the 90th anniversary of the arrival of the first contingent of lumbermen and their families to the West Coast, at Millside Station, Fraser Mills. So many things had come and gone for Maillardville in nine decades. Although its former glory had faded, the community celebrated its blessings as it always had. Organized and presented by Société Maillardville-Uni, the celebratory activities took place at several venues. The commemorative Mass began at the newly opened Heritage Square with a prayer and a procession to Notre Dame de Lourdes on Laval Square. A reception followed with lunch. The "Banquet des Pionniers" was held on October 16, 1999 at the hall at O.L of Fatima followed by a concert.

Longevity notwithstanding, Paroisse Notre Dame de Lourdes was falling on hard times once again. The congregation itself was shrinking, its members aging and there were fewer and fewer young people to bring new life to course through the veins of the community. Sadly, in 1996, École Notre Dame de Lourdes closed its doors as a parish school. The building was let to the Traditional Learning Academy who opened an independent teaching facility.

From the moment the pioneers stepped off the train, the French Catholic education of their children had been foremost in their minds and the building of a school their priority, surpassed in importance only by the building of the church. Built first upon the land at Laval Square, the school was the cradle of community life for generations of Maillardville children. Later, a new building was erected on Hammond Avenue.

A very institutional building, the stucco clad, wood frame "box" was finished inside almost exclusively with fir flooring. The smell of that building undoubtedly remains a vivid memory for many who spent their childhoods there. The classrooms were spacious, the classes full, the Sisters both terrifying and comforting. The large gymnasium with full stage was the site of many floor hockey games, school plays and hot dog days.

At the height of the parish's vigour, midnight Mass at Christmas was celebrated there. But everyone's favourite was the parish bazaars. Gym and classrooms all held activities from fish ponds to craft tables. Baked goodies abounded. Everywhere there were the delighted shrieks of the children and the hubbub of the adults. The sudden cry of "BINGO!" and the clatter of roulette wheels in the Knights of Columbus gambling rooms all blended with the sights and sounds of the day.

The gully to the west of the building was a great place for the boys to get into trouble and the relatively steep slope behind the school was the site of many a toboggan run in the winter. Later, the convent school was built on Rochester in anticipation of continued growth in the parish. Alas, that hope was soon extinguished as the parish began its long, slow decline in the late sixties. Long lines of children from both schools marching down to the church were a regular sight for decades. There never was a lack of altar boys to assist at Masses, baptisms, funerals and weddings. The loss of the parish school slipped by, almost unnoticed. It was the end of an era and a sad loss for Maillardville's church community.

On Thanksgiving Sunday, October 8, 1995, a shocking tragedy occurred. Two long time parishioners, Henri and Céline Roufosse, were brutally murdered in the church parking lot at Our Lady of Lourdes. Moments later the killer, the estranged common law partner of their daughter Annette, was at the family home a few blocks away where he took her life and then left the scene with two of their children. The event was deeply traumatic for the family and for the whole community. It was as though some evil from outside had swept down upon the insular congregation taking not only the lives of three individuals, but also stealing something from the very soul of the community. The Now reported:

"Three Murdered in Maillardville   A Coquitlam man under a court order to have no contact with his common-law wife was charged Monday with her murder. Darcy Richard Bertrand, 29, was charged with the first degree murder of Annette Roufosse, 29, and her parents Céline, 60, and Henry Roufosse, 63 all of Coquitlam. Coquitlam RCMP Cpl. Gil Campbell said two separate calls came in within minutes of each other Sunday around noon. The first call, Campbell said, was reported as a fight at Our Lady of Lourdes church in Maillardville. The second was a 911 call reporting a stabbing outside 324 Therrien Street, just blocks away.

Céline and Henry Roufosse had attended French mass in the bilingual church and died of stab wounds in the parking lot while their 7 year old grandson watched...Police arrested Bertrand Sunday afternoon at his mother's in Burnaby after receiving a 911 call from there. The two younger children who were reported missing from the Roufosse's home, were found unharmed at the Burnaby home. The children are now with the Roufosse family and are receiving psychiatric care. Police said Annette Roufosse and Bertrand had lived together for four years prior to the end of May. Henry Roufosse ran a furnace installation and repair business with his son and Annette Roufosse worked as a house keeping aide at Foyer Maillard."

Annette Roufosse's co-workers and employer placed flowers and a candle outside her home in her memory. The Now:

"The murders shocked residents *of the French-Canadian neighbourhood."Maillardville is a very close knit community." said Doris Brisebois, administrator of Foyer Maillard nursing home where Roufosse worked. "Everyone really cares about everyone and helps everyone. It is difficult to lose three people in our community so violently." Brisebois said in the eight years she was employed as a house keeping aide, Roufosse was well liked by staff and residents. "She was very gentle, that's the easiest way to describe her, very gentle and very caring. We're really going to miss her."*

Their funerals were held on Friday, October 13. Over 500 filled the church. The Now quotes Father Stan Frytek, who had administered last rites to the couple in the church parking lot:

"Not many did I know of that were that devoted in their faith" he said of Henry and Céline Roufosse, longtime members of the church. Frytek spoke of Henry's "quiet, simple, deep faith." During their lives, Frytek said, Henry and Céline Roufosse maintained "intensely close family ties, and became an integral part of their community. Henry and Céline's door was always open and their help, advice and good company was given freely" Frytec said Annette, who worked as a housekeeping aide at Foyer Maillard nursing home, was a devoted mother to her three children. "Her greatest love other than her immediate family was children and the elderly."

Eventually, the charges against Bertrand were reduced to second-degree murder to which he entered a guilty plea. He was sentenced to life in prison with no chance of parole for 22 years.

In a sense, the murders symbolized Maillardville's dramatic change from the French village of its early days to the "new" Maillardville of the nineties. East of Marmont Street, the plan to create higher density residential with "French character" was well underway. The cleaning up of the commercial district west of Marmont had been completed in the early years of the decade. Somehow, the "revitalization" did not occur. Worse, there were signs that a sinister trend was emerging. In 1993, the building at 218 Blue Mountain Street, a block from Alderson Elementary and Our Lady of Fatima School, became home to a sex offender treatment program. Parents and residents were not informed of the development, but when Alderson Parents Advisory Council protested, they were advised according to the News, March 1993 that:

"these offenders are all seductive pedophiles and that none of them are abductive."

That did little to ease their fears, especially when a few days later they learned that a recent "abductive pedophile" was receiving treatment there.

At the west end of Brunette at Lougheed, the shopping experience with "European flair" simply was not happening. Although a few restaurants and services came and went, the hope for revitalization did not bear fruit. One business that did open was the Ultimate Relaxation massage parlour. Council denied them their initial business license application, however as the Now, December 1995 reveals:

*"**Massage Parlour Gets Okay** Council is getting a new massage parlour whether council likes it or not. The B.C. Supreme Court ruled on Monday that the city wrongly refused to grant a license to Ultimate Relaxation, a steam bath and massage facility to be located near Brunette Avenue and Lougheed Highway in Maillardville. The company's original application said the facility would offer "finger pressure holistic therapy" and adult movies. It was turned down by council who felt the business didn't comply with Maillardville's Official Community Plan.*

A second application filed in August, had a revised description of the facility and proposed the inclusion of an oxygen chamber and flotation tanks. The city's permits and licenses director recommended the second application be turned down for the same reasons as the first one. But a B.C. Supreme Court judge ruled the proposal adheres to the land's current zoning. A female voice on Ultimate Relaxation's answering machine said a grand opening is set for December 11."

At the other end of Brunette's commercial district, across from Mackin Park with its children's playground and wading pool, stood the clubhouse of the Hells Angels Vancouver chapter. Its highly visible display of Hells Angels' symbols and logos did little to encourage new businesses with "a European flair" to locate in the area. At that time, marijuana "grow ops" were becoming an increasing problem for Coquitlam. Several large operations in the area surrounding Maillardville were busted by police who stated that the grow ops were connected to the Hell's Angels. The Now, December 1997 reports on one such incident:

"Huge Marijuana Bust Linked to Hells Angels *Three people were arrested in Coquitlam and Port Coquitlam Wednesday in a lower Mainland drug bust linked to the Hells Angels that netted up to $2million worth of marijuana." The Coquitlam residence took place in the 1700 block of Dansey Avenue" The article continues: "All of the drug operations were controlled by the Hells Angels" said Const. Anne Drennan of the Vancouver Police department. Those arrested are suspected of growing pot for "associates" of the infamous biker gang, Drennan said. "There's a huge buffer between the low level growers and the Hells Angels," she said."*

There were several incidents of gunshots. One was the culmination of a high-speed chase from Port Coquitlam, to Digger O'Riley's Pub, the present day Woody's. That incident ended with one of the young fugitives shot to death inside the pub. There was another report in October of 1992, of a drive by shooting in the 300 block of Blue Mountain. Six blasts from a shotgun rang out; the apparent target, an eighteen-year-old male inside the house. He was not hurt. Vandalism and graffiti at Mackin Park was on the rise. A letter to the Now editor in February of 1998 decried the deteriorating condition of the park and called upon the city to install more lighting.

Another serious problem emerged in Coquitlam in 1999: prostitution. The issue was widespread enough that a city task force was struck to deal with it. A group, "Children of the Street Society" was formed to heighten awareness of this growing concern. Meanwhile, prostitutes had begun plying their trade along Brunette west of Nelson Street.

At the corner of Lebleu Street and Brunette, reminiscent of the depressing scene Maillardville from seventies, a house had burned down in 1997. Despite repeated complaints from neighbours, it was 1999 before council issued an order to demolish. In spite of the order, that burned out wreck was to remain for several years more.

With Y2K hysteria reaching fever pitch, the nineties ended. The dream of a revitalized Maillardville remained elusive and the village was once again showing signs of distress. The residential component of the re-building was successful. As a tourist attraction, the newly opened Heritage Square, and especially the museum, would need more time to establish itself. The Festival du Bois certainly did attract much attention. But as an annual event, it could not hope to revive Maillardville single handedly. The French community, through the churches, organizations and principally through Société Maillardville-Uni continued the struggle to survive. At times the challenges were overwhelming.

By far, the major influencing factor of the nineties for Maillardville was the failure of the commercial district to grow. Looking back from the vantage point of almost two decades, it does not seem difficult to see why the revitalization plan did not bear fruit. When the old Maillardville Shopping centre burned down in 1985, no large "anchor" business was built to replace it; there was nothing to attract repeat customers. The new vision called for a pedestrian and bicycle friendly neighborhood centre. The converse of that notion, to discourage the number of shoppers driving to the destination, was highly successful. With no on street parking on Brunette, and parking lot locations that were obscure, there was not much to encourage a vehicle to actually stop and sample the nonexistent European experience.

With the higher density development east of Marmont, perhaps customers would have made the trip by foot or bicycle, if the corridor from the Tower Plaza to Millside proposed in 1995 had been built. The loss of City Hall meant the loss of any reason for people to visit Maillardville other than to take part in a program at Place des Arts. The decision to allow a full-scale commercial development at Lougheed and School-house sealed Maillardville's fate.

Even though the decade was permeated with a spirit of optimism, the nineties are really about the loss of so many ties to the past. Losses that, in most cases were not replaced with viable alternatives to ensure the future growth and health of Maillardville. The village, with its large homes built for large families, had disappeared. The connection to Fraser Mills was severed physically, and modernization of the plant had reduced its work force from over two thousand to a mere two hundred. The mill no longer had a direct impact on Maillardville.

City Hall was lost and with that loss came a disconnect between Council and the local community. The centre of activity that City Hall represented for Maillardville was not replaced with a public facility that might have provided new opportunities for community growth and vitality. The two pubs notwithstanding, little reminder was left of the robust commercial district that once flourished on Brunette. Trev's was one of the few remaining businesses connecting Maillardville to its commercial past and it too saw its last days in the nineties.

The French community, its activities muted in relative anonymity, kept up the struggle for language and culture. Its one strong outward and visible expression, the Festival du Bois, had been relocated outside of Maillardville.

The hope of rebuilding Maillardville that was so alive at the beginning of the decade was by its end frustrated. Quo vadis Maillardville?

Figure 99 Brunette Ave 1970s

Figure 100 Brunette 1970s

Figure 101 Brunette 1970s

Figure 102 Chante Clair

Figure 103 Father G. Chabot

Figure 104 Francofête c. 1979

Figure 105 Francofête c. 1979

Figure 106 Place Maillardville Neighbourhood House

Figure 107 75th Anniversary pin

Figure 108 Johnny Dicaire

Figure 109 Chez Nous

Figure 110 Mayor Lou Sekora

Figure 111 Shopping Centre fire

Figure 112 Shopping Centre fire

Figure 113 Jean Lambert

Figure 114 Napoleon Gareau

Figure 115 Steeple cap being installed

Figure 116 Our Lady of Lourdes

Figure 117 Foyer Maillard

Figure 118 J. Lambert power box art

255

Figure 119 1st Festival du Bois   Figure 120 Festival 2002

Figure 121 Festival 2004

Figure 122 Heritage Square   Figure 123 Heritage Square

Figure 124 Mackin House Museum

Figure 125 Place des Arts

Figure 126 Brunette Ave. c. 2008

Figure 127 Club House

Figure 128 Abandoned trailer park

Figure 129 Fraser Mills deconstruction

Figure 130 100th Anniversary

Figure 131 100th Anniversary

Figure 132 Father Stan Frytec

Figure 133 Fr Maillard's cross.

Ten

New Hope for the Next Century

Τhis final decade of Maillardville's one hundred year history is a
mirror image of the previous one. The high hopes with which the
nineties opened faded as the 21st century began. Maillardville
had become a study in neglect and urban decay. The revitalization effort
that had been initiated in the mid-eighties had failed. This was recognized early in the decade as mention is made several times in Council
minutes of "revitalizing" Maillardville. A third effort was initiated in
2005. By 2009, there were positive signs that the drive to renew the village would finally be successful. There were many influences at play to
encourage this rebuilding effort.

Previous efforts to revive Maillardville's commercial district had failed.
The beautification of Brunette and the building of the mixed-use complex where the Maillardville Shopping Centre once stood turned out to
be mere window dressing. It attracted no "European" businesses. There
was no proliferation of coffee shops, bakeries or boutiques. In fact, the
previous decade saw everything that was a draw to Maillardville taken
away, not to be replaced by other attractions. The major shopping venue
was lost, replaced by a poorly managed mixed-use building. The commercial units, never filled to capacity, would soon be attracting the
"wrong" types of businesses. Activity at City Hall that for so many decades contributed to Maillardville's vibrant life also disappeared when
Council packed up for the move to Town Centre. The benefits of affordable housing notwithstanding, Maillardville lost yet again when Council
chose to create an affordable housing complex on the former site of City
Hall. This decision was made against the strongly expressed wishes of

the community. Those wishes were based on a promise made a decade earlier by Mayor Lou Sekora that a public facility would be located there. Finally, Council failed to carry through with its revitalization plan for Maillardville. While tens of millions were being poured into the development of Town Centre, much of Maillardville's "beautification" money came from either government grants or the good will of businessmen and women along Brunette Avenue. The bicycle and pedestrian corridor from Millside School to Woolridge Street that was supposed to link residents to their own commercial development was never built. Even the clock that was supposed to be installed in the gateway tower was not installed until 2007. It was accomplished with federal grant money.

It would be stated later in the decade, during the third attempt to breathe life into Maillardville's commercial corridor that the failure came because there was insufficient residential density to support a vibrant commerce. While there is truth to that statement, the problem of density alone is insufficient to explain the systemic decline that occurred. The failure on the part of City Council and staff to fully engage in the project and follow through to encourage commercial growth in Maillardville was also a significant contributing factor. Additionally, a high rate of absentee commercial landlords who allowed their properties to decay also fueled the general downward spiral of the area.

Once again, Maillardville was in a state of decay. Its reputation as a low-income area with higher rates of crime contributed to the sense that it was an undesirable place to live. Was this reputation deserved? Was Maillardville a high crime area? Not more so than other areas of Coquitlam at that time. The papers throughout the first half of the decade are filled with stories of the proliferation of marijuana grow ops on Coquitlam's Westwood Plateau and of serious violent crime along the North Road corridor. Maillardville by comparison was relatively quiet. Nevertheless, its reputation as a seedy area was deserved and it was well cultivated. "Crack houses" began to appear. Prostitution, driven by drug addiction, became more visible. Mackin Park was seen as an unsafe place to go at night having become a hangout for the troubled youth of the area. And the sagging commercial strip? With few "mainstream" businesses interested in locating in Maillardville, their opposite numbers began to appear. In addition to side-by-side pubs, unregistered massage parlours, (in at least one case, a front for prostitution), a pawnshop, tattoo parlour, two adult retail stores and a triple x video store all located within a two-block area on Brunette Avenue. The Coquitlam Now, December of 2003 reported on one particular incident and illustrated the general condition of Brunette Avenue:

"Suspected 'prostitution ring' shut down in Maillardville *It employed women called Frisky Brunette, Busty Blond, Spanish Hottie and Chocolate Fantasy, and charged $150.00 for "all inclusive" services. Ultimate Shiatsu, a thorn in the side of Coquitlam City Hall, and at least one former tenant in Maillardville's Village Square strip mall, has lost its supreme court bid to stay open....But while Coquitlam's mayor hopes the closure of Ultimate Shiatsu will spur a renewal of the historic area, empty storefronts in the Village Square shopping centre tell a different story. A sign advertising Karen's Place hair salon is still displayed on the faux heritage clock tower that greets visitors to the green roofed strip mall wedged between the French Quarter and Woody's pubs on Brunette at Lougheed Highway. But the hair salon relocated a year ago according to owner Karen Rogers. Some of the other panels on the sign advertise businesses that have moved on. Others are blank. About half the businesses have "for lease" signs in their windows.....Jimmie Jang and his son Randy, who own the Village Square shopping centre, both declined to comment when reached by the Now...Coquitlam Mayor Jon Kingsbury said the process of shutting down Ultimate Shiatsu has been long and difficult, but that Randy Jang has assured the city "that he's going to clean that area up and become a responsible landlord and do a great job for the community--so we're really looking forward to him living up to his word." Kingsbury labeled Maillardville "an area in transition" but said he feels positive about its future."*

That strip mall continued to deteriorate. With its cracked and delaminating stucco and blue tarps draping its eastern wall, the building was a mockery of the revitalization efforts occurring around it.

The problems surrounding the proliferation of such businesses were recognized by City Council. As early as December of 2001 a motion was put forward to regulate:

"pawn shops, non therapeutic massage parlours, adult video stores, phone sex services and nude entertainment."

These businesses were termed "undesirable", however, no significant change came until 2007. Spurred by an outcry from the community and supported by the Maillardville Residents' Association (MRA), Council passed a new by-law tightening control over pawnshops. In 2009, again at the instigation of the MRA, a by-law governing "undesirable" business was put in place. It banned certain businesses outright and imposed restrictions on others. The measures were too late for Maillardville as most of the above named businesses were already established there, but it was seen as a step in the right direction.

By 2005, the challenges facing Maillardville were undeniable. A grass roots movement of business owners, nonprofit societies and residents began to gain momentum. In its attempt to resolve some of the problems facing the village, this working group paved the way for the formation of a Mayor's Task Force for the Cultural and Commercial Revitalization of Maillardville. This new effort came thirty years after "Plan Maillardville" made the first attempt. Thirty years! Ten to twenty years is a typical period to see revitalization projects to fruition from planning to completion. Here was Maillardville going back to the drawing board in 2005!

In 2006 and 2007, government and businesses partnered to "clean up" Brunette Avenue once again. Generous financial incentives from a Federal Government grant were offered to commercial land owners to paint their buildings and install new awnings. The Gateway Tower finally received its clock and "flower towers" were placed at strategic locations throughout Maillardville. History was repeating itself. Most of these improvements were made possible by grants from the federal and provincial governments.

One significant difference, however, was that all three levels of government, City staff and all stakeholders in Maillardville were represented at the committee table. Council passed a new neighbourhood centre plan for Maillardville in the summer of 2008. The plan was not so very different from the old one. It still envisioned capitalizing on the area's French history and sought to establish a vibrant "Franco/European" commercial district. The "grand boulevard" that was conceived in 1994 connecting Mackin Park and Woolridge Street along Adair Avenue was revived. The same traffic calmed, pedestrian oriented experience was still the goal. Design guidelines that emphasized iron railings, balconies and tall windows were to dominate the streetscape. What was different? Time and density. Most space in Maillardville 2009, commercial and residential, was underutilized. Greater Vancouver included a much broader area than it had in 1974 and Maillardville is, geographically, close to its centre. It is at the junction of the Trans Canada Freeway and the Lougheed Highway. Rapid transit is nearby. In addition, the housing stock is aging and much of it has reached the end of its practical service life. The Task Force, working closely with almost every City department, helped to create a comprehensive revision of the Maillardville Neighbourhood Centre plan, along with changes to the commercial design guidelines. The new plan reinforced the notion of creating a "Franco European" village, but it added something new to the mix: high residential densities. In addition to condominium units over commercial space throughout the area, the new plan allows for a half dozen high-rise towers. Once again, all was in place for the revitalization of Maillardville. One hopes that the same historical error of "waiting" for developers to come to Maillardville will not made in 2009.

Another noteworthy development during this decade was the closing of Fraser Mills in 2001. The plant that had at one time employed over 2000 was now down to fewer than 200. The world of 2001 was very different from that of 1891, when the Ross/McLaren Mill was a new and exciting enterprise for Coquitlam. Modernization, the loss of the mill town and increasing pressure from environmental interests conspired to squeeze the mill out of existence. The sights, sounds and smells that greeted the pioneers in 1909 all now passed into history. The larger machinery had been idle for some years and the entire site would soon be abandoned.

There were many opinions on what should be done with the land upon which the mill stood. The Coquitlam Heritage Society envisioned an interactive historical facility created on the site. Others looked for a major sports complex to be built there. Mayor Jon Kingsbury saw a tourist attraction that would offer tours of a working mill. The site was eventually dismantled, the land remediated. Sadly, very little was saved to preserve the memory of the mill that dominated the land for over a century and whose management was directly responsible for bringing to the area those French men and women who would eventually found Maillardville. In 2003, a major developer, the Beedie Group, bought the entire parcel of 33.4 hectares. After considering the possibility of building an industrial park, BG came to Council with a radically different plan in 2005. The Now, June 2005 offers these details:

"Village Planned For Fraser Mills Site   *Beedie Group hopes to create "vibrant waterfront" The Beedie Group has approached Coquitlam*

265

councilors with an extensive plan for the city's waterfront that would transform the former Fraser Mills site into a self-contained village, complete with open air stage and a community pier....."We're excited" said development manager Dave Gormley, "We think we can create a really unique, active waterfront...The project, dubbed 'The Village at Fraser Mills', calls for 3700 units of mixed housing that would include street level entry condos and high rise towers, Gormley said....about 190,000 square feet of boutique style stores, high end restaurants are planned near the waterfront...About 100,000 square feet would be a business park.....The proposal includes a mill museum, playing fields and community centres."

Council rejected the notion based upon such concerns as the loss of industrial lands, serious traffic challenges and environmental issues. The developer returned with a modified proposal that addressed those concerns. The process was finally completed in 2008 when Council voted in favour of a new land use designation for the site called "waterfront village" The project is to include condominium development, both wood frame and high-rise, commercial and industrial space, a post-secondary facility and a waterfront park. Space has also been set aside for public amenities such as waterfront access, a community centre and a museum facility. Beedie Group sees this as a 15 to 20 year project.

Another major influencing factor for Maillardville as it moves beyond its centenary is the provincial highways project known as Gateway scheduled for completion in 2013. A peripheral project of the work is to create a King Edward overpass. In the early days of Maillardville, King Edward Street was the link between Fraser Mills and the Village. At the north end, where it intersected Pitt River Road (Brunette Avenue) was the archway of the Canadian Western Lumber Company, flanked on either side by the mill manager's house (Ryan House) and that of the sales manager. (Mackin House). This traditional, direct link between mill and village was severed in the 1950s when the Lougheed Highway was built. The overpass will see the present day TransCanada Freeway brought down to ground level, along with the highway and the railway tracks. King Edward will then overpass all of it landing right at the doorstep of the original Fraser Mills site, where it will connect the new Village at Fraser Mills with old Maillardville. The original provincial design saw the overpass curving 150 metres to the west. However, local groups from Maillardville successfully lobbied for the "straight" alignment option, putting forward the argument, among other things, that it was the great desire of the community to preserve the historic link.

The entire Gateway Project will significantly change local traffic patterns and much concern has been expressed about the negative impact such a change might have on Maillardville. According to one study by the Society Promoting Environmental Conservation (SPEC), Maillardville will be one of the hardest hit communities with respect to traffic increase. Only the passage of time will reveal how Gateway will help or harm the historic neighbourhood.

The closing of Fraser Mills was accompanied by another significant loss for the community. Village Credit Union, established in 1946 as Caisse Populaire Notre Dame de Lourdes, was also consigned to the annals of history. In 1999, after 25 years with the credit union, Fern Bouvier announced his resignation from the Board. In 2000, Richard Coulombe was elected as President and Chairman. The financial challenges of the late nineties behind them, CEO Denis Desautels, set the credit union on the path of growth. And grow it did. It was reported at the 2000 AGM that membership stood at 6000, and assets at $67million. By 2002, the credit union boasted 7200 members and assets of $90million. As of 2003, membership had increased to 10,000 while assets climbed to $120million.

If success is measured solely by growth, then Village Credit Union was successful in those years. This growth was the result of an aggressive expansion strategy that included the opening of two new branches. "Northside" in Port Coquitlam was opened in 2000, followed by a branch in distant Chilliwack in 2002. Another aspect of the strategy was to target "*hard working men and women*" to increase the credit union's loan portfolio. This too was pursued with great vigour.

Rapid growth often brings its own profound challenges. By 2003, with management resources spread thin over four branches, the strategy embarked upon 4 years earlier began to bear its true fruit. In 2003, Mr. Desautels resigned as CEO due to health reasons. It was also that year that Al Boire was elected as President and Chairman of the Board. The first task at hand was to embark upon a search for a new executive officer. Eventually, Mr. Ian Cornish was selected. Mr. Cornish was an interesting choice on two counts. Financially conservative, he was part of the management team at Stabilization Central Credit Union, the system watchdog that had Village Credit Union under supervision in the nineties. The other was that he did not speak French, a first in the history of la Caisse Populaire.

The hard work of getting the institution back on track got underway. The board agreed to a change in strategy. It would see a more conservative and controlled approach to the granting of loans and that would, in a sense, return the credit union to its roots of being a smaller community based financial institution, a so-called "boutique" business. But the writing was on the wall. The big vs. small dilemma was what CEOs, presidents and board members of Caisse Populaire Maillardville struggled with almost from the very beginning.

The challenges faced by the credit union continued and by mid-2004 Stabilization Central once again put Village under supervision. After long and painful deliberation, the Board of Directors chose to seek out a merger partner. As the author was Chairman of the Board at the time, it can be accurately stated that it was with very heavy hearts that he and the members of the Board met with stakeholders in the community to inform them of the decision. One meeting was particularly difficult, as it called together many of the older members for whom la Caisse had played such an important role throughout their lives. There was a silver lining. So true to the strong and generous nature of the community at Maillardville, and amidst more than a few held back tears, these humble men and women accepted the situation and wished the Board well in the work that now lay ahead. They demonstrated that with humble hearts, good will and mutual support a community, if not a credit union, can and will survive.

The word went out to the credit union system that Village was seeking a merger partner. Of seven expressing interest, the Board selected three to offer formal proposals. Among other criteria set by the Board, one stipulation was a guarantee that the Maillardville branch would not be abandoned. Another was that the new entity would continue to support and nurture the community's French Canadian heritage. Among the hopefuls was Vancity Credit Union which was eventually chosen to be the "partner". In June of 2005, the last Board of Directors of Village Credit Union faced the membership for the final time. The purpose of the meeting was to vote on the merger proposal and the decision of some 300 members attending was unanimous. The Coquitlam Now, June 2005:

"Village Credit Union Members Approve Merger Maillardville's 60
year old credit union will merge with Vancity Savings Credit Union. At a
special meeting held this week 100% of voting members supported the
change, which will see Village branches in Maillardville, Port Moody,
Port Coquitlam and Chilliwack convert to Vancity outlets by the fall. "I
applaud our members' decision to lead the credit union in this new direction" Village CEO Ian Cornish said in a news release. "We're
confident our members, employees and communities will be welled
served by the merger." Village began as the Caisse Populaire de Notre
Dame de Lourdes in 1946 when it catered only to French speaking residents. The deal includes provision for the creation of a Maillardville
advisory committee which will include members of both Village and
Vancity boards, as well as long time members of the Maillardville community. The group will continue to be active in the Festival du
Bois...."Vancity is helping to ensure that Village's roots in the French
Canadian community of Maillardville are never lost" said Al Boire,
chair of Village's board of directors."*

And so it was that on a quiet Sunday morning, one month later, Mr.
Boire met with Mr. Cornish to sign the documents that formally placed
the assets of the Village Credit Union into the hands of Vancity. It was a
wistful and anticlimactic event, but no less powerful for what it symbolized. Caisse Populaire Notre Dame de Lourdes was established in 1946
to "*consolidate the French community of Maillardville through economic solidarity*". The credit union was successful in that mission for many
decades; indeed it played a key role in much of the development that
Maillardville enjoyed, particularly in the eighties and nineties. Men such
as J.B. Goulet, Victor Muller, Georges Perron, Romeo Paquette, Jean
Aussant and Fern Bouvier, to name but a few, made tremendous contributions to the French community through their involvement with the
institution. But the way was full of challenges from the beginning. Opening the bond to allow non-French, non-Catholic members, the change of
name to the generic "Village", and opening branches in communities
outside of Maillardville were strategies all geared to the preservation of
the credit union. Many from the very beginning stated that a closed bond
French credit union could not survive. History proved them right almost
60 years later, but oh, what a 60 years it was!

As we began this history of the credit union with a list of the founding
members, it is appropriate to include the role of the final Board of Directors of Village Credit Union upon its dissolution in June of 2005. It is

noteworthy that among the founding members, we find the name of Napoléon Gareau. His son Raymond served on the board of Caisse Populaire, and his grandson Richard was on hand as a director in the final days of Village Credit Union.

Al Boire	President and Chairman of the Board
Richard Coulombe	Vice-Chairman
Richard Gareau	Director, Maillardville
Albert Lamothe	Director, Maillardville
Fiona McQuarie	Director, Maillardville
Sylvia Prichard	Director, Port Moody
Gerry Kruchak	Director, Port Coquitlam
Chad Northcott	Director, Chilliwack
Ian Cornish	Chief Executive Officer

The story of Maillardville's credit union does not end there, however. The new relationship with Vancity included keeping the branch in Maillardville and honouring its French heritage. They did this in several ways. Vancity continued to financially support the Festival du Bois, becoming their main stage sponsor. Another significant contribution was that, for the first time in their history, Vancity offered internet-banking services in the French language. Very early on in the merger process, the properties east of the branch along Brunette were purchased. In collaboration with a "transition team" made up of members of the community, Vancity announced that a major development project was in the works. The proposed complex was to be a mix of residential units, commercial shops and a brand new "flagship" branch. It was all to be designed with a French architectural look and the theme of the branch was to focus on the community's French heritage and its links to Fraser Mills and the lumber industry. Here finally was a major project that many saw as being the catalyst needed to spur further development of Maillardville. Sadly, with a change of CEOs both at Vancity and at Vancity Enterprises, their development company, the project was significantly scaled back and eventually stalled altogether in 2007. Economic challenges were cited as the primary reason for the delay.

Heritage Square, completed in 1999, was one of the few remaining attractions located in Maillardville. Place des Arts as an education facility continued to offer a wide range of artistic opportunities that included art, music, theatre and dance classes. The centre had grown in sophistication and it became something of a regional facility. Yet Place des Arts did not forsake its commitment to Maillardville and continued to participate in the life of the community. Special events such as Light up the Square and Fair in the Square highlighted the cooperation that existed among community and nonprofit associations in the village. In 2007, Place des Arts celebrated 35 years of providing young and old with artistic opportunities of every description. They remained faithful to their original mandate of responding to community needs and helping to rebuild Maillardville. Place des Arts has been a true anchor in stormy seas for the village.

In November of 2006, during the early enthusiasm surrounding Maillardville revitalization, the first "Twelve Days of Christmas" campaign was initiated and is a shining example of a community working together. The Now reports:

*"**Maillardville Will Shine During 12 Days of Christmas Campaign**   Maillardville will shine brightly this holiday season as its streets, cultural centres and businesses are animated by both events and dazzling light displays. Over twelve days local arts and heritage groups are hosting events and activities for all ages, many of which are free and offered in both French and English. The festivities kick off with free lantern making workshops at Place Maillardville, Place des Arts and Millside Elementary. Participants can create one of a kind lanterns to adorn both their homes and the streets of Maillardville as they join their community in the carol procession to light up the square and streets of Maillardville. At the stroke of 5pm on Saturday, December 2, a parade of lanterns will proceed from the clock tower along historic Brunette Avenue to Heritage square. At heritage Square guests will be treated to festive performances, seasonal crafts and French fare. Other 12 Days of Christmas events include an early music concert by the Light 'o love ensemble at Place des Arts, breakfast with Santa at Place Maillardville as well as many seasonally themed art workshops to give local residents the opportunity to create unique gifts and keepsakes. Twelve days of Christmas is a community initiative supported by the City of Coquitlam, the Maillardville Merchants' Association, Maillardville Residents' Association and members of the Maillardville Programming the Streets committee."*

For several years there was a great output of energy and ideas to animate the streets of Maillardville. The "Flaunt Your Frenchness" campaign, a series of musical and culinary events culminating with the annual Festival du Bois, the publishing of a guided walking tour of Maillardville and the "Musique Chez Nous" program were all products of the time, creativity and energy of organizations and individuals committed to rejuvenating the cultural life of the village.

Mackin House, the long awaited venue for a Coquitlam museum, finally opened its doors in 2000. The Paré Room, housing hundreds of pictures and artifacts from Fraser Mills and Maillardville had already been established for a number of years in its basement. Soon the rooms of the main and upper floors began to be filled with period clothing, artifacts and a "heritage" kitchen. However, it did not take long for the Board and executive director to shift the focus of the museum in a different and unexpected direction. Antique toys and dolls began to take up shelves and then whole rooms within the museum. Early in the decade, it became known as Mackin Heritage House and Toy and Doll Museum. Over the years, many of the artifacts that were to illustrate Coquitlam's history, including that of Maillardville, were put into storage to make way for the ever-growing collection of toys. Mackin House also organized and ran for a number of years, an "antiques road show" and periodic displays of vintage automobiles. There was even at one time, a display of WWII vehicles including a tank. These events did serve to attract attention and people to Maillardville. The Heritage Society also collaborated in many of the already mentioned events and activities in Maillardville. However, to the dismay of many, after waiting for three decades, there still was no real museum for Coquitlam and Maillardville. In 2007, the Board and executive director encountered organizational challenges. Working with City staff through the summer of 2008, a new Board, mission and vision statements were put in place.

The new mission statement reads, in part:

"The Coquitlam Heritage Society is dedicated, as trustee and advocate, to ensuring the collection, preservation and presentation of Coquitlam's history and heritage assets for past, present and future citizens."

The Paré Room continues to fulfill a part of the mission statement. The community awaits the release and display of many artifacts still in storage and the long awaited opening of a true museum for Coquitlam.

Laval Square had always been the heart of old Maillardville. While many of the original pioneers' houses located around the square had disappeared, a new building, Place Maillardville, had been erected in 1979. Conceived as a neighbourhood house and a drop in centre, Place Maillardville did serve in that capacity for many years. It was also used as a venue for some of the social activity of the community. Yet, as the years rolled by, and with an increasing amount of time and space being devoted to rental activity, Place Maillardville lost its sense of purpose in the latter half of the nineties. Association Habitat Maillardville with the assistance of City staff reviewed and updated their mission statement in 1999. But little changed and in 2001, a City Task Force was established. The findings of the ensuing study highlighted a number of reasons for the failure of Place Maillardville to reach its potential as a valuable community asset. Among the reasons cited were the building's physical limitations, lack of Board training, lack of support by City staff and a high reliance on rental income. The study applauded the Board of Association Habitat Maillardville for its devotion over the years, but concluded that it was unreasonable to expect a residents' association to operate a public facility. It therefore recommended that a new Society be formed with its sole purpose being to manage Place Maillardville as a community centre. On January 1, 2002, the Board of the newly formed Société Place Maillardville Society formally took over management and operation of the building. Place Maillardville Neighbourhood House officially became Place Maillardville Community Centre.

The first Board of Directors included Jean Aussant, president, Jean Lambert, vice president, Arnold Fenrick, treasurer, Blossom Broussard, secretary and Jim Robinson, Shannon Furze and Councilor Maxine Wilson. At the end of January of that year, the Board was completed with the addition of Gerry Kidwell and Carmen Henry. Anne Marie Bouthillette was the first Executive Director. The immediate result of these changes was a dramatic increase in programs being offered at the community centre. Dance, yoga, karate and French classes, boys and girls drop in and adult drama workshops were all available in the first years of the new Place Maillardville. In 2004, a new logo was unveiled. The Now, August 2004 tells us:

"Place Maillardville has unveiled a new logo that reflects the community spirit the centre promotes. A large part of Société Place Maillardville's mandate is to redefine Place Maillardville as a community centre first and foremost." executive director Anne Marie Bouthillette said in a press release. "The new logo absolutely represents

that- it's playful, colourful, just the kind of image Place Maillardville is working hard to project."

An activities coordinator for Centre Bel Age was also hired. The first to fill that role was Suzanne Tkach. Ms. Tkach resigned in 2007, and Diane Johnston was hired to replace her. By 2004, Société Maillardville Uni announced that after conducting its business out of a portable unit for ten years (located outside of Maillardville) it was finally making the move to new offices at Place Maillardville built for that purpose.

With three separate groups now occupying the facility, the building soon became inadequate to handle the increased activity. In 2002, a study was initiated and plans for an addition were drawn up. The expansion project had an estimated $1.5 million cost. The expansion did not take place.

In 2004, Anne Marie Bouthillette stepped down as executive director. Carmen Henry filled in for a short period of time before Jim LaCroix was hired to fill that position. Under the guidance of Mr. LaCroix, the centre continued to grow and in cooperation with SMU, many French programs were offered.

Yet another example of the enthusiasm that existed for a revival of all things French was the renewal of that early festival, the Francofête. The Now, February 2007 announced:

"Francofête fun fair at Place Maillardville On Saturday, February 24, noon to 3pm, Place Maillardville will be showcasing the history of Maillardville at what organizers hope will be the first annual family fun fair. For $1, people can enter a trivia contest on Maillardville history. If you don't know much about history, the answers will be hidden around the building. Everyone who correctly answers all 12 questions will be entered into a draw for a portable DVD player. There will also be a Bingo game using traditional Bingo cards (no bingo dabbers needed), carnival games, a raffle, a 50/50 draw, hotdogs, candy floss, popcorn and snow cones."

However, lack of physical space was not the only factor hampering further program expansion. The high rate of rentals cut deeply into the limited time and space available for community programming. Eventually, the Board directed Mr. LaCroix to begin terminating some of the larger rental contracts. The move did provide some temporary relief.

With the continued success of all three groups, Place Maillardville, Société Maillardville Uni and Club Bel Âge, the facility simply could not support further growth. In addition, the aging building was beginning to decay. Finally, in 2008 a clamor arose from the community demanding a solution to what had become an intolerable situation. Eventually, Mayor and Council established a committee to study the situation. A consulting firm was hired to carry the study into the community, to establish guidelines for what an expanded facility would look like and to make recommendations to the committee. But it was made clear that with continued facility expansion at Town Centre and at the Poirier sports complex, Maillardville would have to wait some time for any new community centre to be built there. As of this writing, there is no confirmation of what the study recommendations were or when the community might hope for the project to get underway.

Even as the community looked to the future, reminders of the past continued to be lost. One by one, those institutions that had helped to form Maillardville were disappearing as the village advanced towards its 100th birthday. The previous decades had witnessed the loss of most of "old Maillardville".

Fraser Mills closed its doors in 2001. Caisse Populaire followed suit in 2005. Another sad loss came in 2007 with the closing of Millside School, the very year of its own centenary. It will be remembered that the school was established in 1907 by Fraser Mills for the workers' children. From the beginning, it was an institution rooted in multiculturalism. Through the years, children of English, French, Chinese, Japanese, East Indian, Norwegian and Greek decent grew up together. However, as Maillardville declined, fewer and fewer children were available to attend the school. For a time, the Programme Cadre, French education for children with at least one parent of French Canadian decent, was located there. The closing was a sad day for hundreds of people who attended Millside School. Its future purpose is unknown.

Société Maillardville Uni continued its work of fostering the French language and culture. When in 2004 Vancouver was chosen to host the 2010 Winter Olympics, SMU announced that the 2010 Festival du Bois would offer an expanded program. The Now, June 2004 quoting an unidentified SMU source stated:

"that by the 100th anniversary of Maillardville in 2009, and the 2010 Winter Olympics, all will be ready to welcome the world to this very unique community and enhance tourism by offering a glimpse of French Canadian culture and heritage."

The Festival du Bois itself continued to draw crowds of 10 to 15 thousand. From its inception in 1990, the grand event was a celebration of the French culture at Maillardville and the historic bond it shared with Fraser Mills and the lumber industry. From events such as the triathlon and various logging competitions to moustache contests and fiddling face offs, the Festival really was a "made in Maillardville" product. In the late nineties, an outreach program to schoolchildren was added. This tradition continued intact into the year 2000 and beyond. But the festival itself was evolving, becoming more complex. While the culinary traditions of maple sugar, tourtière and poutine remained, other aspects of the festival were left behind. By 2004, the connection to Fraser Mills and the lumber industry had all but disappeared. The festival continued to highlight French Canadian music and included performances by artists from Acadia and Louisiana. From 2003 onward, musical offerings from other countries and cultures were also being highlighted at the Festival. The yearly program began featuring Celtic music, throat singing and musicians from Zimbabwe and Chad along with all the old favorites from Quebec and other parts of Canada. Festival du Bois had evolved into primarily a food and musical festival. In 2008, riding the momentum that had been built around the Maillardville revitalization effort, the festival returned to Mackin Park. Over 15,000 attended that year.

Any successful event depends heavily on the good will and generosity of its volunteers. And Festival du Bois has, over the course of two decades, been a stellar demonstration of those very qualities that exist among so many individuals in the community of Maillardville. Reporting on the 2008 Festival, the Coquitlam Now offers us a glimpse of the day from the perspective of those workers without whom such grand events could not be possible:

*"**Prepare 2000 bowls of poutine.** Bake 300 tourtières and ladle out 400 bowls of pea soup. Prepare giant containers full of baked beans, coleslaw and meatballs with gravy. Slice up some French bread. Oh, and don't forget dessert: sugar pies and maple syrup taffy. Congratulations. You now have enough food to feed a hungry crowd of Festival du Bois goers. For volunteers who prepare the French Canadian delicacies*

many of the estimated 10,000 to attend Maillardville's Music Festival this weekend will dig into, slicing and dicing starts early. Gilberte Knapp, one of a "few ladies" who prepare the French Canadian meat pies known as tourtières, bakes them almost year round. She works out of the kitchen at Our Lady of Lourdes parish in Maillardville, from a recipe she inherited from her aunt. The filling is mostly ground pork, but sometime she'll use up to one third ground beef, adding onions, water and a little flour or bread crumbs, as well as her "special spices." "Some people will just taste the meat pies at the festival and they want my phone number," she says, adding that her tourtières have been savoured as far away as Prince George. By starting their Festival du Bois produc-tion five weeks ahead of schedule, volunteers are able to make and freeze 50 pies a week ensuring that they'll have 300 ready to go when the crowds start swarming their tent on Saturday.....Then there's the sugar pies. "No calories at all," the 83 year old jokes, "It's just sugar, some water, butter, a little flour and whipping cream." If sweets are your thing, you'll find kindred spirits at the Cabane a Sucre, French for "sug-ar shack." That's where Raymond Bonneau and other volunteers boil maple syrup on high heat before spreading it over a bed of crushed ice to make tire d'érable, or maple taffy. Like Knapp, Bonneau has volun-teered at the festival for nearly two decades....Volunteers used to drive up Mount Seymour to get real snow to roll the taffy out on, But Bonneau says they simplified the process by crushing ice instead. He'll start at 9:30 Saturday morning, boiling big vats of pure maple syrup for at least half an hour at high heat to get the right consistency. The sticky stuff is ladled out onto the "snow" to form long strips that are cooled just enough to be wrapped around a stick. The trick, says Bonneau, is keep-ing your eye on the syrup when it's cooking. He's cleaned up the mess from a vat of syrup that boiled over, and does what he can to avoid a repeat."

Although the article features Raymond Bonneau in its description of the Cabane a Sucre others, of course, were very much involved, in particular André Beauregard. Indeed, Mr. Beauregard was the heart and soul of the event. He bought and paid for all of the equipment necessary to run "la cabane" and was its prime organizer from the beginning. Sadly, in 2009, this man who was a four time cancer survivor passed away. His funeral at Paroisse Notre Dame de Lourdes was packed to overflowing. A true embodiment of the French Canadian "joie de vivre", André Beauregard left an enduring legacy for Maillardville. The Cabane à Sucre, the fore-runner of the Festival du Bois, has been renamed in his honour as the Cabane Beauregard.

One of the original purposes of the Festival and of SMU was to bring together all of the Francophone organizations of Maillardville. It continued to accomplish that through the decade. Partnering with their member organizations, SMU helped to manifest French culture by sponsoring such programs as the Soirée Jazz/Blues, summer French camps and adult French classes.

In 2008, Société Maillardville Uni changed its name to Société francophone de Maillardville, with a mission to:

"Promote, represent and defend the rights of French speaking in Maillardville and surrounding areas by maintaining the French Canadian language and culture"

With the prospect of Place Maillardville expansion fading once again, the Board of SfM made the decision to relocate on Brunette Avenue in order to have more space and more exposure. Société francophone de Maillardville also assumed the responsibility for organizing the events of Maillardville's centenary in 2009. The activities included a "kick off" New Year's party, and a heritage quilt made of squares from individuals, families and organizations in Maillardville. There were special commemorative photo displays and books, a solemn Mass celebrated on the 27th of September and a gala banquet and play in October. Still, the glory of the fiftieth and seventy fifth anniversaries of Maillardville's founding found only a dim echo in its one hundredth.

In 2005, a new organization made its appearance in Maillardville. In November of that year several residents, tired of watching drug deals take place in front of their homes, banded together to form the Maillardville Residents' Association. After several meetings at which the group was organized, the MRA made its first public appearance at the 2006 Festival du Bois, sharing an information booth with Place Maillardville and the Maillardville Merchants' Association. Membership in the new organization grew quickly, and Maillardville Residents' Association incorporated on November 15, 2006. The members of the first board of directors were: Al Boire, Victoria Boire, John Bergen, Lorraine Bergen, Holly Kirchtag, David Ruckle, Maire Ruckle, Paul Thompson and Jeremy Wright. The group immediately involved itself in many community activities, was invited to participate in several city committees, and offered residents a crime forum and an all candidates meeting. Perhaps the most important contribution of this broad based organization has been its ability to keep residents informed and connected to happenings in Maillardville. As a credible representation of residents in Maillardville, the MRA established a positive relationship with both Council and staff and made a significant contribution to the creation of by-laws governing various adult oriented businesses. The MRA continues to provide residents with many opportunities to have their voices heard and to share in the life of Maillardville.

French culture continued to manifest itself throughout this first decade of the 21st century. Les Scouts francophone de Maillardville celebrated its 50th anniversary in 2005. What a remarkable achievement that from such humble beginnings and operating as an entirely French entity in the far west of Canada, they have survived for fifty years and made such a difference in the lives of so many boys and girls. In fact, les Scouts embodied everything that was cherished by the pioneers who first came to Maillardville. Language, culture, religion, music; all were the building blocks upon which the French scouting movement were founded. Justice, honour and fortitude was its mantra. As the French community at Maillardville owed a great debt to the Sisters of the Child Jesus in the previous decade, so should les Scouts et Guide francophone de Maillardville be honoured in this final decade as the village approached its centenary. So many good men and women have come up through the ranks of the scouting movement to make their contributions to keep alive the spirit of la Francophonie à Maillardville. Hommage aux Scouts et Guides francophones!

Others too were honoured during this decade. Jean Lambert, the Scout's founder, was given the highest honour the City of Coquitlam could offer. He was made a Freeman of the City in 2004. Along with him, recognized for his endless work on City committees and his devotion to the arts in Coquitlam, Fern Bouvier received the same honour. It is a testament to the deep commitment felt by so many residents of Maillardville that since its inception in 1991, 10 people have been named as Freemen of the City and of those, no fewer than 4 have hailed from Maillardville.

Two thousand and four saw another son of Maillardville honoured. At a formal proclamation before Mayor and Council, and in recognition for his significant work with the Coquitlam Heritage Society, Tony Paré was named as Coquitlam's first official Town Crier. The Now, May 2004 recorded that event for posterity:

*"**Historian and author takes on role as town crier** Oyez, oyez, oyez. Let it be known as of this day, the 17th of May, 2004, Mr. Tony Paré is now known to all the people as the official Town Crier for the City of Coquitlam. That's how Paré, a Coquitlam history buff, was introduced at city hall Monday, where he was given a cloak, hat and bell to prepare for his role as the city's first honorary town crier. "I feel I've been very fortunate that I've been recognized for the work I've done." he told the Now Tuesday adding that part of the credit goes to his wife, Teresa, who provided moral support behind the scenes. If anyone is suited to be a town crier it's Paré whose keen interest in preserving Coquitlam's, and especially Maillardville's, heritage is wellknown....Paré was born in a lean to, or annex, at the back of that Brunette house in 1917, about 25 feet back from the jail cells located at the back of the police station. Now 86, Paré has devoted many years of his life to the Coquitlam Heritage Society, including donating more than 700 photographs of early Maillardville life to the Mackin House Museum who named a room after him....Paré is not sure when he will first be called upon to serve as ceremonial town crier, but he suspects it may be in July when Place des Art holds its Fair in the Square. If Monday's meeting was any indication, he will be well received. After addressing the audience in his cloak and hat, he got a standing ovation, a rare occurrence at any city gathering, and was presented with a scroll outlining his duties. His job, the city says, includes making sure the "news" of Coquitlam is heard by all."*

Yet another native of Maillardville was to have an impact on the community. Richard Stewart, MLA for Coquitlam/Maillardville lost his position to Councilor Diane Thorne in the provincial election of 2005. In a quasi-role reversal, Mr. Stewart was elected to City Council. Maxine Wilson unseated Mayor Jon Kingsbury during that same election. In 2008, Mr. Stewart defeated Ms. Wilson to become Coquitlam's new Mayor, the first from Maillardville to achieve that office since George Proulx in 1923.

The Catholic parishes, (once the bastions of French culture at Maillardville), found themselves upon very different paths as the decade progressed. Paroisse Notre Dame de Lourdes, of course, must be recognized as the heart and soul of Maillardville. But as Our Lady of Fatima Parish celebrated its 60th anniversary in 2006, it was she who was now recognized as the "Grande Dame". The bicultural life of Maillardville continued to find vibrant expression in that community. Church and school at Fatima vigorously supported the proud heritage of Maillardville. Knights of Columbus, Scouts francophone, and Dame de Ste Anne also thrived within the fold of the parish. The Now in November, 2006, recorded the parish's 60th anniversary:

"Maillardville Parish Celebrates 60th Anniversary *Our Lady of Fatima started with a small group of Francophones and two tiny houses on Alderson Avenue. The rest of its five acre property was forest, says Jean Lambert, who joined the parish in 1947. All that was there were two little houses and some woods," Lambert recalls, "One building was for the priest the other for the sisters....Today, 800 people attend mass at the church, including those with Chinese, Korean and Filipino roots, and about 400 students attend its school....The Grande Dame of Maillardville is inviting the Tri-Cities to join its 60th anniversary celebrations taking place from December 4 to 9."*

As Our Lady of Fatima was the Grande Dame, N.D. de Lourdes had become the dowager. The decline that had set in during the nineties continued unchecked in the third Christian millennium. Numbers plummeted, and few new parishioners registering were French. The men and women who had laboured for so long at the parish were aging and dying. Those who remained were, perhaps, best represented by that group of dedicated women, the Catholic Ladies of Lourdes. But there was to be no new blood to resuscitate the francophone expression of Catholicism at Our Lady of Lourdes.

One rare happy occasion for the parish came in 2005 with Father Stan Frytek's 60th anniversary of his ordination to the priesthood along with his 90th birthday. The parish fêted him in grand style. Father Frytek continued at the parish until he retired in 1997 at age 92. His departure marked yet another loss for the French community at Notre Dame de Lourdes. First, Father Frytek was the last Franciscan priest stationed at N.D. de Lourdes after 57 years of service to the parish by that Order. Second, and hardly to be believed, he was the last French speaking priest for the parish. The brief interlude between Father Frytek's departure in December 2007 and the arrival of his permanent replacement in July of 2008 was filled with two temporary appointments: Father Bruce McAllister and Father Gabriel de Chadrevian.

So after 100 years of existence, first as a fully francophone parish and then as a bilingual one, French was now hardly to be heard in the venerable old church. Among all of the losses over the decades this was a particularly bitter pill to swallow.

Father Alan Boisclair, a priest of the Archdiocese of Vancouver, arrived as pastor in July of 2008. Father Boisclair entered into his new assignment with great vigour. Taking stock of the parish facilities and anticipating the upcoming 100th anniversary, he organized a refurbishing of the church interior, which would eventually reveal the need for significant structural upgrades. The dramatic changes to the church interior were celebrated on the parish feast day, the Feast of Our Lady of Lourdes with the Rite of Solemn Blessing and Consecration of the New Altar. This most impressive of Catholic rituals is steeped in the deep tradition and symbolism of the 2000 year old church. It was a consolation to some to see that at least on this occasion the church was filled to capacity and that a palpable spirit of joy was felt.

Mass was also celebrated on the day of the 100th Anniversary, September 27, 2009. To honour the francophone heritage of the parish, Michael Miller, Archbishop of the Archdiocese of Vancouver said the Mass in French. During Mass, a delegation from France, three former students of Father Edmond Maillard, presented Father's cross to the parish. A luncheon followed with speeches, acknowledgements, cake cutting and a historical display of pictures and artifacts at Centre Bel Age.

Figure 134 Father Edmond Maillard O.M.I.

Epilogue

Sunday, September 27, 2009. At 12:30pm, I stood at the top of the steps of Our Lady of Lourdes Church, having just attended the 100th anniversary commemorative Mass. A wave of nostalgia washed over me as I tried to imagine the scene at Millside station 100 years earlier. The Columbian newspaper reporting on that day in 1909 announced:

"At 12:30 today a special train composed of nine coaches including baggage cars reached the Fraser River Mills bearing some 250 French Canadians who have been brought out from the province of Quebec to work in the mill. A large number of the employees of the mill were assembled to welcome these new settlers today."

I strained to hear the train's whistle, the hiss of steam and the shriek of metal against metal. I tried to envision the largely Asian group that was there to meet them as Johnny Dicaire first set foot upon the land of his new home. Tried to imagine what these étrangers must have felt and wondered, what fear, anxiety, hopes and aspirations they must have carried with them. As they departed from the east, had they imagined that they would have to carve their homes, church and school out of raw forest? Did they ever imagine that, 100 years later, some of their descendants would stand next to the very foundations of the church they would build?

September 27, 2009. The people are happy. The big day has finally arrived. All year they have immersed themselves in the people, history, character and the very "Frenchness" of Maillardville. Each reflects on memories, perceptions, beliefs. Overall, a feeling of joy and of pride exists; we have arrived, we are still here, we made it...we have not broken the trust, we still bear the torch.

100 years is a short period of time relative to many towns and cities of the world. And Maillardville, not a village in its own right, is modest even as a neighbourhood. Nevertheless, 100 is still a respectable number, and there is something magical in Maillardville that transcends its humble stature and even time itself. Against all odds, the "Frenchtown" founded a century ago still exists today. Its physical body decimated, the need to keep the spirit alive in the hearts of individuals, that flame that was almost extinguished in the nineteen seventies, is kept alive today by the sheer will and determination of those men and women who cannot bear to witness the death of Maillardville, will not let it die.

For 100 years, first as a colourful and even exotic settlement, but above all as a French Catholic village, Maillardville's people have faced the endless challenges with a resolve to overcome and to succeed that would not be shaken. With their hands, the pioneers built the village. With their hearts and minds, they built the community. That determination coursed so purely in them, that the force of it carried them past the birth of their village, isolated as it was, into the full light of the Anglophone world within which they lived. Their unshakeable resolve not only allowed them to survive in that vast Anglophone sea, but their joie de vivre persuaded many to join them on their tiny francophone island. Thus was born the Maillardville of the forties and fifties and so was revealed her true nature. Not only did she live and indeed thrive on the west coast of Canada, but she also made real the existence of that Canadian ideal, a true bilingual community. Maillardville exemplified everything that is truly Canadian; a country based upon two founding nations that recognizes the bilingual nature of their country, yet also cherishes peace and equality for men and women of all races and creeds.

Maillardville, conceived in the racist notions of the day, turned its back on racism. The French Canadians came to Fraser Mills in 1909 and worked side by side with men of all races in peace and in harmony. They themselves would become the victims of racism. But that indefatigable spirit of community, rooted in their Catholic faith, would repeatedly bind them in the face of so many challenges. Maillardville showed her solidarity during the strike at Fraser Mills in 1931, and throughout the depression years. Twenty years later, in a truly remarkable grass roots uprising, Maillardville took up the cause for independent schools and minority rights in BC and stood alone against the government of the day.

Maillardville suffered the sociological ravages of the sixties. It was the village's darkest hour. The flock had been dispersed; the wolf was at the door. Could she survive? By the stubborn determination of a precious few individuals, the tiny flame of francophone culture that sputtered through the seventies was preserved. Maillardville was delivered from her despair to emerge, once again, united. And even as all that came before teetered at the brink of the abyss, still they managed to plant the seeds that would eventually allow for French immersion in public schools and the Programme Cadre enjoyed by so many over the past four decades.

In modern times, as in days gone by, the francophone community has come together in solidarity and with renewed energy and hope for Maillardville. And as in days gone by, the Anglo community has responded favourably and generously to the rediscovery of this rare and precious gem in our midst. The survival of a dream cannot depend on buildings, or even institutions. Those are the vessels which serve to contain and preserve its existence. It is the people themselves who conceive the dream and hold it and forge it into reality.

What fate brought those particular people, the pioneers, to Maillardville? A.D. McRae set the stage when he bought the Fraser River Lumber Company with an aim to making it the largest mill in the world. He also wished to have a reliable supply of lumber for the booming Canadian prairies that he helped to open in 1905. Then there is Théodore Théroux who, as night watchman at Fraser Mills, already had the experience and the dream of building French settlements in the west of Canada. Surely it was fate that brought those two men together, one with a challenge the other the solution to the "labour problems" facing McRae and his consortium. The charismatic Father William Patrick O'Boyle provided the Catholic element that was so necessary to entice the lumbermen to the west. He too was a man of vision and saw far reaching implications in the success of the "experiment" being launched by McRae. The team of Théroux and O'Boyle arrived in Ottawa at the precise moment that they did looking for lumbermen to recruit. And there at that moment they found the young bilingual Johnny Dicaire selling newspapers at the train station. He led them to those he knew, and they chose to brave the unknown and come to the west coast of Canada. It was those particular people who would not start the trip unless they were assured that they could bring their language, religion and culture with them and that they could educate their young in that language and within those values.

And it was the enigmatic Father Edmond Maillard, for whom the village was named, who somehow by force of personality bound those pioneers in the early days so they could create the foundation upon which Maillardville would be built. Through each decade and for every challenge there arose individuals to unite and lead the people in the quest to preserve language, culture and religion.

The fear of assimilation into the Anglophone culture was a real and justified one. Throughout Maillardville's history, time has whittled away many of the supports that were essential to the existence of la Francophonie. The loss of cultural isolation as more and more non-Francophones came and settled in Maillardville. The downgrading of religious influence and authority, the harbour that for so long kept the Francophones sheltered and secure in their community. The loss of the language itself, as it became increasingly difficult to have opportunity to use it in a fully English environment.

What hope then for the future of Maillardville? Success for the village itself seems almost inevitable in 2009. Its geographic position in Metro Vancouver, the age of its structures and the underutilization of its commercial district will all drive a physical renewal of Maillardville. The development of the Fraser Mills land into a waterfront village will also spur new growth. The Gateway highways project and particularly the King Edward overpass will provide new connections and new opportunities. It is hoped that Maillardville's Francophone roots and heritage will be preserved and honoured in the building design guidelines now in place for the neighbourhood centre. All that remains is for the development to commence that will bring many more people to Maillardville. That day is inevitable. The Maillardville of 2020 will be vastly different from that of 2009.

But new buildings and stores, cobblestone sidewalks and lavender themed landscaping does not a culture make nor preserve. As it has always been, people must supply the necessary love and devotion to preserve, in the case of Maillardville, its history, traditions and its bicultural and multicultural nature. And once again, perhaps more so than at

288

any other time in Maillardville's history, the French component is under threat of extinction. So many who have laboured with love over the decades to bring us to this day are aging, passing on. Having made their contributions, they look to see who will rise from the ranks to take their place. To whom will they pass the torch? As it happened during the depression and into the forties and fifties, Maillardville needs another "great migration". According to the 2006 Canadian census the percent of households in Maillardville claiming French as their mother tongue no longer even registers in the top five languages. Outside of specifically French organizations, the language is hardly to be heard. Thanks to events such as Festival du Bois, and groups such as les Scouts francophone, Société francophone de Maillardville, Foyer Maillard, Club Bel Âge, Place Maillardville Community Centre, Les Jammers, Our Lady of Fatima Parish and others, the dream of a vibrant and visible French community still lives.

However, when the fanfare surrounding Maillardville's 100th birthday fades and disappears, the work to rebuild that wonderful dream of a real and visible bilingual community at Maillardville will remain. If that dream is shared by all stakeholders then part of that work must be to attract new Francophones here. The entire community must participate in this endeavor, whatever forms it might take. The support of governments at all levels is vital to success. On the other hand such a dream may not be shared by all. The alternative is to finally allow the dream to fade away into history, leaving only a few pictures and perhaps some street signs to remind us of what once was. It has long been said, for over forty years, that Maillardville offers something precious and unique to the City of Coquitlam. It does.

To quote "Mr. Maillardville", Johnny Dicaire, speaking to a class of schoolchildren in his later years: *"Mon Canada, je l'aime. But don't let Maillardville disappear!"*

Timeline of Significant Events in the Life of Maillardville

1890- Ross/McLaren Mill established on the Fraser River
1903- Ownership changes, mill known as Fraser River Mills
1907- Millside School built
  - Fraser River is dredged, deep water access provided
  - name changes to Fraser River Lumber Company
  - A.D. McRae and Co. buy Fraser Mills
1908- Town site of Millside now known as Fraser Mills
1909- First contingent of French Canadians
1910- Second contingent of French Canadians
  - First Church at Notre Dame de Lourdes Parish
  - Company changes name to Canadian Western Lumber Company
1912- French Settlement granted a post office under the name of Maillardville
1913- Church burns down
  - Port Coquitlam and Fraser Mills secedes from Coquitlam and incorpo rates
  - Temporary Municipal offices located at the home of É. Paré
1914- WWI begins
1917- Les Dames de Ste. Anne founded
1918- WWI ends
1920- New City Hall at Marmont Street and Brunette Avenue
1929- Start of Great Depression; leads to new wave of French Canadians from western provinces
    1931- Strike at Fraser Mills
1938- Present day Church consecrated at Notre Dame de Lourdes Parish
1939- WWII begins
1940- Coquitlam's first May Day
1944- Fraser Mills donates the land south of Brunette to create Mackin Park
1945- WWII ends
  - Féderation Canadienne-Francaise de Colombie-Britanique founded.
  - First "Frenchman's Frolic"
1946- New French parish of Notre Dame de Fatima founded
  - Caisse Populaire de N.D. de Lourdes founded
  - c1946 "Teen Town" is organised
1948- Fraser River Floods
  - c1948 Catholic Youth Organization (CYO) is founded
1950- Caisse Populaire de N.D. de Lourdes changes its name to "Caisse Populaire de Maillardville"
1951- Catholic School strike in Maillardville
  - Sisters of the Child Jesus leave after serving the community for 42 years
1952- Schools reopen
1955- Scouts de Maillardville founded

1957- Mouvement de Guide Catholique founded
1958- New Church at Fatima consecrated
1959- 50th Anniversary of Maillardville
1963- Société Biculturelle de Maillardville founded
1966- Death of Father Edmond Maillard
      Branch 86/ Club Bel Âge founded
1968- French immersion at Alderson Elementary
1969- Foyer Maillard opens
1972- Fraser Mills becomes a part of Coquitlam
      Place des Arts opens
1973- Les Échos du Pacifique (choral) founded
1974- First attempt at Maillardville revitalization, Plan Maillardville
1977- Francofête in Maillardville
   - Provincial recognition of Independent Schools
   - Full implementation of French Immersion Program
1979- Place Maillardville Community Centre built
   - Maillardville Uni founded (incorporated 1983)
1984- 75th Anniversary of Maillardville
1985- Second attempt at Maillardville revitalization
   - Maillardville Shopping Centre burns down
1990- First annual Festival du Bois
   - Caisse Populaire changes name to "Village Credit Union"
   - Village CU opens a branch in Port Moody
1998- City Hall abandons its historic location at Brunette and Marmont
1999- Heritage Square: Place des Arts, Mackin House, Railway Museum
2000- Place Maillardville expansion
   - Village Credit Union opens a branch in Port Coquitlam
2001- Fraser Mills ceases operations
2002- Village Credit Union opens a branch in Chilliwack
2005- Village CU sells assets to VanCity CU…end of a significant aspect of
life in Maillardville
   - Maillardville Residents' Association founded (incorporates 2006)
2006- Third attempt at Maillardville revitalization
2008- Société Maillardville Uni changes name to "Société francophone de
      Maillardville"
   - Beedie group, owners of the Fraser Mills site will develop as the
     "Village at Fraser Mills
   - After 17 years Festival du Bois returns to Mackin Park
2009- Bonne Fête Maillardville!!!----Happy Birthday Maillardville!!!

Bibliography

The Coquitlam Star
The Coquitlam Herald
The Coquitlam Times
The Coquitlam Enterprise
The Coquitlam Now
The TriCities News
The Fraser News
The Columbian
The Vancouver Sun
The B.C. Catholic

Communism in British Columbia   Citizen's League of British Columbia 1935
British Columbia Provincial Police Veterans' Association website

"Un pionnier se raconte" Chotikan, Patrick. , Le Soleil de Colombie
(Colombie-Britannique), Vendredi 14 Janvier 1977, p. 6. (Johnny Dicaire)

British Columbia Magazine 1911

Harold Pritchett: Communism & the International Woodworkers of America Timothy Kilgren

A Study of the French Vocabulary of School Children in Maillardville B.C. Jaqueline van
Campen 1970 Simon Fraser University

Prohibition in British Columbia Albert John Hiebert 1969 Simon Fraser University

Ethnicity And Class Conflict at Maillardville/Fraser Mills The Strike of 1931 M. Jeanne Meyers Williams 1982 Simon Fraser University

The Asahi Baseball Team Remembered CBC News in Review September 2004

Statements of significance   City of Coquitlam, 2007
Notre Dame de Lourdes, 830 Laval Street

Statements of significance   City of Coquitlam, 2007
Mackin Residence, 169 King Edward Street

Statements of significance   City of Coquitlam, 2007
Millside Elementary School, 1432 Brunette Avenue

Statements of significance   City of Coquitlam, 2007
Fraser Mills Manager's Residence 1120 Brunette Avenue

The Story of Maillardville   City of Coquitlam website

Archives of Council Minutes   City of Coquitlam

Programme Souvenir du 60 Anniversaire La Federation des francophone de la Colombie Britannique

La Federation des francophone de la Colombie Britannique
Website: History of the Francophone Community in British Columbia and of its Official Organization

Japanese Internment; British Columbia wages war against Japanese Canadians from Canada
A People's History CBC website

Scouts Francophone de la Colombie Britannique website

A 75 Year Chronicle Jean Riou 1984

The History of Metropolitan Vancouver website vancouverhistory.ca

The Merchant Prince Betty O'Keefe and Ian MacDonald

A History of Coquitlam and Fraser Mills 1858-1958 H.A.J. Monk and John Stewart

French Canadian Settlement in British Columbia John Ray Stewart

Regard Sur Maillardville Alexandre Spagnolo

History Atlas of Vancouver and the Lower Fraser Valley Derek Hayes

Programme Souvenir; Notre Dame de Lourdes/Maillardville 1909-1959

Programme Souvenir; Notre Dame de Lourdes/Maillardville 1909-1984

Programme Souvenir; Notre Dame de Fatima/Maillardville 1946-2006

Programme Souvenir; Scouts francophone de C.B 1955-1995

L'Histoire de La Caisse Populaire de Maillardville Roméo Paquette

My Memoirs of le vieux (old) Maillardville Antonio Paré

Vancouver Oral History Project (recorded interviews)

Mrs. Oméra Paré (Yvonne)
Mr. Johnny Dicaire
Mr. and Mrs. Léo Hammond
Mr. Arthur Coutu
Mr. Arthur Laverdure

Mr. Hercules Lamoureux
Mr. Harold Pritchett

The Mansions on the Hill Antonio Paré

Historical List of Coquitlam's Mayors and Councilors Coquitlam Public Library

Coquitlam, 100 Years, Reflections of Our Past Pioneer Tales Book Committee, District of Coquitlam

Caisse Populaire de Notre Dame de Lourdes minutes

Caisse Populaire de Maillardville minutes, financial statements, newsletters

Caisse Populaire de Maillardville Twenty Fifth Anniversary booklet

Société Place Maillardville minutes 2001-2009

Plan Maillardville Documents and Studies, District of Coquitlam 1974

Maillardville Revitalization Documents and Studies, District of Coquitlam 1985-1987

Maillardville Streetscape & Pedestrian/Bicycle Corridor Design Guidelines City of Coquitlam 1994

Maillardville Revitalization-Documents and Studies City of Coquitlam, 2005-2009

Index of Photos and Credits

*Société historique francophone de la Colombie-Britanique

*Société historique francophone de la Colombie-Britanique

Fig107 p253 Lourdes 75th	Uncredited
Fig108 p253 Johnny Dicaire	Centre bel Age
Fig109 p253 Chez Nous	Centre bel Age
Fig110 p253 L.Sekora	City of Coquitlam Archives
Fig111 p254 Maillardville fire	C.Hodge/Coquitlam Archives
Fig112 p254 Maillardville fire	C.Hodge/Coquitlam Archives
Fig113 p255 J. Lambert	Centre bel Age
Fig114 p255 N. Gareau	Uncredited
Fig115 p255 Lourdes steeple	Centre bel Age
Fig116 p255 Lourdes steeple	Centre bel Age
Fig117 p255 Foyer Maillard	Centre bel Age
Fig118 p255 J Lambert art	A. Boire
Fig119 p256 Festival du Bois	Uncredited
Fig120 p256 Festival du Bois	Uncredited
Fig121 p256 Festival du Bois	Uncredited
Fig122 p257 Heritage Square	A. Boire
Fig123 p257 Heritage Square	A. Boire
Fig124 p257 Mackin House	A. Boire
Fig125 p257 Place des Arts	A. Boire
Fig126 p258 Brunette c 2008	A. Boire
Fig127 p258 Brunette c 2008	A. Boire
Fig128 p258 Brunette c 2008	A. Boire
Fig129 p258 Fraser Mills c 2001	Centre bel Age
Fig130 p259 100 anniversary	Centre bel Age
Fig131 p259 100 anniversary	Centre bel Age
Fig132 p259 Father Stan Frytec	Centre bel Age
Fig133 p259 Fr Maillard's cross	Centre bel Age
Fig 134 p 260 Fr Maillard	SHFCB*

*Société historique francophone de la Colombie-Britanique

Index

ABOUT THE AUTHOR

Al Boire grew up in Maillardville where he still resides with Victoria and Angel the furry white monster. Al is a home inspector by day. Over the years he has been very active in the neighbourhood serving as a founding member and president of the Maillardville Residents' Association and assisting with various community initiatives and committees. Al is a recipient of the Queen Elizabeth II Diamond Jubilee Award.

On his time off, he enjoys walking Angel, reading, music and riding his motorcycle. Of course, research and writing is his passion.

Made in the USA
Charleston, SC
13 October 2016